D1525278

Addiction:

A Personal Story

Written by Lacy Deane Enderson

www.personaladdiction.com

Published by Bennett Deane Publishing
Simi Valley, CA

Co-published by Bettis Publishing
Simi Valley, CA

Forward

If you have taken the time to purchase this book, I must assume that you have begun your journey towards lifelong sobriety. Congratulations! I have never been an alcoholic so I will probably never understand Lacy's story the way that you will. I must admit that until I read through the pages of this book I had no idea how much my sister had been through.

I have watched in amazement as Jesus has transformed her life through the writing of these stories and the reading of His word. Scripture is powerful when it is applied to your life. Lacy has applied God's Word to her daily life and the work He has done in her spirit has truly been miraculous.

But you will not be transformed by simply reading through this book. You will gain nothing by peeping into Lacy's past and grimacing at her embarrassments. You will not grow by marveling at her faith or relating to her pain. You must approach this book as a project in introspection, prayer and application if you are to be changed.

I recommend that you read a page each day. Begin by reading the scripture several times and meditating on what it means to you. Then, read the story. Some stories will offer deep thoughts for contemplation. Other stories were simply written for Lacy's own sake. Hopefully, you will be able to relate to them and learn something from them.

After reading the "Thought to Meditate on," spend some time in prayer. Sometimes, when we sit in silence before God, He tells us what we need to hear. When you have finished talking to God, write what is in your heart under Thoughts and Revelations. You may want to write a story of your own or how the scripture makes you feel about your own journey. If you need more space, use a separate sheet of paper.

My prayer for you is that you will submit yourself totally to the love and care of God. He has the power and desire to transform your life. He is an overcoming God and He can keep you on the road to recovery. You simply have to trust that He wants to.

Trisha Lee

Introduction

Addiction: A Personal Story enters into a world where God is in control and your only job is to trust in Him. Easier said than done, I know. If you have ever struggled with an addiction than you know the mental torment and the driving force behind it. God says if you will trust in Him, He will set you free. God will remove the obsession from you so you no longer desire the thing you crave. Whether you are controlled by alcohol, cigarettes, food, relationships or some other addictive behavior, God can and will deliver you.

Insatiable cravings are hard to ignore and harder to resist. And what about feelings of anger, rage, fear, guilt and shame. Do you not turn towards the substance you have grown to love and trust to quench the pain of these awful feelings? Do you not run to food or alcohol to drown out this pain? Is your life so difficult you must seek to escape from your reality through food, drugs, or even a relationship? Addicts use anything that might relieve their discomfort. They seek a quick fix, a place of secret euphoria where uncomfortable feelings are not allowed to exist.

Addiction: A Personal Story was written as a quide to help anyone who suffers. If you are addicted, or you know someone who is, you will find comfort and guidance in the pages of this journal.

Now, for those of you who aren't sure if you are addicted. Have you ever been in a blackout and woke up the next morning with no recollection of the night before? Have you ever ate a whole gallon of ice cream and when it was gone looked for something else to eat? Have you met a guy or gal in a bar and wondered why you weren't living together by the second week? What about the bottle of codeine for the toothache? Was the prescription gone days before they should have been and were you calling the doctor for more telling him the pills were lost or stolen? These might be signs pointing to a potential addiction. These behaviors are good indicators that there might be something else wrong.

Have you ever thought about the damage done to those around you? Have you ever taken into consideration the damaging effects your drunken episode might have had on someone else? Maybe a child? You wake up thinking the night was so innocent because you don't remember what you did, but did you ever stop to think, they can? The kids do remember what you did, and they will for the rest of their lives. And we wonder what is wrong with the children.

Maybe your addiction doesn't seem so devastating because it doesn't qualify as a narcotic or a substance that impairs perception. Do you think the family is any less affected by that behavior?

Don't underestimate the power of addiction and it's harmful effects on those you love. Don't ever fall under the deception that your addiction isn't hurting anybody; it hurts everyone around you.

Take some time and read my story. It is my hope that you too will overcome every addiction just as I have. It is my prayer that you too will find the life of peace and serenity I have grown to love. It is my strongest desire that you too can escape the mental torment and driving force behind all addictions so nothing will ever master and control you again!

- Lacy Enderson

Table of Contents

*"Thank you to all my family and friends for
all their love and support"*
Lacy Enderson

When I was drinking, I used any excuse I could think of in order to justify my drinking. "Even Jesus drank wine," I would say. "Wine was served at every Holy meal," I would argue. But the Bible is very specific when it comes to drunkenness. I have included verses below that make it very clear how the Lord feels about alcoholism. Read them often. Read them on days when you try to convince yourself that one drink couldn't possibly hurt.

Isaiah 56: 11,12

They are dogs with mighty appetites; they never have enough. They are Shepherds who lack understanding; they all turn to their own way, each seeks his own gain. "Come," each one cries, "let me get wine, let us drink our fill of beer! And tomorrow will be like today, or even far better. "

Isaiah 24:11

In the streets they cry out for wine; all joy turns to gloom, all gaiety is banished from the earth.

Isaiah 24:9

No longer do they drink wine with a song the beer is bitter to its drinkers.

Isaiah 5: 11,12

Woe to those who rise early in the morning to run after their drinks, who stay up late at night till they are inflamed with wine, they have no regard for the deeds of the Lord, no respect for the work of his hands.

Proverbs 23:29-35

Who has woe? Who has sorrow? Who has strife? Who has complaints? Who has needless bruises? Who has bloodshot eyes? Those who linger

over wine, who go to sample bowls of mixed wine. Do not gaze at wine when it is red, when it sparkles in the cup, when it goes down smoothly! In the end it bites like a snake and poisons like a viper. Your eyes will see strange sights and your mind imagine confusing things. You will be like one sleeping on the high seas, lying on top of the rigging. "They hit me," you will say, "but I'm not hurt! They beat me, but I don't feel it! When will I wake up so I can find another drink? "

Haggai 1:6

You have planted much, but have harvested little. You eat but never have enough. You drink, but never have your fill. You earn wages only to put them in a purse with holes in it.

Proverbs 20: 1

Wine is a mocker and beer a brawler; whoever is led astray by them is not wise.

Proverbs 23:20,21

Do not join those who drink too much wine or gorge themselves on meat, for drunkards and gluttons become poor, and drowsiness clothes them in rags.

Proverbs 31:4,5

It is not for kings, 0 Lemuel not for kings to crave wine, not for rulers to crave beer, lest they drink and forget what the law decrees and deprive all the oppressed of their rights.

Isaiah 5:21,22,24

Woe to those who are wise in their own eyes and clever in their own sight. Woe to those who are heroes at drinking wine and champions at mixing drinks... their roots will decay.

Isaiah 24:7

The new wine dries up and the vine withers; all the merrymakers groan.

Isaiah 28:7,8

And these also stagger from wine and reel from beer: Priests and prophets stagger from beer and are befuddled with wine; they reel from beer, they stagger when seeing visions, they stumble when rendering decisions. All the tables are covered with vomit and there is not a spot without filth.

Joel 1:5

Wake up, you drunkards, and weep! Wail all you drinkers of wine; wail because of the new wine, for it has been snatched from your lips.

Luke 21:34

Be careful, or your hearts will be weighed down with dissipation, drunkenness and the anxieties of life, and that day will close on you unexpectedly like a trap.

Ephesians 4: 19

Having lost all sensitivity, they have given themselves over to sensuality so as to indulge in every kind of impurity, with a continual lust for more.

Nahum 1:10

They will be entangled among thorns and drunk from their wine; they will be consumed like dry stubble.

Habakkuk 2:5

Indeed wine betrays him; he is arrogant and never at rest. Because he is greedy as the grave and like death is never satisfied.

Habakkuk 2:15,16

Woe to him who gives drink to his neighbors, pouring it from the wineskin till they are drunk, so that he can gaze on their naked bodies. You will be filled with shame instead of glory. Now it is your turn! Drink and be exposed!

Romans 13:12,14

The night is nearly over; the day is almost here. So let us put aside the deeds of darkness and put on the armor of light. Let us behave decently as in the daytime, not in orgies and drunkenness, not in sexual immorality and debauchery, not in dissension and jealousy. Rather, clothe yourselves with the Lord Jesus Christ, and do not think about how to gratify the desires of the sinful nature.

Ephesians 5:18

Do not get drunk on wine, which leads to debauchery. Instead, be filled with the Spirit.
I thought God would open up the gates of heaven and let me in; instead he opened up the gates of hell and let me out.
My prayer for you is that through these pages you find hope, strength, deliverance, peace and most of all the love God has for you.

by Lacy Enderson

I Surrender All

♥

Exodus 15:26

He said, "If you listen carefully to the voice of the LORD your God and do what is right in his eyes, if you pay attention to his commands and keep all his decrees, I will not bring on you any of the diseases I brought on the Egyptians, for I am the LORD, who heals you. "

I woke up one morning after a two month drunk and knew I had to quit drinking. I had experienced one too many hangovers. This morning was the worst. I called my friend and asked for help. She told me to be ready by 6:00. She was taking me to a meeting. I felt such a sense of relief. But the obsession was greater than my desire to quit. Immediately, I went to the store for a beer. If I was going to quit drinking, and today would be my last drink, I needed a drink. This is a perfect example of an alcoholic. Before the meeting I consumed six beers. At 5:30 I panicked! She was on her way and I wanted more alcohol. I ran across the street to my neighbor's to get a beer. His wife had just left for the store to buy more so he had nothing to offer. The entire time I sat in that meeting, I thought about drinking. I planned what I would drink when the meeting was over. In desperation, I stayed for the late night meeting. Again, I thought about drinking through that meeting. I was taken home at 10:30 that night. And only by the grace of God, I went to bed. I was done. I have not taken a drink since that day, August 17th, 1999.

Thought To Meditate On:

God is our redeemer. He is our healer and our salvation. He is all we will ever want and need. We must let the Word of God dwell in us richly. Forget not his benefits and blessings. His Word is gospel. Every Word from beginning to end has been promised to us. Let us hold those Words close to our heart and never let them go. He will never let us go.

Thoughts and Revelations:

His Mercies are New Every Morning
♥

Jude 1 :22,23

Be merciful to those who doubt; snatch others from the fire and save them; to others show mercy, mixed with fear, hating even the clothing stained by corrupted flesh.

A friend from school and her family were going on a camping trip and I was invited. Her family consisted of parents, aunts, uncles, cousins, siblings and grandparents. It was a big family. We camped at the beach for a week. They had a motor home we slept in and the campsite offered bathrooms and showers. It was a nice setup. I always loved camping and the beach. Lying out in the sun was my favorite thing to do. It could not have been a better vacation, until the last night. Somehow I got a hold of the family alcohol without getting caught. I can't remember exactly how I got it or what it was, but I set out to get completely drunk. Taking my friend and her little sister with me, we took a walk up the road where we ran into some other teens. They were smoking pot. I was never a big pot-smoker but since I was already drinking I thought I'd have a better party and proceeded to get wasted. I wasn't doing very well. I went back to the campsite and carried on like a teenage drunk. It was obvious I was not in my right mind. But I think all the adults were drunk too, because no one seemed to notice that I was. That night when I went to sleep I wet the bed in the motorhome. It was drenched, and I was so embarrassed. Wetting the bed was common for me when I was drinking. As an adult, wetting my own bed was bad enough, but wetting someone else's was horrifying. Today, I don't wet my bed. In sobriety I found that I am perfectly capable of getting up and using the bathroom. What a concept.

Thought To Meditate On:

It breaks my heart when someone I love is struggling with drugs and alcohol. Compassion overwhelms me and I wish there was something I could do to help. I am filled with the same compassion and mercy God has for me when I struggle.

Thoughts and Revelations:

by Lacy Enderson

Light Unto My Path

♥

2 Peter 1 :3,4

His divine power has given us everything we need for life and godliness through our knowledge of him who called us by his own glory and goodness. Through these he has given us his very great and precious promises, so that through them you may participate in the divine nature and escape the corruption in the world caused by evil desires.

When I think about some of the things I did when I was drunk, I get very embarrassed. I thought I was so funny all the time. But when I woke up the next morning and realized how not funny I was I wanted to dig a hole and hide in it. I remember when my first husband left me. My sister thought it would be fun for us to go dancing. She thought it would help me if I dressed up and got out for a little while. She said I needed to feel good about myself. But when we got to the club my husband was there. Talk about putting a damper on the evening. But us alcoholics know how to fix minor inconveniences. I got drunk. I got embarrassingly drunk. I thought I was so beautiful. I just knew every head in that room turned when I walked by. At one point, I was dancing with this guy and I took off my jacket and did this little twirly thing with it as I threw it into the air. He walked off the dance floor and left me standing there alone. So I drank more. And eventually I puked all over the back seat of my sister's car. I still cringe when I think about that night. But I own it. I can learn through it. And with God's help I will never have to be that embarrassed again.

Thought To Meditate On:

God never told us we would have to walk through this world alone. In fact, he gave us his Son Jesus, who then sent the Holy Spirit so we in confidence would always have a helper by our side. In our own strength we are failures but with God's strength we can do anything. He said we would be more than conquerors with His help.

Thoughts and Revelations:

Slow to Anger

♥

Proverbs 16:32

Better a patient man than a warrior. A man who controls his temper than one who takes a city.

There was a time in my life when I was a RAGEaholic. I could yell and scream louder than anyone. I hadn't been taught good communication skills so I either gave people the silent treatment or I shouted. When I was a child I was told not to talk back. You probably were too. In the olden days children were not encouraged to have an opinion. I learned to stuff my feelings rather than to share them. When I became an adult I still had a hard time saying how I felt. The response I got from sharing my feelings always made me feel so badly about myself. The problem with stuffed feelings is that you will eventually explode and I was very good at exploding. I used old issues to attack my husband and I often took my anger out on my children. My anger turned into rage and I was uncontrollable. Over the years, through lots of prayer and working with others, I have learned to communicate and I don't hold anything in. If there is a problem with me and I feel it is important I will share it immediately. People don't like confrontation. But if I have something I need to say, I am going to say it. Most of the time, I can do this with patience and love. Communication has become an important part of my life. The damage that was caused because of my fear to communicate was far more destructive than sharing my feelings. Today I talk, I don't yell. If you have a problem with rage, find a good class on communication. And don't forget the self esteem.

Thought To Meditate On:

When the storms of life are crashing down around us, remember the one who said He would calm the storm. Sit quietly and wait on God. He will take care of it, if we let him. Or we can fight, scream, argue and explode. Forget the battle and turn to Him first. He is all we need.

Thoughts and Revelations:

by Lacy Enderson

Firm Foundation

♥

Psalms 40:1-3

I waited patiently for the LORD; he turned to me and heard my cry. He lifted me out of the slimy pit, out of the mud and mire; he set my feet on a rock and gave me a firm place to stand. He put a new song in my mouth, a hymn of praise to our God. Many will see and fear and put their trust in the LORD.

Towards the end of my drinking I found it was taking less and less alcohol to make me sick. Some nights I would drink what I considered to be a small amount of liquor, but I would still wake up with the shakes. So I would run to the store for more alcohol to make me feel better. Once, when I was living with my parents, I was sitting at the table with my mom trying to hide my hands from her because they were shaking so bad. She saw them and told me I needed to be careful. Her Aunt Joanne used to shake like that and she died emaciated and used up. I felt such shame. I started to get weak. I felt tired all the time. I could hardly wash my hair because raising my arms over my head was tiring. I went to the Doctor and the blood tests revealed liver disease. I was warned I had to quit drinking or I would die. It took at least two more years until I heeded his warning. It is amazing to me how much I suffered because of alcohol. Yet I continued to drink. I cried out to God with my mouth on a daily basis. But until I was willing to call out to God with my heart I wasn't ready to receive. It was then that He gave me the help I needed. He picked me up out of that pit and gave me a solid place to stand. Today I don't suffer self inflicted pain. Today I feel good waking up in the morning. Today I am sober.

Thought To Meditate On:

When we fell down, and couldn't get up on our own, we put our hand out to God. He took our hand and picked us up. He pulled us up and placed us on his firm foundation. A place that no wind can blow us over and no wave can knock us down. He is truly the solid Rock on which we stand.

Thoughts and Revelations:

We Came to Our Senses and Escaped

♥

Psalm 124:7, 8

We have escaped like a bird out of the fowler's snare; the snare has been broken, and we have escaped. Our help is in the name of the LORD, the Maker of heaven and earth.

I never meant to take college for granted. My father gave me every means available to get an education, but I didn't want one. He bought me a new car, put me up in an apartment, and paid my tuition and all of my expenses. This was every student's dream. But I was an alcoholic. I didn't think like normal kids. When I quit college my family was so disappointed. But I believe God had a hand in that decision. If I had continued going to school I would probably have ended up dead. Fraternity parties were an alcoholic's dream. I went to every party I could find. Most nights I fell asleep in strange places and woke up not knowing where I parked my car. One night, a boy slipped a drug into my drink. When I woke up I had no idea where I was. My college career quickly became dark and dangerous. I had to quit. At the age of eighteen it isn't easy to understand emotional problems. It's even harder to try to tell your parents about them. I could not have put into words what I was going through. So I got pregnant, quit school, got married and had babies. It was exactly what I needed at that time. Had I not been an alcoholic, my school experience would have been wonderful. But today, I live to tell about it.

Thought To Meditate On:

When we finally make the decision to quit drinking, God intervenes and breaks those chains of bondage to alcohol that hold us captive. He picks us up out of the dungeon of despair and puts us in a Royal Palace He created just for us. He called us to be priests and kings. Let us desire to live like one.

Thoughts and Revelations:

At the Name of Jesus Every Knee Will Bow

♥

1 John 5:19,21

We know that we are children of God, and that the whole world is under the control of the evil one. We know also that the Son of God has come and has given us under-standing, so that we may know him who is true. And we are in him who is true even in his Son Jesus Christ. He is the true God and eternal life.

It is every abnormal drinker's greatest desire to be able to drink like a normal person. Alcohol is cunning, baffling and powerful. I've heard it said that alcoholism is waiting outside the door of every alcoholic doing pushups, getting stronger and stronger until the next time that person takes a drink. The disease progresses whether we take a drink or not, but when we do, we are far worse off than before we ever quit. It gets worse, never better. I have a friend who was struggling to stay sober. She would get some sobriety and then drink again. The alcohol continuously lied to her and told her she could have just one. She had friends over for dinner one night who liked to drink beer, so they brought a six pack with them. When they went home they left two beers in her refrigerator. Everyday, she opened her refrigerator and saw those two bottles of beer. And one day that beer called her name and she answered. She told me she had one. Then she drank the other. And then she went to the store to buy more. When I saw her that night all she could say was, "I don't know what happened." We are all children of God, but we are under the influence of the evil one. We must never turn our backs on the dangers that lie waiting. They can hit us hardest, when we least expect them. My friend should have poured those beers down the drain as soon as her guests walked out the door. Unfortunately she had to learn this the hard way.

Thought To Meditate On:

God sent His son Jesus into the world to save us from evil and corruption. He became our Savior and our hope, but we must accept him first if we are to receive all He has to offer us. God saw fallen men and provided a way out, for Jesus is the Way, the Truth and the Life. So accept him today. He has already accepted you.

Thoughts and Revelations:

God of All Comfort
♥

Psalm 121:1-3,5-8

I lift up my eyes to the hills, where does my help come from? My help comes from the Lord, the Maker of heaven and earth. He will not let your foot slip, he who watches over you will not slumber; The Lord watches over you. The Lord is your shade at your right hand; the sun will not harm you by day, nor the moon by night. The Lord will keep you from all harm, he will watch over your life; the Lord will watch over your coming and your going both now and forever more.

Not only am I an alcoholic but I have been bulimic, I smoked cigarettes, and I know what it's like to be addicted to prescription pills. I have experienced the horrifying feelings of trying to find comfort and solace in a carton of ice cream or a bottle of Vicodin. I know the pain of being so uncomfortable in my own skin that I wanted to drown out the pain and make it go away. I have experienced the pure misery of the narcotic pill. I convinced myself that if I took three instead of one I'd feel even better. Then I would go through days of constipation and nausea only to turn around and do it again and again. I thought I was taking the pills to get rid of my pain. Now I know that what I was really trying to get rid of were the painful emotions. I didn't want to walk through them alone. But I have been delivered into the hands of a competent God. He can heal me from every discomfort. He can carry me over rough water or He can be my bridge. He offers me a firm place to stand and a loving place to rest my head when I want to cry. And when the day has come to an end, I am headache free. I am not constipated. I am not nauseous. I sleep restful and wake up feeling refreshed. I would not trade His peace for any substance in the world. He is a cool drink of water.

Thought To Meditate On:

When the trials of life become too heavy, we willingly lay them down before God. He takes each and every one of them from us so we don't have to carry them anymore. Let go of the troubles that overwhelm you and let God deal with them. Let them all go. Choose today to experience His freedom.

Thoughts and Revelations:

by Lacy Enderson

God is in Control

♥

Psalm 37:3-7

Trust in the Lord and do good; dwell in the land and enjoy safe pasture. Delight yourself in the Lord and he will give you the desires of your heart. Commit your way to the Lord; trust in him and he will do this: He will make your righteousness shine like the dawn, the justice of your cause like the noonday sun.

I know what it's like to fight the world and everyone in it. I'm good at it. I've spent a lifetime giving people advice. Don't people know that I know what is best? "How to be Happy According to Lacy," would have been a best seller. But nobody ever listens to me. They continue to do as they please. Then one day somebody told me that I am powerless over people, places and things. They said that I need to get off the director's chair and quit trying to run the show. That chair belongs to God. He really is an intelligent God. He really does know what I need. He even knows what is best for my husband, my children, my friends and all of the people I disagree with. They told me my only job is to pray. I pray that he would guide me. I pray for wisdom in helping those around me who are still sick. I trust that he has a plan and that I can be part of that plan. But he is the director and I am simply a servant. Use me God. Guide me and show me the way; your way.

Thought To Meditate On:

If God could do anything for his people, it would be to do everything.

Thoughts and Revelations:

He Stands By Me
♥

Psalms 6:7

In the day of my trouble I will call to you, for you will answer me.

I am not a pretty alcoholic. Some drinkers become charming and are the life of the party. I simply lose all of my inhibitions and become a raving maniac. I have experienced more "morning after" regrets than I care to remember. It was usually then that I called out to God, "Lord, if you get me out of this one I will never drink again." But by afternoon I would be on my way to the store to buy another bottle. When I look back at all of the shameful things I did I cannot believe I continued the crazy behavior for so long. But then maybe I continued in the craziness because of all the shameful things I did. Being sober meant I had to be aware. Awareness meant I had to feel the shame. Alcohol let me forget. I was really good at calling out to God after the mistakes were made, but God wanted me to call on Him before I took that first drink. In the day of trouble I will call to Him, for He will answer me. And I believe His answer will be "I love you, my child, very much. Abide in me and I will give you strength." What an awesome God we serve!

Thought To Meditate On:

No matter how bad it gets, God still sits on the throne. So come before His throne of grace and find mercy to help you in your time of need.

Thoughts and Revelations:

Just Say No

♥

2 Timothy 2:22

Flee the evil desires of youth, and pursue righteousness, faith, love and peace, along with those who call on the Lord out of a pure heart.

If I had been paying attention when I was a teenager I would have known from my very first drink that I was an alcoholic and an addict. But at the age of fifteen my thinking was that alcoholics were all old men who lived on the street and drank alcohol out of brown paper bags. My brother took me to my very first party in the summer before my first year of high school. I was so excited. I thought my brother's friends were so cute. When we got to the party I immediately found the wine sitting on the counter. You know the kind, Boonesfarm, a teenagers favorite. I sat on that counter next to that wine and I did not move until the wine was gone. My brother was so embarrassed and angry with me. He swore that he would never take me to another party again. That was the beginning of my alcoholic adventure. Whether drinking or sober, alcohol had been in the center of my thinking since that party. And it began when I was only fifteen. So if you think you are too young to have a problem with alcohol, think again.

Thought To Meditate On:

One of the hardest things we can do at a young age is to stand up for what we believe, and just say no. If we are raised with God in our lives we have a much better chance of walking away. If we are not, then God help us.

Thoughts and Revelations:

In Desperate Need

♥

Psalms 18:4-6

The cords of death entangled me; the torrents of destruction overwhelmed me. The cords of the grave coiled around me; the snares of death confronted me. In my distress I called to the LORD; I cried to my God for help. From his temple he heard my voice; my cry came before him, into his ears.

I woke up one morning from a blackout to discover I had consumed two full bottles of vodka. I am lucky I ever woke up at all. It amazes me how a person in a blackout can walk, talk, and function, and never remember doing any of the things that were done. I've been told some bizarre things I've done in a blackout, that I had no recollection of the next day. One morning I woke up and found my husband's shorts on the floor filled with lettuce. I could come up with no logical explanation for this and absolutely no remembrance of it either. I heard one lady talking about a blackout she had experienced. She was sitting on her bed with a gun in her mouth. Somehow her friends talked her into putting the gun down, but the next morning when they told her what she had done, she was mortified. They say alcoholism is a killer disease. I am amazed that more of us do not die while drinking and using drugs. I am grateful to God that he delivered me, before my luck ran out. Or maybe I should call them blessings. I truly believe he was watching over me even when I was drinking. Probably even more so.

Thought To Meditate On:

Death and destruction lurk around every corner looking for an alcoholic to destroy. We tried to find happiness in a bottle and all we found was emptiness and heartache. God is waiting for us to call on Him for help. And when we do, He will come to our rescue.

Thoughts and Revelations:

by Lacy Enderson

Give Them All to Jesus

♥

John 14:1

"Do not let your hearts be troubled; Trust in God; trust also in me.

I have suffered with some serious depression in sobriety. I know if I work on my sobriety to the best of my ability and work with other alcoholics, I am not supposed to get depressed. Maybe I am doing something wrong. When my second husband left me I called my girlfriend over and we shared a bottle of vodka. That's what I did when my heart ached. I drank. When Saturday night came and I was alone and lonely, I would fill my sipper cup up with beer, and I would go to the bowling alley and watch the people bowl. Alcohol took away the lonely space. When I became sober, even though I believed and trusted in God, the lonely place was still there sometimes, without alcohol to fill it, I found myself depressed. I try not to sit in my loneliness for long. I know it's not healthy for me. Today I try to imagine a happy place and then I go there in my thoughts. I stay only long enough to find the peace I need and then I return to my world ready to go on. It is comforting to know that depression always lifts in time. At least it always did for me. Sometimes it's best to simply read a good magazine and eat a hot fudge sundae. In the morning, everything seems brighter.

Thought To Meditate On:

Bad news we can't do anything about can be very frustrating. But God says to trust in Him and He will replace our troubled minds with peace and serenity. When there is absolutely nothing we can do, we must let God deal with it. He knows what to do. He can fix it for us. But we have to let Him.

Thoughts and Revelations:

My Mind is Stayed on Thee

♥

Isaiah 26:3,4

You will keep in perfect peace him whose mind is steadfast, because he trusts in you. Trust in the LORD forever, for the LORD, the Lord , is the Rock eternal

I have lived in nineteen different places in my life, and I am not very old. The first two homes were with my parents. I moved away from them when I was seventeen. For the next twenty years I moved seventeen times. I feel sorry for my kids when I think of how many times they have been uprooted. I attended one elementary school, one Jr. High and one High school. They went to different schools every year. I didn't give them much stability. I found a problem with each home I had. There was always something wrong. One house was in a neighborhood that had no sidewalks. I felt my children needed a safer place to play. One house had too many earwig bugs. Fumigating did not get rid of them. The apartment didn't have a washer or a dryer. I got tired of laundry mats. I could go on and on. After some sobriety and clarity, I came to realize it wasn't the homes that had problems, it was me. I was not happy. I was looking for happiness in my surroundings and when my home didn't provide my inner peace, I moved. Everywhere I went, there I was. I took myself with all my problems each time I relocated. It wasn't until I became OK with myself that my home became OK. When I changed my life, and I found joy and happiness within, it didn't matter anymore where I lived. I am just grateful to have a home.

Thought To Meditate On:

It is nearly impossible to think about problems when I am singing a song of praise to God. If my mind is troubled or worried, and my thoughts are not what they should be, I start praising God. My mind cannot think two thoughts at one time.

Thoughts and Revelations:

17

by Lacy Enderson

Hate What is Evil. Cling to What is Good

♥

1 Corinthians 10:21,22.

You cannot drink the cup of the Lord and the cup of demons too; you cannot have a part in both the Lord's table and the table of demons. Are we trying to arouse the Lord's jealousy? Are we stronger than he is?

In the summer of my sophomore year, a friend and I went to a fourth of July party. The crowd was older because they were friends of her eldest brother. There were quite a few people at the party. They were playing volleyball in the backyard. They were drinking and cooking food on the barbeque. I felt out of place. I was too young to be there and I wanted to drink. But I was afraid. I had already had my share of hangovers and I was afraid of what would happen if I drank too much. And I knew I'd drink too much because I always did. I found a book on a shelf in the living room and I sat down in a big chair to read. I felt safe. I planned to sit in that room and read until it was time to go. But I was an alcoholic. That beer started calling my name from the moment I sat down until three hours later when I heeded its call. I began to drink. The evening was mellow. I never did anything I'm ashamed to talk about. What shamed me was the fact that I could not say no to that beer. I was not able to go anywhere alcohol was served without getting drunk. Now that I am older I understand the disease of alcoholism. When I was in high school I didn't. I was not able to have a good time without drinking and I could not drink without getting drunk. I know teenagers who have sobered up. I am happy someone showed them the way to sobriety at an early age. I wasn't so lucky. I was thirty when I first saw the advertisement for recovery on TV. But that's not important now. What is important is I am sober today. For every situation I went through as a teen, I have a story that might help another teen to get sober sooner.

Thought To Meditate On:

The Bible says that we should either be hot or cold in our relationship with God. He wants all of us, not just part of us. And rightfully so, since we are His. Choose God today. Choose all of Him.

Thoughts and Revelations:

Fear Not For I Am With You

♥

Psalm 46:1-3,10

God is our refuge and strength; an ever present help in trouble. Therefore we will not fear, though the earth give way and the mountains fall into the heart of the sea, though its waters roar and foam and the mountains quake with their surging. Be still, and know that I am God.

I remember when I first got sober. I would sit and contemplate all of the good reasons I could come up with for taking a drink. What if my pet rat were to die? That would be a good excuse to drink. What if my parents were to divorce? Wouldn't that be a good excuse for drinking? What if my mother died? That would surely be a good excuse to drink. I really wanted to stay sober but I couldn't imagine that it would actually be forever. But then my pet rat did die, and I didn't drink. I cried and cried but was able to get through it. My grandpa died and I stayed sober through that too. My father even died and drinking was never an option. Life happens, but there isn't one situation that will ever be better because of alcohol. Sometimes the pain is great and I find myself crying uncontrollably. But in time the pain subsides. God is greater than my grief. He is bigger than my pain. Imagine it this way: I can either reach out and grab that bottle or I can reach out and grab the hand of God.

Thought To Meditate On:

No matter what circumstances we face, God is always with us. His love will protect us from every adversity and His perfect love casts out all fear. There is nothing in life that will ever feel better to an alcoholic than being sober. I speak from experience.

Thoughts and Revelations:

Run to Obtain the Prize

♥

2 John 1 :8,9

Watch out that you do not lose what you have worked for, but that you may be rewarded fully. Anyone who runs ahead and does not continue in the teaching of Christ does not have God; whoever continues in the teaching has both the Father and the Son.

I had looked into alcohol recovery a few years prior to actually making an honest attempt at getting sober. I attended Alcoholics Anonymous meetings every Wednesday night for four weeks. What the people talked about didn't make much sense to me, so I didn't hang around them for very long. I managed to stay sober on my own for about four months. During that time I read a book called "Twelve Steps to Happiness." This was the greatest book on how to live life. It wasn't based on recovery from anything in particular. It was generalized. It could have applied to any bad habit. I attended co-dependency anonymous meetings for a while with a friend. At first she thought she might be an alcoholic so she went to AA. After a few months she decided she was co-dependent and not an alcoholic. I liked that idea. I didn't want to be an alcoholic either. So I joined a co-dependency group also and set out to tackle all of my emotional problems. I went every week for six months. I learned about control issues and how I allowed other people's choices to affect my life in negative ways. I was taught about relationships and how to allow others to be themselves and make their own decisions. I actually learned a lot of very important information. It helped me tremendously. But the bottom line was, I was still an alcoholic. My drinking progressively got worse and eventually I had to quit. I am still very co-dependent, but an alcoholic just as well.

Thought To Meditate On:

Cherishing my sobriety, I fight hard not to take my new gift for granted. Continuing daily in prayer, I seek God's strength to get me through every temptation. Victorious living has become my new way of life. What a shame to have gotten this far just to have to start all over again.

Thoughts and Revelations:

I Want to be More Like Jesus

♥

Galatians 5:24-26

Those who belong to Christ Jesus have crucified the sinful nature with its passions and desires. Since we live by the Spirit, let us keep in step with the Spirit. Let us not become conceited, provoking and envying each other.

My second husband's greatest passion was his guns. His friends would come over and they would clean their guns for hours. They would go shooting often. They were like little boys with toys. One summer we took a trip to the desert. We brought his friends, my children and a friend of mine. The whole purpose of the trip was to shoot guns. We drove all night and when we arrived I was exhausted. My children were already asleep. But the men had other plans. They began shooting their loud guns with no regard to my feelings whatsoever and I was angry. Trying to sleep with the guns going off was impossible. So I got up and began drinking. I must have had eight beers within an hour. The more I drank, the madder I got. Before long I was letting him know how angry I was. Being tired and drunk himself, he didn't care what I thought. He basically told me to go away. Upset and distraught, I drank a bottle of cough syrup and took a bottle of aspirin. I'll show you, was my attitude. If I had to die to get his attention, that's the way it had to be. Of course I didn't die. I slept all day. What a poor victim I was. I didn't get my way, so I pouted. To this day the insanity of my behavior baffles me. Why would I place so much importance on what someone else thought about me that I would destroy myself? Today, nobody has that kind of power over me.

Thought To Meditate On:

We turned to God and asked Him to heal and deliver us. He set us free from addictive behaviors as well as destructive personality disorders. Anger, rage, and envy begin to disappear. In order to truly become what God wants us to be we must let Jesus do a complete change in us, from the inside out. Tell Him today, "I surrender all to thee."

Thoughts and Revelations:

by Lacy Enderson

A New Creation

♥

Isaiah 43:18,19

"Forget the former things; do not dwell on the past. See, I am doing a new thing! Now it springs up; do you not perceive it? I am making a way in the desert and streams in the wasteland."

I am not proud of the person I used to be. At times, when I allow myself to think about the past and the horrible things I've done, I become so depressed I can hardly function. So, needless to say, I don't dwell on the past very much. I know, in order to completely heal, I have to go back through my past and deal with some issues. But this can be painful. I don't like to believe that I really caused people that much pain. But I did and I spend each day trying to mend what I have broken. There isn't anyone in my life who has disowned me because of the wrong I have done to them. I would not blame them if they did. The people in my life have accepted me exactly the way I am, as hard as that is for them at times. They love me no matter what. They don't always agree with me but they support me the best they can. I sometimes feel like they treat me as if I am a fragile porcelain doll who is easily broken. That is probably because I am.

Thought To Meditate On:

God advises us not to look back on what we have done but to look forward at what He is doing. We can allow our mistakes to hinder us, or we can forgive ourselves and move on. God promises to make our lives better than we ever could have hoped for. Isn't that exciting?   .

Thoughts and Revelations:

Spiritual Nourishment

♥

Joel 2:26

You will have plenty to eat, until you are full, and you will praise the name of the LORD your God, who has worked wonders for you; never again will my people be shamed.

The stomach is for food and food is for the stomach, but the heart is to be filled with the spirit of God. We were born with an innate natural instinct to satisfy our physical hunger with food. God put this human desire and need within us because He knew we needed food in order to survive and stay alive. But man was not created with a natural desire to satisfy his spiritual hunger. We are born spiritually empty and we must learn how to fill this void with God. Sometimes we get confused and we try to fill this spiritual void with everything but God. We eat because we think that food will fill the emptiness, but the heart still remains empty. We drink, we smoke, we have sex, and we take drugs, all in an attempt to satisfy our spiritual need. But we end up dissatisfied every time. God has given to each man the ability and resources necessary to find Him. All we need to do is seek to find Him, and He will be found. He will provide for every need we have, both physical and spiritual, but we must first make the decision to follow Him.

Thought To Meditate On:

God provides food for every animal. How much more will He provide for His children whom He loves. We must not worry about what we will eat or what we will drink. God will meet every need we have. Not only our physical needs but our spiritual needs as well.

Thoughts and Revelations:

by Lacy Enderson

Mind of Christ

♥

1 Corinthians 2:11,12

For who among men knows the thoughts of a man except the man's spirit within him? In the same way no one knows the thoughts of God except the Spirit of God. We have not received the spirit of the world but the Spirit who is from God, that we may understand what God has freely given us.

It is embarrassing to know that God can read my mind. It is not that I am always thinking bad thoughts, but when I do I wish I could hide them. But as we all know, nothing can be hidden from God. I try to control my thinking, but every now and then I get mad at someone and anger and rage enters my mind, sometimes uninvited. Before I know it my thoughts are inappropriate. Knowing that my thinking affects my behavior I practice dwelling on the thoughts of God. When I do, my days and my attitude are better. It isn't that I want a polluted mind, but my humanity and sinful nature somehow gets in the way. Because I know that the corruption found on television is powerfully ineffective for my spiritual growth, I watch as little as possible. If I do find myself in front of the TV it is usually to view an old I Love Lucy, or Andy and Mayberry episode. These programs are safe. It is important for me to be pleasing to God in every area of my life. This includes my thoughts. So I pray this prayer on a daily basis. "May the words of my mouth and the meditations of my heart and mind be pleasing to you, Oh God." Just remember, part of being able to stay sober is staying serene. Serenity starts in the mind.

Thought To Meditate On:

God's Holy Spirit reveals to us the thoughts of God. God will tell us everything we need to know, if we ask Him. We will be given the mind of Christ and the wisdom of God.

Thoughts and Revelations:

Thy Will Be Done

♥

Psalms 131:1

My heart is not proud, oh LORD, my eyes are not haughty; I do not concern myself with great matters or things too wonderful for me.

It was when I allowed God to be the boss of my life and I quit thinking I knew what was best all the time, that I was given real peace of mind. I had to quit trying to control everyone around me and learn to accept people as they were. I met a man in recovery who had a hard time trusting God. He was never a Bible reader and he only attended church on holidays, but he knew God existed. Because he couldn't trust God, he drove the car and God sat in the passenger seat. He trusted in his own ability above God's. He feared the consequences of turning his life over to God and giving up his control. His head spun all day long in crazy confusion and he was constantly explaining his way out of the trouble he caused. His life was filled with daily chaos and he soon found that his very need to control, was out of control. One day, he decided to give God a chance. And when he finally got out of God's way, he experienced the peace of God he had never known before. God began to manage his life and he was restored to sanity. God will restore you to sanity too. But you have to get out of the driver's seat. If you have to, lock yourself in the trunk!

Thought To Meditate On:

Pride is the character defect that sets us up against God. When we take matters into our own hands and think we know what is best, we set ourselves up for a fall. No matter how smart or wise we think we are, compared to God, we're really not.

Thoughts and Revelations:

by Lacy Enderson

Powerful Witness

♥

1 Peter 2:11,12

Dear friends, I urge you, as aliens and strangers in the world, to abstain from sinful desires, which war against your soul. Live such good lives among the pagans that, though they accuse you of doing wrong, they may see your good deeds and glorify God on the day he visits us.

I was sitting in an alcohol recovery meeting listening to a man share every detail of his horrible life to all of us who were listening. He was obviously having a bad day because he had nothing nice to say about anything or anyone. He was especially down on recovery. He was a man who had seventeen years of sobriety. He should have had a better story to tell, even if just to give thanks to God for keeping him sober for so long. The problem was that there were newcomers in that meeting. These were lost souls who were trying very hard to find God and sobriety. But here they were in a meeting listening to a man share about how miserable his life was. All I could think was if I had been one of those newcomers, I would have went out and drank. The man made it sound like there was nothing good about being sober. What a shame to be so ungrateful for such a great gift. It is so important that we live our lives as an example to all who are lost and in need of hope. If we depict misery and depression it isn't too likely anyone will want what we have. We are all entitled to have bad days, but maybe those days are better left at home.

Thought To Meditate On:

Some people have a hard time believing that there is a God. It is up to us to show unbelievers that God is alive and real in us by our behavior. Peace, patience, kindness, and tolerance can be powerful and effective tools to show that God is real to those who don't believe. We must live lives filled with joy so others might see and want what we have.

Thoughts and Revelations:

Prayer of Deliverance

♥

2 Corinthians 1:10,11

He has delivered us from such a deadly peril, and he will deliver us. On him we have set our hope that he will continue to deliver us, as you help us by your prayers. Then many will give thanks on our behalf for the gracious favor granted us in answer to the prayers of many.

We are told until we are ready to quit drinking for ourselves, we will not ever fully recover. I had a friend who finally admitted he needed to quit drugs and he needed to taper off his alcohol consumption. His habits were causing his children sorrow and heartache and were interfering with the amount of time he chose to spend with them. He decided to quit for the kids. But a few days later he reasoned with himself; the children were still young and he had their whole future to spend time with them. He began to drink and use again. He decided that his deceased mother would have been ecstatic if he quit. She never saw him sober and he owed it to her to try one more time. But again, a few days later he convinced himself she was not around to keep him accountable and was back to his old habits. He thought he should quit for his wife. She had tolerated his addictions for years. He felt he owed it to her. But the bottom line was, she had never asked him to quit, so it must not have been that important to her. It wasn't until four years later he finally quit for himself and hasn't had a drink or drug in seven years. It is important to value ourselves as worthy. It is amazing what we can accomplish when we place value on our own lives.

Thought To Meditate On:

God saves us from sin and destruction. He works in us, giving us the ability to live according to His good purpose. God loves us too much to leave us the way we are. And we should love ourselves just as much as He does.

Thoughts and Revelations:

by Lacy Enderson

The Greatest of These is Love

♥

Ephesians 3:16

I pray that out of his glorious riches he may strengthen you with power through his Spirit in your inner being.

There are two types of drinkers. The happy drinker is friendly and social. He jokes around and has a good time. He slurs his words but manages to have fun and to be fun to be around. My husband was the other kind of drinker. He was nasty, foul mouthed, antagonistic, and always ready to fight. He was not fun to be around, but people stuck close to him because when he was drunk he bought everyone's drinks. The last bar fight he can remember was with an entire male softball team. They beat him to a pulp and he couldn't eat solid food for two weeks. At the end of such an evening, when he returned home, he would fight with his family, justifying and defending himself. Home didn't change his attitude. He was a bad drunk wherever he was. He ripped phones out of the wall and threw them, he punched holes in walls, and he verbally threatened the ones he loved. After years of this alcoholic rage and many attempts at sobriety, he has actually quit drinking. Does this sound like you or someone you love? The hardest part of sobriety is admitting you are an alcoholic and need help. But once you can honestly admit your need, help is on the way.

Thought To Meditate On:

Some people find it hard to understand the depth of God's love. Some people find it difficult to think God loves them at all. God's Word assures us that His love is for everyone. All we have to do is accept it. No matter what we have done in the past, God's love is for us all.

Thoughts and Revelations:

Be a Doer of the Word
♥

Hebrews 4:1,2

Therefore, since the promise of entering his rest still stands; let us be careful that none of you be found to have fallen short of it. For we also have had the gospel preached to us, just as they did; but the message they heard was of no value to them, because those who heard did not combine it with faith.

I thought it was strange how God set out to get my attention one day. I was walking around the grocery store looking for a few items when God told me to buy a dustpan. You may be thinking, "How did she know it was God and why would God care about a dustpan?" I know! I know! It sounds a little wacky. But when you hear God's voice, you know it is God. And who am I to question what God cares about. I really didn't need a dustpan because I used an electric broom. So I kept shopping. But the thought to buy a dustpan stayed with me until I was ready to pay for my purchases. So just to amuse myself I bought a dustpan realizing it couldn't hurt me to own one. The very next time I used my electric broom, it blew up. I was amazed. I couldn't believe it. God knew my electric broom was going to blow up so He prepared me in advance for my need of a dustpan. He loves me so much that He wanted to show me that even the simple things in life matter to Him. Now I try to listen carefully to every thought I have. After that experience I never quite know what God will be trying to tell me next.

Thought To Meditate On:

We can hear God's message of love and we can see the love of God in the lives of others. But if we do not take that message we hear and apply it to our own lives then its value to us is worthless. If we want to experience the joy of knowing God we must make it a priority to live as His message instructs. Only then will we truly understand how powerful God's love is.

Thoughts and Revelations:

by Lacy Enderson

Divine Inheritance

♥

1 John 2:29

If you know that he is righteous, you know that everyone who does what is right has been born of him.

My grandfather and his sister were alcoholics. Their mother, my great grandmother was also an alcoholic. The disease skipped a generation and landed directly on me. Out of my three siblings and myself I was the only unlucky recipient. I don't remember as a child ever imagining that I'd grow up to be an alcoholic. I don't remember ever being given the choice. I liked alcohol from as early as I can remember. When I was as young as six my father would allow me the first drink whenever I brought him a beer. I always made sure it was me who got the privilege. But who would have guessed I'd grow up to crave it? I have to say I feel blessed to know I am not diabetic. Nor do I have polio, multiple sclerosis, or any other crippling disease. I have the disease of alcoholism. My disease does not have a cure. My disease does not come with a badge of honor. My disease does not elicit sympathy from onlookers. My disease will destroy my liver, discolor my face, kill my brain cells, break apart my family, drain my bank account and hurt my children. The beautiful thing about my terrible disease is that it can be overcome by a power greater than myself. I call Him Jesus.

Thought To Meditate On:

Once we make a decision to accept Jesus as our savior we are invited into His family and He knows us by our names. Once God has us in His family he will fight hard to keep us with Him. He says he will never let us go. Isn't that nice to know.

Thoughts and Revelations:

I Will Rescue Him

♥

2 Timothy 4:18

The Lord will rescue me from every evil attack and will bring me safely to his heavenly kingdom. To him be glory for ever and ever. Amen.

I was invited to a dear friend's birthday party. I was excited because she had moved away after graduation and I had not seen her in quite a while. I invited another friend to go with me and promised her I would control my drinking. She knew about my alcohol problem and did not want to be put in a compromising situation. I had driven her home drunk before and it frightened her to think I would do it again. Being the alcoholic that I was I began to hide beers in the bathroom and drink them without anyone knowing. As far as my friend knew, I had only consumed one beer all night. When it was time to leave, my lack of common sense due to my intoxication took over and I drove her home drunk once again. I could barely see. My vision was completely blurred and yet I risked both of our lives because of stubborn pride and an addiction to alcohol. I was self centered, dishonest, and didn't care who got hurt when I was drinking. By the grace of God we made it home safe. I cringe at the thought of what could have happened.

Thought To Meditate On:

The devil's job is to weaken God's people. The Bible tells us that Satan comes to steal, kill and destroy. He knows our weakness and attacks us accordingly. God can and will protect us from every evil attack. He sees it before it ever happens and prepares the way for our victory every time.

Thoughts and Revelations:

by Lacy Enderson

Pride Comes Before a Fall

♥

Zephaniah 3:11,12

On that day you will not be put to shame for all the wrongs you have done to me, because I will remove from this city those who rejoice in their pride. Never again will you be haughty on my holy hill. But I will leave within you the meek and humble, who trust in the name of the LORD.

Most of us alcoholics, when reflecting back over our lives, are appalled by what we see. We see self centered, manipulating, egotistical, proud, afraid human beings. We were so full of pride that there was no room for anyone or anything else. After all, who wouldn't have wanted to be me? Richard was one such person. He built a successful business as a practicing alcoholic, (drunk all the time). He had a good income, a home, nice cars, and a family. He was married for seventeen years and had two daughters. Two years after he got sober his wife left him and filed for divorce. It took getting sober to see how much he was doing for her financially which left him completely amazed at her lack of appreciation. (He was so drunk all the time he didn't even know how much money he was making) It took a while for her to admit how tired she was of him. She hadn't married the home, or the cars, or any of the other material items. What she wanted was a little bit if her husband's time. And even in sobriety he wasn't giving her much of it. He finally came to the understanding that had it been him, he would have left too. And probably a whole lot sooner. Alcoholics tend to be blind to reality. We think we know what's going on, but really we haven't got a clue. And deep down inside, as long as we're drinking, we really don't care.

Thought To Meditate On:

If anyone knows how hard it is to completely follow the ways of the Lord, it is me. It seems no matter how hard I try to obey God and be good I am right back to my old bad habits falling flat on my face once again. As discouraged as I get from my complete lack of victory I know that if I keep trying eventually I will win. And when I do, it will be a victory very much worth fighting for. So, what is my point you ask? Don't give up.

Thoughts and Revelations:

Humble Thyself

♥

Micah 6:8

He has showed you, 0 man, what is good. And what does the LORD require of you? To act justly and to love mercy and to walk humbly with your God.

If I were to take a poll and ask how many people really like themselves just the way they are, I would guess that most people would want to change at least one thing about themselves. I have heard rude people justify their rudeness by saying, "I was born that way. It's just the way I am." So they live under the false belief that they are rude because God made them that way. I believe God loves us just the way we are. But he also loves us so much that he wants to see us change into kind, loving people. We have all had bad things happen to us. And we all live in a sinful world that brings out the worst in us. But Jesus made a blind man see. He made a crippled man walk. He gave a prostitute a cool cup of water and said that she would never thirst again. If he can do all these things, he can change a bitter person's heart. He can soften the spirit of a cranky drunk and he can break the chains of alcoholism. He wants to create in us a new thing. And if he tells us we will be like Him, He must be able to deliver us from being mean and nasty people. God wants to change our characters and dispositions. He wants us to be happy. But we must first want to change.

Thought To Meditate On:

God doesn't expect us to read His mind. He has laid all of His thoughts out for us in His Word as our guide for living. God tells us exactly what we need to do for Him in order to partake of His glorious blessings, and He also informs us of what will happen if we choose to reject Him. He leaves nothing to the imagination. God doesn't play mind games. If you want to know God's will, read His Word.

Thoughts and Revelations:

by Lacy Enderson

Patiently Waiting

♥

Romans 8:24,25

For in this hope we were saved, But hope that is seen is no hope at all. Who hopes for what he already has? But if we hope for what we do not yet have, we wait for it patiently.

I love the desert. The warm winds, the smell of sage in the air and the large open spaces bring a calm, serene feeling deep within my soul. There is something awesome about looking across an open field to see the sun actually coming up where the earth meets the sky. The desert has nothing blocking my view. If anything, I see a few Joshua trees, but they are never tall enough to block the full view of the mountains. Some people experience serenity surrounded by green trees and blooming flowers. Others find their peace in the sound of the ocean and the smell of the sea. God has blessed us all with different desires. That is what makes us each unique. One of the similar characteristics of God's people is the need to have something to hope for. We are told that without hope we would die. Our hope is the driving force we need as we trudge the busy road of our lives towards our individual goals. God wants us to have a hope and to live in constant expectation of what he is about to do. Instead of reaching for the drink, reach for hope.

Thought To Meditate On:

Sometimes we wait for what seems like an eternity. Deep down inside we want to be prettier, or thinner, or richer, or smarter but sometimes those innermost desires never manifest and our waiting seems endless. If we put our hope in something we know God wants to do for us, like set us free from alcoholism, we can be rest assured our waiting will not be in vain. If you hope for sobriety you will not be disappointed.

Thoughts and Revelations:

Gently Restored

♥

Galatians 6:1,2

Brothers, if someone is caught in a sin, you who are spiritual should restore him gently. But watch yourself, or you also may be tempted. Carry each other's burdens, and in this way you will fulfill the law of Christ.

I met a girl in recovery who was struggling to stay sober. I felt sorry for her because I saw how tormented she was. She was a drug addict. Her boyfriend was also an addict and every time she visited him she would give in to the temptation to use drugs. I asked her why she continued to see him and she said he was as much of an addiction as the drugs. I could relate. After a few months and no sobriety time, she left town. She said it would be easier for her to stay clean if she got away from him. She managed to put together four months without using, but when she came home her desire to use became greater than her desire to stay clean and she was back to using drugs again. I have been told that if I am not spiritually fit I will not be able to stay sober. It doesn't matter where I go. If I do not have a conscience contact with God everyday, I will drink. I suppose her lack of spirituality was the problem. Maybe she wasn't connected to God like she needed to be. Actually, it was none of my business. God put her in my life to love and encourage, not to judge or to fix. So I prayed for her that she would find the relationship with God that she needed to stay clean. I prayed that one day God would become more important to her than the drugs.

Thought To Meditate On:

One of the biggest obstacles in helping others is my need to control people. I know if they would just listen to me and do what I say everything would be all right. But I should know better. I had plenty of people telling me what to do and I never listened to them either. I got sober only when I made the decision to do so. Today I remember, prayer changes people, not me.

Thoughts and Revelations:

by Lacy Enderson

I Will Never Leave You

♥

Malachi 3:7

Ever since the time of your forefathers you have turned away from my decrees and have not kept them. "Return to me, and I will return to you," says the LORD Almighty.

I wish I could have put down the alcohol long before I did. I wish I could have saved God, my family and myself years of pain and misery. Towards the end of my drinking I was consuming more than a twelve pack of beer a day. When I was bloated and tired of beer I would start drinking the vodka because I needed something stronger to keep me drunk. Not to mention it helped me sleep at night. The only problem was the hard alcohol got me drunk too quickly and I'd have to start drinking the beer again. Looking at my face in the mirror and seeing how bloated and swollen I was I would then swear off the beer one more time. It was just a vicious cycle. I have pictures that were taken of me during this time. I looked horrible. I am so grateful that when I finally made up my mind to quit drinking, God was right there for me. He said he'd never leave me and he never did. And it is funny how my mind played tricks on me. What did it really matter, beer or vodka? In the end it is all just the same destruction.

Thought To Meditate On:

God waited patiently for me to come to my senses and put down the drink. It wasn't until I finally made up my own mind to quit drinking that He was ready to help me. Now that I am sober and drinking isn't an option, I sure wish I had listened to Him long before I did. But like they say, better late than never.

Thoughts and Revelations:

The Rock on Which I Stand

♥

Deuteronomy 32:4

He is the Rock, his works are perfect, and all his ways are just. A faithful God who does no wrong, upright and just is he.

My son went to school with a boy whose mother loved to drink even more than I did. She was definitely an alcoholic. She could drink me under the table. One night, she invited my kids and I over to visit. I thought it would be fun to have a friend to party with, so I agreed. It was perfect. My children could play with her children while we drank. It took no time at all before I was so drunk I couldn't keep my eyes open. I was not prepared to stay the night so I asked her boyfriend to drive me home on his motorcycle. I left my children and my car at her place. When I got home, I left the door wide open and passed out in my bed. The next morning my parents came by and saw my door open but my car gone and they panicked. They came inside and saw me sleeping so they went home. When I woke up I had to walk to where I had left my kids and my car. I hated myself that morning. I felt completely helpless. It wasn't too much longer before I discovered my need for God. I was so tired of my life, and I was disgusted at who I had become. When I asked Him to, God became my rock, my fortress and my deliverer. He helped me quit drinking and I haven't had a drink since.

Thought To Meditate On:

God doesn't make mistakes. His ways are honest and His intentions are good. We don't know what tomorrow holds, but we know God holds our tomorrow. He is solid as a rock and a strong fortress for us when we need Him.

Thoughts and Revelations:

by Lacy Enderson

Transforming Power of God's Spirit

♥

1 Samuel 10:6

The Spirit of the LORD will come upon you in power, and you will prophesy with them; and you will be changed into a different person.

God's power is awesome. I have seen downtrodden men and women transformed into well respected members of society by the power of God. There was a man who used to wander the streets of my town with a shopping cart. He was a homeless man and collected trash to make money. He obviously had mental problems. He rambled on and on to anyone who would listen. If nobody would listen, he would talk to himself. He wore the most outlandish outfits and hats. Sometimes he wore layers of unnecessary clothing. One Sunday I saw this man at my church singing in the choir. I couldn't believe it was the same person. God had taken a hopeless man and transformed him into a new creation. He was nicely dressed and very well behaved. I learned a lesson when I saw him up on the stage giving praise to God. No one is too difficult for my God to change.

Thought To Meditate On:

God's Spirit is powerful and effective. He can change obstinate, stubborn, hateful people into kind, loving, patient, and tolerant members of society. We ask God to send us His Spirit so we too can experience these changes in us.

Thoughts and Revelations:

Faith is Believing

♥

Hebrews 11:1

Now faith is being sure of what we hope for and certain of what we do not see.

I had to trust in the people who told me that my life would get better after I quit drinking. That is hard for an alcoholic to believe. I couldn't imagine a day without a drink, let alone a lifetime! Before alcohol quit working for me, it was relaxing and enjoyable to have a few beers around the pool, or to have a few drinks at dinner. Sometimes, cleaning my house with a six pack of beer was what I needed to get the job done. When the alcohol quit working and my drinking became a problem, I remember trying everything possible to get the good ole feeling back. It never came back, and it seemed the harder I tried the worse it got. The only solution was to quit. I was the skeptical one who came in doubting. But today I am living proof that life without alcohol has been everything and more than I was told. Faith and a power greater than myself have given me a life I never thought possible.

Thought To Meditate On:

Faith is knowing that God is working in our lives, even when we cannot see Him. It is faith that keeps us moving forward. It is faith that pleases God. By faith we can wake up each morning and know we will make it through another day.

Thoughts and Revelations:

by Lacy Enderson

The Door to My Heart

♥

Luke 11:9,10

"So I say to you: Ask and it will be given to you; seek and you will find; knock and the door will be opened to you. For everyone who asks receives; he who seeks finds; and to him who knocks, the door will be opened."

Jesus is referred to as the light of the world. His light shines on my darkest sin. His light exposes the darkness so that I might be aware of it's existence. Alcoholics live in denial. I don't like to admit it when I am wrong. If I were to own up to the sin in my life then I would have to acknowledge my need to change. For a long time I was not ready, nor willing, to do this. God was knocking on the door of my heart for many years before I opened it. I used to peer at Him from the window, letting Him know I was OK. I would say hello every now and then. But letting Him actually come into my life and change me took a long time. Now that I have experienced the marvelous life of living sober, the door to my heart is never closed. I welcome the changes He wants to make in me. When I finally accepted Jesus into my heart to be my Lord and savior, He brought me the power and strength to overcome all of the sin in my life. Today, I hate what is evil and I cling to what is good.

Thought To Meditate On:

Be persistent in your prayers because God promises to answer every one of them. Make your requests known to Him and He will make your paths straight. You might not get the answer that you want but you will definitely get the answer that you need. Sobriety is about learning to trust that God actually knows what is best for you.

Thoughts and Revelations:

My God is An Awesome God

♥

Malachi 2:5,6

"My covenant was with him, a covenant of life and peace, and I gave them to him; this called for reverence and he revered me and stood in awe of my name. True instruction was in his mouth and nothing false was found on his lips. He walked with me in peace and uprightness, and turned many from sin."

I have experienced the serenity and hope that was promised to me when I gave up alcohol. I was told if I quit drinking God would give me a life better than any life I could have imagined. I remember when I had nine days of sobriety and I went to my parent's house to tell them. I was so excited! My brother was there and his comment was, "Nine days sober, big deal". For him, nine days without a drink was no big deal. He probably went longer without a drink all the time. But for an alcoholic even one day without a drink is a miracle. Each day that I did not drink offered me new opportunities. I began to look forward to each new day to see what plans God had for me. My life took on a whole new meaning. Life began to unfold and excitement at what God would do next became my new outlook. No longer do I live in the fear and dread of the next problem I will face. Every night I go to bed and thank God for one more day sober.

Thought To Meditate On:

I am incredibly grateful to God for giving me the gift of sobriety. I could never have dreamed of a life this good. If you are still drinking I highly encourage you to give sobriety a chance. What you don't know, can hurt you.

Thoughts and Revelations:

by Lacy Enderson

Child-like Faith

♥

Matthew 18:3,4

And he said: "I tell you the truth, unless you change and become like little children, you will never enter the kingdom of heaven. Therefore, whoever humbles himself like this child is the greatest in the kingdom of heaven."

It is not until we experience the pain of despair that we begin to doubt. If every promise made to us was kept, and every prayer we prayed was answered, we would have no problem believing. But unfortunately as we grow older we experience disappointments. Our ability to trust becomes hindered as promises are broken and dreams are smashed. I was blessed to have parents who honored their word. If they told me we were going somewhere, we went. If they promised to buy me something, they did. It has not always been that way as an adult. I have been promised places and things that never materialized. The feeling of despair is overwhelming. Fortunately, we have a God who keeps his promises and honors his Word. In fact, the Word tells us, "Hope does not disappoint us." God wants us to trust and believe in His promises. He wants our hope to be only in Him. Unlike people, He will never let us down.

Thought To Meditate On:

Children are gullible. They will believe just about anything. It is not until they get older that they will experience the pain of un-kept promises. God wants us to come to Him, believing as a child does. We learn that people do fail us, but God never will.

Thoughts and Revelations:

Deliver Me Oh Lord

♥

Isaiah 38:17

Surely it was for my benefit that I suffered such anguish. In your love you kept me from the pit of destruction; you have put all my sins behind your back.

If my drinking produced good things, I would still be drinking. If I managed to drink and still function normally, I never would have had a need to quit. If the Doctor had not told me my liver was damaged, then alcohol would not have been a problem. But alcohol never produced anything good, and I never functioned normally while intoxicated. My liver was so impaired that I was told if I didn't stop drinking I would die. I went through a lot of anguish in order to see my need for God. But if all my anguish brought me to God, then I'm thankful for it. I made an appointment with a mental health Doctor because I thought I was going crazy. I thought I was having a nervous breakdown and I was losing my mind. After the Doctor evaluated me and told me I was mentally fine, he asked me if I had a drinking problem. Of course I said no. I finally realized that it was the alcohol that was making me crazy. It was time to quit drinking and turn to God. My imagined insanity proved to be a blessing. God got my attention in order to save me from the pit I was quickly falling into. He pulled me out of the darkness and despair, and restored me to sanity.

Thought To Meditate On:

We hear people say they are grateful for the trials in their lives. They say it was the hard times that led them to God. If all the anguish of all the mistakes we have made lead us to God, then they are all worth it.

Thoughts and Revelations:

by Lacy Enderson

Hiding Behind A Wall Of Darkness

♥

Galatians 5:19

The acts of the sinful nature are obvious: sexual immorality, impurity and debauchery; idolatry and witchcraft; hatred, discord, jealousy, fits of rage, selfish ambition, dissensions, factions and envy; drunkenness, orgies, and the like. I warn you, as I did before, that those who live like this will not inherit the kingdom of God.

When I got sober it was amazing how many character defects I had. I wasn't aware of most of them because I hid them behind a mask of deception. I remember someone told me that I was a manipulator. I could not believe how stupid this person was. I was not a manipulator! I hated manipulation in other people, and I swore I would never behave like them. But when I began to look at myself more carefully I discovered that not only was I a manipulator, I was good at it. Getting sober was just the first step of sobriety. Without the alcohol I was left with me, and I wasn't a very nice person. I wanted to be more like Jesus. Though I was willing to do anything to become a better person, I was very good at justifying my behaviors. Justification stands in the way of change. So God showed me that sin is never justified. When I realized this, God began to change me. It took a lot of hard work and lots of defeat, but today I can honestly say I am not a manipulator, and I'm proud of it!

Thought To Meditate On:

It took a long time to become the person I really wanted to be. Natural instincts caused me to behave in ways that were very unattractive. No matter how hard I tried I just couldn't be tolerant, patient or kind. But then one day when I wasn't paying much attention I noticed I had changed. Thank you, God.

Thoughts and Revelations:

God Has All Power

♥

Colossians 1:11,12

being strengthened with all power according to his glorious might so that you may have great endurance and patience, and joyfully giving thanks to the Father, who has qualified you to share in the inheritance of the saints in the kingdom of light.

The Word says God is omnipotent. That means He is all powerful. If I rely on Him and His power working in me, I can do anything. The Bible tells me, "I can do all things through Christ who strengthens me." My problem is, I continue to rely on my own strength instead of God's. God told me I could never drink again, but I didn't believe Him. I believed that I had strong enough will power to stop drinking after 2 drinks. So I played this game with myself over and over again. Some days I actually won. I would drink a few drinks and stop. I convinced myself that God was wrong and I could drink if I wanted to. But then I'd go on a binge, get really drunk and cause a lot of damage. I played my game for a long time until I was completely beaten up. When I finally submitted to God's instructions and gave up the drinking, I felt ten times better, and wondered why I ever wanted to drink in the first place. God wants me to live in his kingdom of righteousness. He wants me sober. He wants me to experience the freedom I found in Him, not in alcohol. He wants me to quit playing games and just trust that He does know what is best for me.

Thought To Meditate On:

We are no longer prisoners in the devil's dominion of darkness. We have been transferred into God's kingdom of light. In this perfect kingdom we are given the power to overcome every temptation we are faced with. No longer do we stand alone unprotected in the dark.

Thoughts and Revelations:

He Has The Answer

♥

2 Timothy 3:16,17

All Scripture is God breathed and is useful for teaching; rebuking, perfecting and training in righteousness, so that the man of God may be thoroughly equipped for every good work.

God makes it perfectly clear in His Word that nothing should master or control our lives. He doesn't want us to be obsessed with anything other than Him. A hot fudge sundae once a week is harmless, but a hot fudge sundae everyday is a potential problem. The same goes for sex and alcohol. I knew a man who did nothing in moderation. When he drank, he drank a lot. When he smoked, he smoked continuously. One day, while he was quite drunk, he decided to ride his bike to the store for more cigarettes. While he was riding, he passed out, fell off of his bike and hit his head. He was in a coma for three days before he finally died. If my friend had been asked how he would have liked to spend his last three days on earth, I'm sure he would have chosen time with his family. He may have wanted to tell them how sorry he was for his lifestyle. He might have even wanted to make things right with his God. But my friend chose to drink himself into a stupor and end his life before his time. God did not create our bodies to be able to withstand the punishment we inflict upon them with our compulsive and destructive behaviors. Although we are tough, we are still fragile in many ways. We were built for moderation. When I forget this, I remember my friend and how much he lost that day on his way to the store.

Thought To Meditate On:

For every problem, God has a solution. The answers are in His Word. The Bible is our manual for life. He knew our needs before we were ever born and He provided a way to meet those needs in His Word. For every struggle, problem or trial we face, He has the answer.

Thoughts and Revelations:

Choose Life

♥

1 Peter 1:22,23

Now that you have purified yourselves by obeying the truth so that you have sincere love for your brothers, love one another deeply, from the heart. For you have been born again, not of perishable seed, but of imperishable, through the living and enduring word of God.

When my children were younger I taught preschool to make some extra money. One of my favorite stories to read to the children was "The Giving Tree" by Shel Silverstein. It is about a boy and his relationship with a tree. At first, the boy enjoys the tree. He swings from the tree's branches. He eats the tree's apples. He climbs up the tree's trunk. But as the boy grows older, he begins to want other things. He begins to see the tree in light of what it can give him. Throughout his life, the boy takes the tree's apples and sells them for money and he cuts down the tree's branches to build a house. He takes the tree's trunk to build a boat and in the end, the tree is left with only a stump. This book reminds me of how an alcoholic can treat his family. We take and take, always justifying in our minds why we deserve all we take. The people in our lives are like the tree. They give and they give until they have nothing left to give. And then they wait and wait and pray that we will come back to them. And in the end they offer us a shady place to rest when we finally come to our senses and get sober. If you have the chance, read this book. Depending on where you are in your recovery, it will either make you feel really good, or really sad.

Thought To Meditate On:

I have never quite been able to figure alcoholics out. For some reason we feel like we are so much better than everyone else. And we honestly believe that other people should do everything we expect of them. When I got sober I had a rude awakening. Nobody owed me anything. In fact, it was the other way around.

Thoughts and Revelations:

by Lacy Enderson

Let your Life Shine

♥

1 Thessalonians 5:5-7

You are all sons of the light and sons of the day. We do not belong to the night or to the darkness. So then, let us not be like others, who are asleep, but let us be alert and self-controlled. For those who sleep, sleep at night, and those who get drunk, get drunk at night.

I used to live for the night life. I couldn't wait until after dark so I could go out. It became such a habit it was near impossible to stay home. I remember when I was in high school. On friday nights my friends and I would pile into a car and drive around all night looking for a party. If I could find a party, I could drink. Other kids went roller-skating and to the movies. But those activities were not appealing to me. I wanted alcohol. If I couldn't drink, I went home. When I got older I hung out in the places that served alcohol. I went to nightclubs at least five nights a week where I could dance and drink until 1:30 in the morning. I would get home at 2:00 am, wake up at 6:00 am, and go to work. I basically lived on four hours of sleep each night. I did this almost every night for quite a few years. (It wasn't until later that I began drinking at home.) My alcohol dependence developed slowly. It took a long time to develop a need for the alcohol. But once the want turned into a need I knew I had to stop drinking. Today I welcome my sleep. No, I cherish my sleep. I could not imagine getting less than 8 hours of sleep each night. How I ever managed to function throughout my day on four hours of sleep, I will never know. What a joy it is to stay home, read a good book and fall asleep early.

Thought To Meditate On:

It's funny when I think about all the so-called "fun" I thought I was having when I was going out drinking every night, because to be perfectly honest, their wasn't anything fun about it at all. In reality, I was absolutely miserable. I was looking for something to fill the emptiness inside. I have to admit, in those nightclubs, nothing was ever found.

Thoughts and Revelations:

I Shall Not Want

♥

Psalms 34:6-10

This poor man called, and the LORD heard him; he saved him out of all his trou-
bles. The angel of the LORD encamps around those who fear him, and he delivers
them. Taste and see that the LORD is good; blessed is the man who takes refuge in
him. Fear the LORD, you his saints, for those who fear him lack nothing. The lions
may grow weak and hungry, but those who seek the LORD lack no good thing.

When I was a teenager I suffered from depression. I knew something was wrong
with me because I never felt well. I could not deal with my feelings. I hated how I
felt. Most of the time I wasn't even sure what I felt. I just knew I felt uncomfortable
most of the time. One afternoon when I was fifteen I went on a binge, eating anything I could find in my house, trying to make myself feel better. The bad feelings
would not go away. I got tired of eating so I started drinking the rum my dad had
under the cupboard. I remember every emotional pain I felt instantly disappeared. It
was the answer I had been looking for. I was standing drunk in the kitchen when my
dad came home and told me that my sister had broken her arm and we had to go to
the hospital. What? My dad had no sense of smell, but I was horrified that someone
in that hospital would smell the alcohol on my breath. I walked as far away from the
people as I could, and lucky for me, I never got caught. I often wonder if my life
would have gone differently with counseling. Maybe someone could have helped
me with my problems and spared me years of torment. Unfortunately, no one knew I
needed help. I never told anyone about my feelings. My secret of bulimia, alcoholism and depression stayed only with me. As a sober adult I have learned it is
quite normal for a teenager to have some depression. Nowadays they have many
programs available to young girls who suffer. It would be easy for me to lament
about all those wasted years. But I am far too grateful for the way I feel today to
give much thought at all to those horrendous years of my past.

Thought To Meditate On:

I often hear people say they would love to go back and be a teenager again. I can't
think of a worse thing I would rather do. In fact, I thank God everyday that I don't
ever have to relive those years again. But for those who suffer, please get help.
There is help for you no matter what it is you suffer from.

Thoughts and Revelations:

by Lacy Enderson

Seek First the Kingdom

♥

1 John 2:15-17

Do not love the world or anything in the world. If anyone loves the world, the love of the Father is not in him. For everything in the world—the cravings of sinful man, the lust of his eyes and the boasting of what he has and does—comes not from the Father but from the world. The world and its desires pass away, but the man who does the will of God lives forever.

Giving up the comfort of alcohol and drugs without a God to help you is a very bad idea. I have seen non-believers suffering with withdrawal symptoms, spinning out of control. The comfort they were used to getting from the drugs was gone and they had nothing to fill the void. They were miserable. There is a very good reason 12-step programs require that you replace the addiction with help from a power greater than yourself. One man I know replaced his addictions with other bad habits. He loved to gamble. He gambled every chance he got. He bet on sporting events, he played the pyramid scams, he played pool and of course Vegas was his favorite vacation spot. Money became his obsession. He couldn't get enough. He bought a new car every six months. Every year he moved into a bigger house. Nothing he purchased satisfied his desires and he was always seeking to buy something new. He had more shoes than any woman I know. And his closets were overflowing with new clothes. The corruption in the world became his master. He allowed lust and perversion to entertain him. He got caught up in the immorality of having other women. An affair was second nature to him. He was a smoker and enjoyed his food. It seemed there was nothing he would not try for satisfaction. Nothing, except for God. It is sad for me to see someone run so far away from the only thing that will truly satisfy. God, I pray you will open their eyes. Extend your mercy to them, as you have done for me. Allow them to know you. Once they do, they will never need anything of this world again. I can attest to that.

Thought To Meditate On:

I will be the first person to admit, this world is not an easy place to live in. Everywhere we go there is desire and temptation that sometimes is just to great to resist. But I will also gladly be the first one to tell you that God can and will get you through it if you ask Him to. Since I gave up drugs and alcohol, there is nothing in this world that will ever get me to use and drink again. But until I quit, I did not know this.

Thoughts and Revelations:

Robe of Righteousness

♥

Ephesians 4:22-24

You were taught, with regard to your former way of life, to put off your old self, which is being corrupted by its deceitful desires; to be made new in the attitude of your minds; and to put on the new self, created to be like God in true righteousness and holiness.

After getting sober and learning how to live a fairly peaceful life it amazes me how I ever survived the chaos my life was in when I was drinking. It frightens me to think I could fall right back into that old lifestyle with just one drink. I am convinced it would take only one small moment of insanity and I'd be floundering all over again. And believe me, I never want to go back to that horrible place. There is comfort in knowing God is near. As long as I wake up every morning and make a conscience decision to follow God I know I have a real good chance of staying sober that day. I also know if I allow anger or resentment into my mind I face a strong possibility that I might drink. Drinking was a substitute for God. Instead of seeking God when life got hard, I had a beer. My comfort came in a bottle. (Maybe yours comes in a pint of ice cream.) My answers were found in a pill. I turned to a substance for temporary relief and the despair in my soul grew bigger and bigger. The pit I was digging grew deeper and deeper. Morning after morning I lay on my couch unable to move. The nausea and the headaches were debilitating. My children scurried around me and I could hardly find the strength to feed them. Only by the grace of God was I able to pick myself up. I cried out to God and he heard me. He gave me the help I needed. Now I revel in my moments with Him. I am completely consumed by His love. I wouldn't trade the relationship I have with God today with any mind altering chemical.

Thought To Meditate On:

It is easy to think that a beer or a box of cookies will make you feel better, I mean time after time it worked. But imagine a time when you don't need anything to make you feel better because you already feel good. I know it seems impossible but when you fully surrender to God and trust in Him completely food and alcohol will be the last thing on your mind. Imagine that.

Thoughts and Revelations:

by Lacy Enderson

I Will Follow Where He Leads

♥

James 4:13-15

Now listen, you who say, "Today or tomorrow we will go to this or that city, spend a year there, carry on business and make money." Why, you do not even know what will happen tomorrow. What is your life? You are a mist that appears for a little while and then vanishes. Instead, you ought to say, "If it is the Lord's will, we will live and do this or that."

I never asked God what He thought about me getting married. I never inquired if it was His will or not. I married three times without His permission. During a pre-marriage counseling session the pastor asked my first husband if he believed in God. He said no. God was telling me something, but I wasn't listening. Or maybe I was listening, but I just didn't want to hear what was being said. The Bible tells us that people should not be unequally yoked. Believers and unbelievers do not mix, just as light cannot mix with the darkness. We didn't mix. We were headed in opposite directions. We had nothing in common. And eventually he left me for another woman. My second husband was a daily drinker. This was before I had become one. While we were dating he would come over after work smelling of alcohol. Each time I asked him if he had been drinking, he would say no. I had a fear of being alone. I liked it when he came to see me so I turned my head to his drinking and refused to look at it. I was in denial. I guess I thought if I ignored the problem it would go away. It didn't. My only request of him was he not drink on our wedding day. I told him if he did I would walk off the altar. He had been drinking. The smell was embarrassing, as I was sure the pastor could smell him too. But I stayed and we exchanged vows. I began drinking more after that marriage. His drinking was an open door for me to drink whenever I wanted. Divorce was inevitable. I married based on what I felt I needed, not based on God's best for me. Today I ask God to direct my decisions. Today, I listen.

Thought To Meditate On:

I know sometimes we skip asking God's approval because we are afraid He might say no. But wouldn't it be better to find out something is not going to work out before we take the plunge. This principle works not only for marriage, but in business, in buying a home and even with the kids. God sees into your future. Ask Him what He thinks. You will be glad you did.

Thoughts and Revelations:

Selfish Ambition

♥

Proverbs 30:7-9

"Two things I ask of you, O LORD; do not refuse me before I die: Keep falsehood and lies far from me; give me neither poverty nor riches, but give me only my daily bread. Otherwise, I may have too much and disown you and say, 'Who is the LORD?' Or I may become poor and steal, and so dishonor the name of my God."

When I was younger I had an imaginary weight problem. I call it imaginary because it was all in my mind. I thought I was fat, but I wasn't. I can see now when I look at pictures of myself, I was not fat at all. I remember thinking, "If only I were thin, then I'd be happy." I focused on my weight daily. I thought of little else. I took diet pills and ran miles everyday. I walked when I could have driven. I was bound and determined to be thin. Because of this obsession I missed out on a whole period of my life. I was not happy, because my happiness was determined by what I looked like. At times I have the same problem with money. If only the bills were paid, then I'd be happy. If only I had extra money in the bank so I could feel financially secure, then everything would be all right. I cannot believe how much money I spent when I was drinking. The cost of the drinks was one thing, the baby sitter so I could go out was another. Money was never an issue when I was drinking. I always had enough money to buy alcohol. I made sure I had the resources available to fund my alcoholism. Now that I'm not drinking I can't imagine how I ever paid for my booze. I barely have the money to pay the car payment, or the rent. I try not to focus too much on what I don't have. I trust God enough to know he will provide. But sometimes it gets scary. So, today my happiness is not based on money or how thin I am. I refuse to live my life that way. Today I am content with exactly the way God made me and I am comfortable with what He provides.

Thought To Meditate On:

Someone told me once I should thank God for the bills. I couldn't imagine thanking God for something I despised so much. But when I did, those bills no longer had power over me. I started thanking God and all my financial fear subsided. I don't always know how He does it, but every month, each and every bill gets paid. So instead of worrying, I thank God for the good things He will do for me when I let the problems go and trust in Him.

Thoughts and Revelations:

by Lacy Enderson

Seek and Ye Shall Find

♥

Acts 17:27,28

God did this so that men would seek him and perhaps reach out for him and find him, though he is not far from each one of us. 'For in him we live and move and have our being.' As some of your own poets have said, 'We are his offspring.'

One night a group of my friends and I got together for a night on the town. We went to a local club to dance. They had a lotto game being played that night so I picked my six numbers. I had just as good a chance to win as anybody else. I drank, danced and had a great time. After a few hours I left the club to visit a friend who was bartending in a restaurant across the street. She served me free drinks and we talked. The friends I had gone out with didn't like it when they couldn't find me so they left. I didn't care. That was their problem. I went back to the first club in time for the lotto game to begin. By this time I was completely intoxicated. They began calling out the numbers to the lotto. Each time they called a number I had, I screamed (I was a loud drunk). I had all the numbers. I won. They set me on a chair in the middle of the dance floor and gave me lots of neat prizes. When they asked me what my favorite song was I requested a song that was special to my husband and I. We were separated at the time and I was sad. As the song played I sat on that stool and cried. I told everyone about my husband and how sad I was because we were apart. I blubbered like a drunken idiot. Talk about making a public spectacle out of myself. The next morning I felt like such a fool. I hid under my pillow for hours from my embarrassment. What a sight I was, drunk and crying. I will never forget that night. It is the remembering that helps me stay sober. It reminds me of where I never want to be again.

Thought To Meditate On:

I thank God everyday for giving me such a great memory. It is the remembering that has proved to be one of my greatest allies. There is no greater remedy for alcoholism than the remembrance of humiliation. All I have to do is think back over my past and it almost 100% guarantees that I will never drink again.

Thoughts and Revelations:

Suffering Servant

♥

1 Timothy 6:18,19

Command them to do good, to be rich in good deeds, and to be generous and willing to share. In this way they will lay up treasure for themselves as a firm foundation for the coming age, so that they may take hold of the life that is truly life.

I met a girl in a meeting who needed a ride home. She was a nice person so I gave her my phone number and told her to call me sometime. I wanted to be helpful and driving her around was something I could do for her. She called me a lot. Not always for rides. Sometimes just to talk. She had a lot of anguish in her life and she didn't have many friends. It seemed she ended friendships before people could get too close. I felt sorry for her. The wall around her was a mile high. She told me stories about people in her life and what they had done to hurt her. What she said led me to believe the relationship problems were her fault. But I never told her that. I just listened. A few months and many rides later, she called to see if I would take her to a meeting. I told her I wasn't going to a meeting that night. I had planned on going, but my husband wasn't feeling well. Her response was very rude. Her words were, "You can't go to a meeting because your husband isn't feeling well? Whatever." And she hung up. I was shocked. What kind of appreciation was that for all I had done for her? I let that hurt my feelings for about five minutes and then I let it go. My intuition about her was right. She was lousy at friendship. She got too close to me and burned the bridge before I could. Not that I ever would have, but her fear was based on what other people had done to her in the past. Nothing I did could erase her fear. She never called me again. When I see her, she won't even look at me. That is OK. Today I know if I do my best for others and I treat them well, then I've done my part. What others choose to do in return, is none of my business.

Thought To Meditate On:

I learned a long time ago that I cannot control other people. I cannot make them behave the way I want them to. I must allow people to be who they are. People are not always nice. But when I step back and allow them to be who they are I no longer find myself feeling responsible for them. I can love them just the way they are or I can choose to walk away from them knowing that I did my best for the relationship. I am not responsible for everyone else's reaction towards me. What freedom there is in knowing that.

Thoughts and Revelations:

by Lacy Enderson

Tempted but Without Sin

♥

1 Peter 2: 21-23

To this you were called, because Christ suffered for you, leaving you an example, that you should follow in his steps. "He committed no sin, and no deceit was found in his mouth." When they hurled their insults at him, he did not retaliate; when he suffered, he made no threats. Instead, he entrusted himself to him who judges justly.

For my birthday one year my second husband and I took a trip to Las Vegas. It was one of many. It was a lot of fun. We usually had a good time. The relationship wasn't going well, but we always managed to put the problems behind us when we went on our trips. We were actually very good friends. We just didn't do well being married. The financial part of the trip didn't go well. We lost quite a bit of money. Something we were used to. But this time my husband seemed especially upset. I asked him what was wrong. He said to me, "I was praying we would win a lot of money so I could afford to get you counseling". I was mortified. Me need help? I didn't have any problems. What was he talking about? I didn't speak to him the whole drive home. It was him who needed help, or so I thought. I honestly could not see my faults. I was so focused on what everybody else was doing wrong I never had time to look at myself and see what was wrong with me. I feel sorry for my husband. I did have problems. Some were devastating to him and our marriage, but I couldn't see them. Looking back I recognize the problems I had, unfortunately, a little too late. I have since allowed those problems to teach me. I have looked at them as growing experiences. I have used my knowledge to do things differently this time. When my new husband has a problem with me, I tell him, "You should have known me before I met you, this is nothing compared to how I used to be". Of course I am still growing. I will never be perfect. But at least today I'm willing to try.

Thought To Meditate On:

I wish it were easier to live righteous all the time because I so desire pleasing God. I cannot explain fully the feeling of knowing that God is happy with me. But on those days when I feel I did my best and my attitude towards others is good, it just feels right. And with right living comes peace, quietness and assurance forever.

Thoughts and Revelations:

Faith Without Works is Dead

♥

James 1:21,22

Therefore, get rid of all moral filth and the evil that is so prevalent and humbly accept the word planted in you, which can save you. Do not merely listen to the word, and so deceive yourselves. Do what it says.

I had been suffering stomach pains that went on for a month or so. I wasn't sure if they were associated with drinking. I would expect they could have been since I was heavily drinking every night. The pain would wake me in the night and I'd sit in a bath full off hot water to alleviate the discomfort. This was the only relief I could find. In the evenings friends would come over to visit. They'd be drinking in the front room with my husband, and I'd go to bed. I would lie there in pain knowing the beer would aggravate my stomach, but angry that I couldn't drink. And angry that my husband was having a party without me. I felt he should have stayed sober for my sake. He was making it very hard for me. On Thanksgiving we went to my parents for our annual gathering. I felt OK and decided to have a beer. I made the comment, "I hope this beer doesn't hurt my stomach". My mother asked me why I was drinking it if I was afraid it would hurt me. I was so mad. What do you mean why am I drinking it? How dare you ask me, was my response. I didn't even know why I was drinking it. But in my anger and rebellion (probably at myself) I left my family's Thanksgiving meal. There were many days during my drinking when I was confused. I did not understand much of what went on inside me. For a long time I did not know why I did what I did. Today, I know. And today I understand. I am forever grateful to God for the knowledge he has given me, about myself.

Thought To Meditate On:

I spent a lot of time reading God's word and memorizing scripture but was drinking alcohol every night. The Bible says we should hide God's word in our hearts so we might not sin against God, but I found myself following my sinful nature even with a heart full of God's word. Alcoholism is a disease. And once I treated it like a disease I was able to quit. So in spite of all your failure, never give up on your daily pursuit of God and His word. Never give up on yourself because God never will.

Thoughts and Revelations:

Make it Ever True

♥

2 Corinthians 10:17,18

But, "Let him who boasts boast in the Lord." For it is not the one who commends himself who is approved, but the one whom the Lord commends.

I have a friend who is always talking about his accomplishments. In practically every conversation I hear about what he has done, where he has gone and what he has acquired. Lately he has had a streak of bad luck. He can't quite measure up to who he once was. His abilities are not producing the same results. Step three of the twelve steps is a hard one for him. He is finding it hard to turn his life over to the care of God. He believes in God, but trusting Him has not been easy. Relying on his own strength and ability made him a huge success. Now that he has God in his life his own power isn't working for him anymore. God requires more from us when we claim to believe in Him. Doing things our own way has to be smashed. My friend shared with me some fear he was having about work. He was afraid there wouldn't be any work lined up when his present job was complete. So I mentioned to him, he should just trust God and go forward one step at a time. One day on the job-site a realtor was driving by and stopped to look at the property. The house they were building intrigued him. This man was looking for a contractor for a development and asked if my friend was interested. Within three days he had seven sets of plans for future work. This was an act of God. Nothing my friend did offered him this opportunity. It is the little "God shots" like these that help grow our faith and enable us to believe that God is working in our lives to bring about good results. It is very important that we give credit to God for our success without boasting in ourselves. We wouldn't even be alive if it were not for Him.

Thought To Meditate On:

The Bible tells us not to boast or brag about anything but God. We should never look at success and prosperity as an accomplishment of our own. It is God who gives us the ability to succeed. It says in His word, it is God who gives us the ability to get wealth. Make sure that God is glorified in all you do and He will bless your life.

Thoughts and Revelations:

Once and For All

♥

Hebrews 10:17,18

"Their sins and lawless acts I will remember no more." And where these have been forgiven, there is no longer any sacrifice for sin.

When I was a teenager I played on a softball team in a league I had played in for seven years. The team was made up of other teenage girls and some really fun coaches. We had a good time. Our team was invited to a three day tournament in Buena Park. I couldn't wait. I lived across the street from a man who bought me alcohol. He was the father of a good friend of mine and obviously wasn't playing with a sound mind. To this day I do not know why he did it, but when I wanted alcohol, he bought it for me. Did he not know how much trouble he could have been in had my parents found out what he was doing? I thought it would be fun to bring alcohol with me to the tournament, so I had him buy me two bottles of wine. I packed the bottles carefully in my suitcase and off I went. It was the second night when I decided it would be fun to pull out my bottles of wine, so I rounded up my little group and we set out to get drunk. Our hotel was next to a bowling alley where we hid to consume our wine. We had fun, until the coaches found us. The next day we were all hungover. We could not play ball no matter how hard we tried. Needless to say we lost the tournament. Our coaches were so disappointed. Our parents were not happy with us either. Alcohol always seems so innocent before it is consumed. Afterwards it reaps nothing but destruction. And the only thing innocent are the lives of those it hurts.

Thought To Meditate On:

The Bible tells us that Jesus was the final sacrifice for our sin. He took our sins from us and gave us His righteousness. But it is up to us to make the decision to stop sinning. There is only so much God can do for us since He gives us a free will to make our own decisions. It is true we are told He will forgive every sin we commit, but how much better would life be if we just stopped committing them. Aren't you tired of saying you're sorry? God knows I am.

Thoughts and Revelations:

by Lacy Enderson

Peaceable and Considerate

♥

Philippians 2:3,4

Do nothing out of selfish ambition or vain conceit, but in humility consider others better than yourselves. Each of you should look not only to your own interests, but also to the interests of others.

Because of some tooth pain my husband was having the dentist prescribed for him Tylenol with Codeine. I had already developed an unhealthy obsession for pills, and having narcotics around made me crazy. After the prescription for the pain killers was filled he brought them home and put them on top of the dresser. I yelled, "If you don't want me taking your pills, you need to hide them!" So he put them in a drawer under some things and thought they were safe. But an addict looks everywhere for the drugs. If they are not under lock and key, they will be found. The tooth pain was caused by a gum problem that required surgery. This meant more pills. The mental torment of having those pills in my home was unbearable. My husband was not a pill addict. He had overcome an addiction to a much harder drug, and he knew the obsession, and how hard it was to battle. I actually blamed him for my torment. I did not need to know those pills were in the house. Out of respect and consideration for me I felt he should have kept the whole situation to himself. Maybe he could have told me the prescription was for Motrin. Anything to spare me from what I went through. Today I am delivered from the obsession for narcotics. You could put a bowl full of Vicodin on the coffee table and I will not touch them. I used to love the feeling I got from a narcotic pill. Today, the thought of that feeling makes me sick to my stomach.

Thought To Meditate On:

One thing I have learned over the years is that not everybody considers others. I think it is a natural human response to think about ourselves first. I mean, aren't we so important? The Bible tells us not to be a stumbling block to others. We are told it is a crime to cause others to sin. We should have that same goal in mind for every area of our life. If someone is on a diet, don't order chocolate cake. If somebody is trying to quit smoking, don't light that cigarette. It is just common courtesy to care about other people. And it is just plain rude when we don't.

Thoughts and Revelations:

Call Upon Me and I Will Answer

♥

Mark 11:24

Therefore I tell you, whatever you ask for in prayer, believe that you have received it, and it will be yours.

I believe God answers prayer. I am convinced He knows the depth of my soul and hears my heart cry out to Him before I ever utter a word. But He still asks me to come to Him in prayer, believing that I will receive from Him when I pray. When my eldest son was four he was walking along the top of a brick wall when he lost his footing and fell on his head. A neighbor came running into my home frantic to tell me my son was knocked out. As I approached him he regained consciousness but informed me he could not see. He was dizzy and his walk was tilted sideways. I rushed him to the hospital and they immediately put him in for a CAT scan. They were concerned he would have brain damage. After he was admitted I called the prayer chain of the most dynamic church in town and the people started praying. When my son came out of that machine he was fine. His vision was perfect and his walk was straight. He was healed. I will never know the extent of the damage that had been done. But I do know that God came on the scene immediately when we called out His name.

Thought To Meditate On:

Faith is believing in God. For such a small word it has a very powerful meaning. What good is it for us to pray to God if we don't believe He is going to answer us. It seems ridiculous to me to say the least. The Bible tells us to lay our requests down before the Lord in the morning, and then to wait in expectation. If you have a request for God, tell Him what it is and do yourself a favor; believe He is going to answer you.

Thoughts and Revelations:

by Lacy Enderson

Blessed are the Pure of Heart

♥

Deuteronomy 28:1-3,6

If you fully obey the LORD your God and carefully follow all his commands I give you today, the LORD your God will set you high above all the nations on earth. All these blessings will come upon you and accompany you if you obey the LORD your God: You will be blessed in the city and blessed in the country. You will be blessed when you come in and blessed when you go out.

A few years ago my sister won a radio contest. When the song of the day was played the first person to call in won the prize. She was the winner! Her prize was $2,000.00. My sister is a believer in God and inquired what God wanted her to do with the money. God told her to fly our grandfather out here for Christmas. My grandpa was a preacher of the Word. He was my hero. I admired him very much. We wrote letters to each other often. I loved his letters. In fact I still have every letter he ever wrote me. He lived in South Carolina and didn't have much money to afford a trip to California to visit his family. My sister was obedient and put my grandpa on a plane for the holidays. He came to stay with us for two weeks. I cherished his company. During his visit we had the opportunity to talk about God. I loved to hear him preach. He was definitely a man of faith. He used to call me his little evangelist. I am completely convinced I have the relationship with God that I have today because my grandpa prayed for me. My grandpa died the following September. It was a sad time for everyone. But the joy of having that one last chance to spend time with him was the greatest gift we could have been given. I am grateful to my sister for her generosity. Because she was obedient to God, we were all blessed.

Thought To Meditate On:

Don't forget to pray for others. We might not always see those prayers answered but we can be confident that they are. Everyday I pray that God will keep my children safe and protected from all harm. I pray everyday for God's protection over my granddaughter. I am so blessed to know that my grandparents prayed for me. I am determined to give back by praying for others. I know sometimes our prayers feel small, but it could be that one small prayer that you pray that makes all the difference in the world to someone else.

Thoughts and Revelations:

Ask That You May Receive

♥

Psalms 20:4,5

May he give you the desire of your heart and make all your plans succeed. We will shout for joy when you are victorious and will lift up our banners in the name of our God. May the LORD grant all your requests.

When I decided to get sober for the umpteenth time, my husband wasn't ready yet to quit and continued to drink. For a month I stayed sober and tried my best to stay out of his way. Allowing him to make the decision to quit drinking on his own was extremely important. If he was not ready, his sobriety would be short lived. We can't get sober for anyone but ourselves. Any other motive is futile. I knew this. I had loved ones telling me for years I needed to quit drinking. I couldn't quit until I was ready. During that month that I stayed sober my marriage quickly took a turn for the worse. My husband was spending a lot of time at the bars, and on a few occasions he was out all night. I realize an alcoholic lives a very selfish life. We behave in ways others would never dream of. His behaviors were unacceptable to me in a marriage. Alcoholic or not, he had choices, and he was making the wrong ones. So I planned to leave. When I made the decision to go, it was amazing how God intervened and took over. I was provided with a house and my sister offered me a cash gift. All my needs were met. All my plans succeeded. God saw to it every detail was in order. But in the end I never left. I never needed to. The threat of my leaving woke him up to reality. He quit drinking and we remained together. I know God's will is not divorce, so it was hard for me to call it quits. But God was still there, working on my behalf. He saw into the future and He knew the outcome. He took a bad situation and turned it into good.

Thought To Meditate On:

Sometimes what we think we should do isn't what we should do at all. And sometimes those things we absolutely know we shouldn't do is exactly what we need to do. God has a strange way of turning bad situations into good but we must be obedient to what he is telling us to do, even if it seems wrong to us. God is smarter than we think.

Thoughts and Revelations:

by Lacy Enderson

The Works of His Hands

♥

Job 37:5,6

God's voice thunders in marvelous ways; he does great things beyond our understanding. He says to the snow, "Fall on the earth, and to the rain shower, Be a mighty downpour."

I often questioned the ability of God to bring to me what I needed, when I needed it. I had this strange notion if I had a husband in my life all would be well. I depended on a husband to take care of me. I came from the old school where women married and stayed home. My mom always stayed home. My dad went to work and provided for the family. I grew up thinking that my job was to clean house and raise children. Somewhere in our society that concept has been lost. The economy actually demands that women work also. We have patterned our lives to have bigger houses, better cars and more toys. A one-income family has become a thing of the past. My problem is I am still old fashioned. I still think I need a husband to provide for me. But why is this? As a single mother between my second and third husbands every bill was paid on time, I always had food to eat and gas for my car, and I still ordered pizza occasionally for my kids. God was a perfect provider. I had every single one of my needs met. I don't know why I ever doubted His ability. I am not saying that a husband can't provide. I'm saying my trust should never have been placed in one. I have been shown over and over, people can and will fail me. If I had remained focused on the 'Great provider', most of my difficulties today might have been prevented. Don't get me wrong, I love my husband. But today I put my trust in God. He is the one who ultimately provides.

Thought To Meditate On:

It took me a long time to learn that worrying was a waste of time. I don't know why I always felt the need to sit and worry about things when time after time nothing was ever accomplished that way. I was told to wake up in the morning raise my hands towards heaven and shout,"Thank you God for all of your provision today". So every morning that is what I do. And strangely enough, for that day, I have everything I need.

Thoughts and Revelations:

At My Right Hand

♥

Joshua 1:8,9

Do not let this Book of the Law depart from your mouth; meditate on it day and night, so that you may be careful to do everything written in it. Then you will be prosperous and successful. Have I not commanded you? Be strong and courageous. Do not be terrified; do not be discouraged, for the LORD your God will be with you wherever you go."

Did you know that if you don't pay your car payment, they will repossess your car? Unfortunately I had to learn this the hard way, twice. I could point the finger and blame, but I have learned to be responsible for my mistakes. Blaming others doesn't get me anywhere, and it never solved the problem. People are defensive. Nobody likes to accept responsibility for the bad things that happen. So I accepted responsibility and set out to fix the problem. I knew someone who owned a used car lot. I told him my situation and he gave me a car. A real cute '87 Excel. I was pleased to see the body was in good shape, but had it not been, I was still grateful. But the car had an oil leak and I could not afford to get it fixed. No problem, he gave me another car. This time it was a great big, 1986, yellow, 4-door Cadillac. This time I didn't feel so grateful. This was the type of car I made fun of. I vowed I would never be caught dead in a car this size. But here I was without a choice. I was shocked at how many people loved my car and stopped me on the road to tell me. I guess I was driving a classic. But that didn't change my mind. I was embarrassed and I hated that car. Three years later and by the grace of God my sister bought me a new car. It was the perfect size. And then I was free to sell the Cadillac, the car I never got used to. But now that it is gone I am happy to say it taught me a few lessons. Today I have humility. I am more accepting of others and more compassionate towards their misfortunes. And I am grateful. Even for a gift I do not want, I have learned to be appreciative.

Thought To Meditate On:

You know the old saying, beggars can't be choosers? Well, that is a great saying as long as you don't apply it to me. I mean, I don't want to sound ungrateful if you have something for me I really don't want, but sometimes that is the case. With so much arrogance and pride running lose on the earth it is a wonder anyone gets along. Everyone is always trying to be better than the next. It makes me grateful that I have a God who teaches me humility. There is freedom in acceptance and peace in gratitude. And humility brings contentment in who we are and what we have.

Thoughts and Revelations:

by Lacy Enderson

God is Able

♥

Numbers 14:7-9

"The land we passed through and explored is exceedingly good. If the LORD is pleased with us, he will lead us into that land, a land flowing with milk and honey, and will give it to us. Only do not rebel against the LORD. And do not be afraid of the people of the land, because we will swallow them up. Their protection is gone, but the LORD is with us. Do not be afraid of them."

It is unfortunate how spoiled children are these days. I blame the parents, myself included. Children are given whatever they ask for, and kids are never satisfied. Most teenagers nowadays have pagers. I never knew what a pager was when I was younger. I hear them asking for cell phones and some parents have actually bought their children one. My father raised me to be conservative. I never went without anything. But I was also taught to be happy with little. When I was a kid I remember wanting something because my friend had one, and my mom telling me I didn't need to have everything everybody else had. She was right. Unfortunately there are some very wealthy people. Rich kids are intermingled with the not so well off kids. It is hard for the less fortunate to see their friends with so much more than they will ever have. And they can't understand why they too can't have these luxuries. I have seen kids pout and manipulate their parents until they get what they want, and everyday there seems to be something else they think they need. I hate to see so much materialism amongst our young folk. And the worst part is when the parents really can't afford the extra expense, the children are angry and resentful. What is this world coming to? God help the children realize their value is not based on what they own, it comes from within. It comes from the satisfaction of knowing God. Everything they think they need will be destroyed someday, but the knowledge and blessings of God will last forever.

Thought To Meditate On:

It is not easy wanting something I cannot have. In fact, sometimes it is downright difficult. Wanting isn't going to cause something to materialize. And the only thing I am left with when I want something I cannot have is a lot of frustration. That frustration leads to drinking, drugs, smoking, and overeating, all in an attempt to feel better about what I can't have. Learn to be content. Contentment feels good all the time.

Thoughts and Revelations:

Let the Words of My Mouth be Acceptable
♥

1 Peter 3:10-12

For, "Whoever would love life and see good days must keep his tongue from evil and his lips from deceitful speech. He must turn from evil and do good; he must seek peace and pursue it. For the eyes of the Lord are on the righteous and his ears are attentive to their prayer, but the face of the Lord is against those who do evil."

My third husband was afflicted with Attention Deficit Hyperactive Disorder, Obsessive Compulsive Disorder, Neurotic Behaviors and my favorite, Tourette's Syndrome. He didn't run around screaming obscenities like they show on TV, but he would say inappropriate things at inappropriate times. This was greatly increased when he was nervous. When we first started dating it was hard for me to get used to the way he talked. It was easy to get my feelings hurt. One day we went over to visit my mom. He walked in her house and said, "I must like pain, I'm dating your daughter." I was mortified. I couldn't believe he just said that about me. And to my family. I don't think I spoke to him for 3 days. Over time I came to realize these were uncontrollable words. He never meant any harm. I read a book on Tourette's Syndrome and learned a lot of information about the disease. Gaining knowledge helped our relationship. I learned not to take his words so personally. In the time that we've been together I have developed an awesome sense of humor. I taught myself how to be quick with my own words so I could turn the situation into something fun. I had to learn to joke in order to maintain my sanity. I realize not every rude person is suffering from a disorder. In fact, most people aren't. But it is still important not to allow other people's words to offend me. If I hold on to my confidence of who I am in Jesus I can allow other people's words to roll off my back.

Thought To Meditate On:

I remember when I was drinking, I always felt so sorry for myself. I couldn't understand why people were so mean to me and how they could be so nasty. Everyone was out to get me and I wanted sympathy. There is a saying I have heard in sobriety: poor, poor, poor me another drink. Alcoholics are always looking for a reason to drink. And what a perfect reason, a personal offense. You know what I say about that today? Forgive, and get over it.

Thoughts and Revelations:

by Lacy Enderson

I Once Was Lost, But Now I'm Found

♥

Matthew 18:12-14

"What do you think? If a man owns a hundred sheep, and one of them wanders away, will he not leave the ninety-nine on the hills and go to look for the one that wandered off? And if he finds it, I tell you the truth, he is happier about that one sheep than about the ninety-nine that did not wander off. In the same way your Father in heaven is not willing that any of these little ones should be lost.

Why did God choose me? Why did God hear my cries for help? If I really stop to think about the millions of people on this earth who suffer the torment of an addiction it brings me to my knees. I was spared. God counted me worthy of His mercy. He saw me wandering down a dark road of misery and destruction going nowhere fast. He pulled me out of the hole I had dug for myself and gave me a second chance. God loved me enough to choose me for Himself. He broke the bondage of addiction off me and gave me a life I had only ever dreamed of. I have many friends who are still suffering with addictions and I wonder sometimes, why me? I think it is because I became willing. God called my name and I said yes. I believe He has the same hope available for everyone. But God can only help those who want His help. When I had had enough, and I was sick and tired of being sick and tired, I was ready for God to intervene. His divine intervention rescued me and provided me with the help I needed. When others who suffer are ready, God will help them too.

Thought To Meditate On:

It's hard for someone who is not an alcoholic to understand how hard it is for an alcoholic to quit drinking. For normal people, you just don't drink. For alcoholics all we know how to do is drink so to quit drinking is very difficult. Sometimes it takes an alcoholic years and many attempts at sobriety before they really get sober for good. Keep this in mind if you have a loved one who drinks. The worst thing you can do is give up on them. With each failed attempt they move one step closer to victory. Don't give up before the miracle happens.

Thoughts and Revelations:

Be Still and Know That I Am God
♥

John 14:27

Peace I leave with you; my peace I give you. I do not give to you as the world gives. Do not let your hearts be troubled and do not be afraid.

Changes are hard. I don't like change. I like my world to go the same way every day. I have my comfort zone and I don't want any interference. But sometimes God has different plans. He can see into the future and he knows what's best for me. So I pray and ask Him to help me face the changes with confidence and courage. I run on a schedule. I plan my life accordingly. I am not spontaneous. It doesn't matter what my schedule is as long as it is planned. This drives my family crazy. But I tell them, just give me at least a days notice and I will schedule it in. What is so difficult about that? I remember when I quit smoking, I did not know what to do with myself. It seemed I always had a cigarette in my hand and now I don't. It took me months to get over that habit. I think the change in my schedule was harder than the nicotine withdrawal. Giving up alcohol was another big change. A friend told me to picture myself standing on the edge of a cliff with nowhere to go. My only option available was to wait on God. So I waited. And God provided comfort and solutions for every dilemma I faced. I often wonder how people go through change and difficult times in life without God. I absolutely think I'd fall apart if God were not by my side. The circumstances would be completely unbearable. But God gives me peace and removes the fear. And He tells me everything is going to be all right. One of the hardest changes I have gone through has been the loss of my father. Nothing could have prepared me for that change. Everything in my life changed when my father passed away. But, by the grace of God I have survived. Life is different. But I have adjusted. And the good thing is, I always do.

Thought To Meditate On:

Using cigarette smoking as an example, I remember swearing I would take those cigarettes with me to the grave. I loved smoking and I was never going to quit. But having been a non-smoker now for quite a few years, I thank God everyday for taking the desire away from me. We kick and scream to avoid change even when it turns out to be the best thing that ever could have happened to us.

Thoughts and Revelations:

by Lacy Enderson

Treasures in Heaven

♥

Jeremiah 9:23,24

This is what the LORD says: "Let not the wise man boast of his wisdom or the strong man boast of his strength or the rich man boast of his riches, but let him who boasts boast about this: that he understands and knows me, that I am the LORD, who exercises kindness, justice and righteousness on earth, for in these I delight," declares the LORD.

My eldest son was in a very bad car accident. He was driving about fifty miles a hour and ran into the back of a parked car. He was not wearing his seat belt and was thrown into the windshield. Had it not been for his visor he might have gone through the window. The visor actually cushioned the blow. The man he hit was more concerned for my son than he was for himself. He had a phone and let my son call his father who came to pick him up. My son's car was demolished, but his physical damage was minimal. He had a headache for a few days and a cut on his head. A few weeks later a friend of his was also in a similar car accident. My son had the opportunity to see his friend and the damage that his face received. His friend was not so lucky. I shared with my son my prayer of protection I pray over him every night, and the gratitude that should be given to God for his life. My son should have died. But God saved him. God performs miracles everyday. Some are big and obvious and some are so small we never see them. If you have ever seen a drug addict come clean or an alcoholic give up drinking than you have witnessed one of God's biggest miracles. People who do drugs or drink usually do so to escape from reality. Life is too difficult, and they are trying to run away from it. When a person gets sober they must learn how to live in reality without a means of escape. It takes a lot of hard work, sheer determination and complete trust in God. Just because the drugs and alcohol are gone doesn't mean the problems disappear too. But, giving up the drugs and alcohol let the miracles begin. These people should have died, but God saved them. A miracle indeed.

Thought To Meditate On:

We miss out on a lot of great things God does because we don't pay attention, but it doesn't stop God from doing great things. Once the alcohol is removed we can clearly see how much God is working in our life. And oh how great He is.

Thoughts and Revelations:

God Loves a Cheerful Giver

♥

1 Chronicles 28:9

"And you, my son Solomon, acknowledge the God of your father, and serve him with wholehearted devotion and with a willing mind, for the LORD searches every heart and understands every motive behind the thoughts. If you seek him, he will be found by you; but if you forsake him, he will reject you forever.

I knew a man who loved to give extravagant gifts. But the motive behind the gift-giving was to gain much needed attention. He had a need to be validated. He needed people to like him. He lacked self esteem and had very little confidence in himself. To feel better about himself he not only gave things away, but he boasted and bragged to everyone else about all the nice things he did for others. He loved the praise. When he gave gifts he spent as much money on the wrapping and the ribbon as he did on the gift. He said presentation was important. He wanted others to be impressed by his kindness and generosity. If he gave cash to a friend, he made sure his other friends knew about it. If he put a tip in a tip jar, the person behind the desk had to be looking. It didn't matter if he could afford to be generous, he neglected his responsibilities in order to look rich. The instant gratification he got from impressing others was more important to him than paying the bills. He was constantly patting himself on the back. Praise and recognition is what he lived for. He loved God and even talked to God, but he never listened to God. Because he wanted to do things his own way, God stepped aside and let him. Before long his resources dried up and he had nothing left to give. His ability to impress others vanished. His so-called friends vanished too. He was left all alone with nothing and no one but himself. And since he didn't like himself, he was miserable and afraid. Confidence comes in knowing who we are in Jesus, not from what others think about us. And we learn, if someone doesn't like us for who we are, then they aren't worthy of our friendship anyway.

Thought To Meditate On:

We cannot live our lives based on what other people think about us. We will end up pleasing some and turning others away. We can't please everyone. But if we strive to please God we can't go wrong.

Thoughts and Revelations:

by Lacy Enderson

God is Stronger Than Man's Strength

♥

1 Corinthians 1:8

He will keep you strong to the end, so that you will be blameless on the day of our Lord Jesus Christ.

When God says He can keep me sober I must remember to rely on His strength and not my own. Considering I am an alcoholic and I don't have any strength against alcohol, I have to let God do it for me. I remember one morning waking up with the worst hangover I had ever had in my whole life. It was so bad I did not think I would make it through another day. I literally lied on the kitchen floor and moaned for what seemed like hours. So I prayed, "Dear God, I am so sorry I drank so much last night. I promise I will try harder not to drink. Amen." I felt I was sincere. But later on in the afternoon, when I started feeling better, beer wasn't sounding so bad anymore. I just didn't get it. I wanted to quit drinking more than anything. But I must have been trying to use my own strength because each time I tried, I failed. I prayed and asked God countless times for help but in the end I always drank. Day after day, week after week I grew more and more discouraged. Over and over again, no matter how I felt the next day, by the afternoon I was drinking. Through will power and determination I was able to stay sober for maybe a few days. But through God's power I will stay sober forever. I am so grateful that God removed the obsession for alcohol. I can actually get through an entire day without thinking of drinking. But only by the strength that comes from God and His power. It was never and will never be by my own.

Thought To Meditate On:

We can do anything one day at a time. Eventually, all of those one-day-at-a-times will add up to weeks, months, years and then to the rest of our lives. Alcoholics are real good at complicating things. We must keep it simple if we want to stay sober.

Thoughts and Revelations:

Wholesome Thinking

♥

Philippians 4:8

Finally, brothers, whatever is true, whatever is noble, whatever is right, whatever is pure, whatever is lovely, whatever is admirable—if anything is excellent or praise-worthy—think about such things.

It only takes one thought to change my whole attitude, good or bad. If I think about the ocean or the desert I feel peaceful and serene. If I think about alcohol or ciga-rettes I find myself craving them. If I think about an offense done against me I feel angry and defensive. I see and hear things throughout my day that cause me to lose control of my thoughts. It is my choice whether I will let those thoughts control my actions. I must never be in bondage to bad thoughts. I must be able to change my thinking to good thoughts at anytime, anyplace. Only then will I ever learn to master my thinking and stay sober. The Bible says not to look back, so I try not to dwell on the past. But sometimes I struggle with an awful memory that causes anguish in my soul. I often find myself thinking angry thoughts. And then I feel really bad and I have to repent. I mean, what kind of a person am I anyway. Try thinking an angry thought without feeling frustrated...it is absolutely impossible to do. The battle that goes on inside my head is like a war zone at times. I wish I had an on/off switch that I could turn to shut it off. Jesus tells me I am transformed by the renewing of my mind. My thoughts must be pleasing to God. The Bible tells me to think about things that are true, pure, lovely and excellent. I wish this were easier to do. But I always try to remember, if God asks me to do something, He will provide a way.

Thought To Meditate On:

Sooner or later my thoughts will effect my actions. If I think about chocolate cake or a hot fudge sundae it might be days before I eat them but eventually I will. When I quit smoking the hardest part was I could not stop thinking about cigarettes. Probably a good reason it took me ten years to quit. Once I learned how to think about other things, instead of the one thing I was suppose to be forgetting about, I found letting go was a whole lot easier to do.

Thoughts and Revelations:

by Lacy Enderson

Lead Me on a Straight Path

♥

Isaiah 58:11

The LORD will guide you always; he will satisfy your needs in a sun-scorched land and will strengthen your frame. You will be like a well-watered garden, like a spring whose waters never fail.

I met a man one night in recovery who was forced to be there by the judge. You know, part of the sentence for a DUI is alcohol school and recovery meetings. He was required to attend eight meetings and had his card from the court which had to be signed. His face was purple and bloated yet he claimed that he drank very little. He said he was in the wrong place at the wrong time when he got his drunk driving citation. Typical behavior for an alcoholic. Even after getting in trouble we still can't accept the fact that we have a problem. I believe that God allows us to get pulled over in order to get our attention or maybe even to save our life. Maybe God saw into the future of this young man and an accident was prevented by getting him off the road. God does know our futures. God is always in control. And He knows that an alcoholic driving drunk is nothing but trouble. God knows what we need. Unfortunately we don't always want the same things as God. All we know is how inconvenienced we are because we lost our driver's license. Every situation we encounter leads us one step closer to God. Some of us take a little longer to get to Him because we can't stop complaining. Instead of facing our problems, we deny they exist. We might not always be grateful for God's intervention, but God knows that one day we will thank Him; one day hopefully when we are ready.

Thought To Meditate On:

Sometimes it takes an alcoholic more than one drunk driving citation to stop driving drunk. It is the nature of an alcoholic to drink. And more times than I can remember I swore I would never drink and drive. But as soon as I was drunk all those great plans went right out the window. We do things while intoxicated we would never dream of doing while we are sober. That is why it is just a good idea to stop drinking. Instead of placing a band-aid on top of the splinter, take the splinter out.

Thoughts and Revelations:

Do Not Be Deceived
♥

1 John 2:20,21

But you have an anointing from the Holy One, and all of you know the truth. I do not write to you because you do not know the truth, but because you do know it and because no lie comes from the truth.

Alcoholism is a funny disease. It is a deceptive disease that lies to its victims. If you listen real close you can hear the alcohol say, "Come on, you can drink, I bet you can have just one!" Now of course I have never really heard that outright. Maybe I was just hoping, like I did every time, that this time I really could have just one. But it never happened that way for me. One drink always led to a six pack or more. I have watched as my friends drank outrageous amounts of alcohol night after night and swear they did not have a problem. But we all knew they did. My husband told me a story about a weekend when he was a teen. His parents went out of town and he decided to have a party. At that time he was working in a grocery market so he had access to as much liquor as he wanted. His party was a big hit. He and his friends played cards and drank all weekend. They placed a large bucket in the center of the table just in case one of the guys needed to vomit. If they threw up then they could drink more. This particular party lasted for three days. They drank until they could drink no more. My husband tells me that not one of those boys thought they had a problem with alcohol. To them, this was a perfectly normal and acceptable way to spend a weekend. My husband felt the same way and continued to drink for the next thirty years. Now that he is sober, he admits he knew he was an alcoholic at a young age. But quitting drinking was always the last thing on his agenda.

Thought To Meditate On:

Living in denial is what alcoholics do best. We love to pretend our alcohol problem doesn't exist. We learn it is beneficial to deny the existence of a bad habit we aren't ready to give up. It is funny to me how long us alcoholics will drink even when it makes us feel bad. Why in the world would we want to do something that makes us feel bad? But we do. And we continue drinking. Go figure that one out!

Thoughts and Revelations:

by Lacy Enderson

A Kind Man Benefits Himself

♥

1 Peter 2:1

Therefore, rid yourselves of all malice and all deceit, hypocrisy, envy, and slander of every kind.

When my children were little my sister attended a college in another state which was quite a distance from my home. She called often to see how we were doing and to check on my oldest son. She called him her "Little Sunshine." She said there was something about him that lit up her life. One night she called the house and my husband answered the phone. She heard me in the background yelling viciously at my children. When I was done reprimanding my kids I picked up the phone and she started to yell at me for my behavior. It angered her to hear me talk to her nephews that way. Instead of being sorry, I proceeded to tell her it was none of her business. I slammed the phone down and cursed her for thinking she was better than me. And what did she know anyway? She didn't have any kids and what did she know about my life? I mean, if she had my life, then she would understand. When she called back, I refused to talk with her. My husband's comment to my sister was, "Now you know what I put up with on a daily basis." I was a miserable human being for a long time. I was the victim of circumstances. I always had something to complain about and I always felt people were out to do me wrong. I was your typical victim and victims tend to victimize others. I feel bad about the way I used to speak to my kids. I hurt them emotionally. I am told it was because I was emotionally troubled. Today, I praise them and tell them how wonderful they are. It is my prayer that someday I might undue the damage I caused.

Thought To Meditate On:

Just because we make an honest decision to change, does not mean everything about us will be different overnight. Sometimes our character defects go unnoticed for years before we are aware of them. It is like a domino effect. As soon as we get rid of one personality flaw another will surface, and so on and so on until one day we might actually like who we are. And maybe, if we are lucky, others will too.

Thoughts and Revelations:

Dream in the Night

♥

Psalms 16:7,8

I will praise the LORD, who counsels me; even at night my heart instructs me. I have set the LORD always before me. Because he is at my right hand, I will not be shaken.

I have had several "Drunk Dreams" since I quit drinking. I am not sure exactly what they mean. But I do know that they are very real reminders of my alcoholism and how much I never want to drink again. I remember one very vivid dream early in my sobriety. In this dream I wasn't sober for very long and I got drunk. I wanted to keep it a secret. I didn't want to lose my sober time. In my dream, I was afraid somebody would find out that I had drank alcohol and I would have to start my sobriety all over again. If you have ever been in recovery than you know the amount of time sober is a big deal. We pick our sober dates and they become more important than our biological birth dates. I was grateful when I woke up to realize it was only a dream. Sobriety is very important, and I didn't want to get drunk. But it isn't about losing time. It's about the lives that were destroyed. It's about the children that were neglected, and unpaid bills. It's about the spouses who wondered where we were, and the parents who cried for us at night. It's about ruined health, damaged livers and smashed cars. God uses my dreams to remind me of what alcoholism can do. I am able to experience the insanity of the alcohol without actually drinking. This way, nobody gets hurt. This way, I can remember how much I never want to drink again. This is God's instruction for me at night.

Thought To Meditate On:

Drunk Dreams can be very important for a sober alcoholic. Nothing is better at keeping a drunk sober than the reminder of the alcoholic insanity.

Thoughts and Revelations:

by Lacy Enderson

Leader of the Pack

♥

Deuteronomy 28:13

The LORD will make you the head, not the tail. If you pay attention to the commands of the LORD your God that I give you this day and carefully follow them, you will always be at the top, never at the bottom.

I was a cross-country runner in school. I started running in eighth grade and continued until I graduated high school. My coach told me I ran like a deer. And I did. I had a great talent for running and enjoyed it very much. But my dad was very competitive. He used to tell me I needed to do better. He said I didn't practice hard enough. Because I was stubborn and rebellious, I just quit trying. I always did the opposite of what my parents said, even if it hurt me. I had a hard time accepting adult instruction. I did not like being told what to do. I experienced the same opposition with drinking. The more I was told I needed to quit drinking, the more I drank. People who told me to quit drinking just didn't understand. I was certain that life would be much better if people would just leave me alone. But they wouldn't. Everyone always had an opinion about what they thought I should do. As soon as someone mentioned that I shouldn't drink, the rebellious Lacy would take over. I would drink more. Why was everyone bothering me? Why did it seem like everyone thought they knew what was best for me? I wasn't stupid. I knew what I was doing. And I didn't need their help. When I finally got sober I realized the importance of obedience. I realized people only cared about me. Today I welcome opinions. Today I realize I don't know everything. God tells me if I humble myself and follow Him I will be the head and not the tail. I brought up the rear long enough. Now I choose to follow God with my head held high.

Thought To Meditate On:

What is constructive criticism anyway? To an alcoholic it is just another way of saying you are disappointed in me. I have learned that if I tell someone what to do I have to make sure my intentions are good. I must have their best interest at heart and not my own. If an alcoholic needs to quit drinking it must be because I care about his well being and not just about how much he is ruining my life. Sometimes it must be about others and not always about me.

Thoughts and Revelations:

Master of Everything

♥

Romans 6:16

Don't you know that when you offer yourselves to someone to obey him as slaves, you are slaves to the one whom you obey—whether you are slaves to sin, which leads to death, or to obedience, which leads to righteousness?

I was a slave to alcohol. Alcohol ran my life. It told me what I would do, and when I would do it. It told me how I would treat my husband and my kids. It was my master. I was its slave. I tried desperately on a few occasions to run away from the alcohol, but it always found me. I would break the bottles of vodka and pour the cans of beer down the drain, but it would always show up again. I lost my control over alcohol and my power of choice. I could no longer choose when I would drink and how much I would consume once I got started. Alcohol had a hold on me, a very tight hold. If I could go to the grocery store and get out without buying alcohol, it was a miracle. I would walk in the door and begin the conversation with myself, "I can buy just one beer." "No! You don't need a beer." "Only one. One won't hurt." "No! You won't have just one, and you know it." The conversation went on until I left the store. Some days I would win. Other days, the alcohol was victorious. This was a daily battle. Until one day, God had mercy on me and removed the obsession to drink. Alcohol lost its control over me and the victory was mine. Today, I am a slave set free. I still have a master. His name is Jesus.

Thought To Meditate On:

For the longest time after I got sober there were certain stores I could not go into. Stores where I frequently purchased alcohol became slippery places for me to go. Stores where I battled against the desire to drink carried far too many bad memories. It was best just to stay out of those places. Today I don't have that problem. I can go anywhere and not be tempted. But it took awhile. In the beginning of your sobriety do yourself a favor and listen to yourself. You will know what to do.

Thoughts and Revelations:

by Lacy Enderson

What a Wonder You Are

♥

Revelation 3:12

Him who overcomes I will make a pillar in the temple of my God. Never again will he leave it. I will write on him the name of my God and the name of the city of my God, the new Jerusalem, which is coming down out of heaven from my God; and I will also write on him my new name.

I bet you don't have any idea how proud God is of us. I know I can't fathom His love. I am told His love for us is a million times greater than a parent's earthly love for a child. Although I love my children dearly I know my love is not perfect. God's love is. When I was sober for two years my parents bought me a gold chain with two gold hearts. Each heart signified one year sober. They said they would add a heart for each additional year I stayed sober. My parents were very proud of me. They had witnessed me drunk on many occasions and anguished over my situation. My mother came from an alcoholic home and understood what I was going through. She knew I had a disease. So she was always very patient with me. I'm certain I will be just as compassionate towards my children if they ever find themselves addicted. I will understand and love them through it. My mom taught me how. Alcoholism is a disease and must be treated as such. Addiction is powerful and also must be dealt with. Although sometimes I wish I had never been an alcoholic, most of the time I am grateful that I am. It is easier for me to understand others who suffer because I too suffered. Instead of looking down on alcoholics I can teach them to look up. God teaches me how to love and although it will never be a perfect love as He loves us, it is growing stronger everyday.

Thought To Meditate On:

I don't think God ever required that I love others the way He loves me but He does ask that I at least try. God is perfect and His ways are perfect. As perfect as I might wish I was, unfortunately I will never be. But God knows that and He loves me anyway. I am told God loves me just the way I am and there is nothing I could ever do or not do that will change that. Remember that, when you feel unworthy of God's love. That is all in your mind, not His.

Thoughts and Revelations:

Be Patient and Stand Firm

♥

James 5:7,8

Be patient, then, brothers, until the Lord's coming. See how the farmer waits for the land to yield its valuable crop and how patient he is for the autumn and spring rains. You too, be patient and stand firm, because the Lord's coming is near.

The definition of patience is not, "One who sits around doing nothing while waiting for something to happen." We are not to sit in a chair and hide our faces until the time comes to do something. God wants us doing something while we are waiting. In the Bible there is a story about those who believed Jesus was returning soon. Because they thought it would be any day they quit work, and sat down to wait. But Jesus never said He would come back that soon and these people were doing nothing while waiting. I knew a man who had five years sober and then made a decision to go out drinking. He only drank for one day and then he came back into recovery. He was so upset he had given up his five years of sobriety that he lay in bed and watched TV. He wanted time to go by quickly. But the more he thought about his failure, the more he lied around doing nothing, and the slower time went by. He finally got involved with a fellowship and began his own support group. Before he knew it, he had a year sober. God wants us to be busy and productive members of society while He is preparing our future. After we pray, we are to thank him for the answer and then get busy. Remember, time will not go by any faster just because we want it to. Time flies by when we are having fun.

Thought To Meditate On:

When a farmer plants his crops he must wait for them to grow before he can harvest them. It is the same with our Christian walk and sobriety. We must pray and read God's Word. We must love others and be willing to help. We must continue moving forward, growing stronger and teaching others and then we will see the fruit of our labor.

Thoughts and Revelations:

by Lacy Enderson

Your Dedication Will Not Go Unnoticed

♥

Hebrews 6:10

God is not unjust; he will not forget your work and the love you have shown him as you have helped his people and continue to help them.

My sister volunteers her time at a local nursing home. She gets great pleasure from visiting these people who might not otherwise have visitors. She listens to their stories and in turn tells them stories of her own. One day a week she has a Bible study. She meets in a room with the patients who are interested and she teaches them the Word of God. Another day in the week she sets up a 'Mommy and Me' class. She invites parents to bring their small children to interact with the older people. She sets up activities such as playdough, and paints. She has story and dance time. The elderly residents enjoy watching the children play. This is more interaction than some of them ever receive. My sister is very dedicated to her ministry. She loves the idea that God is pleased with her. And I'm sure He is. It only takes a little time out of her schedule to help someone else, and God cherishes her obedience to Him. I was never as fortunate as my sister. She had a gift I never had. She had the ability to talk to strangers. I have social anxiety. Because I was always drinking to fit in, visiting the needy was never an option. I was always too drunk or preoccupied with myself to think of others. But since I got sober that has all changed. Although I still have social anxiety and talking to strangers is hard for me, I have been given the gift of caring for others. Maybe I don't spend a lot of time with people, but I definitely pray for them daily.

Thought To Meditate On:

Do you ever wonder why you are with the spouse God has partnered you with? Do you ever wonder what kind of sense of humor God must have to have given you your spouse? I know I question God often on His choice for me. But God is smart. He knows who will compliment our life and who will encourage us to grow. Don't look at His choice as a poor decision, but as one purposefully and uniquely made.

Thoughts and Revelations:

Unity of the Spirit

♥

Ephesians 4:2,3

Be completely humble and gentle; be patient, bearing with one another in love.
Make every effort to keep the unity of the Spirit through the bond of peace.

I have a friend who could not stay sober. Her problems at home were so frustrating for her that she kept turning to alcohol for comfort. After years of drowning her problems in alcohol she committed herself into an alcohol recovery home. It was too hard for her to get sober while living in the chaos of her life, so she removed herself from her life. Sobriety became more important than anything else. It was hard for her husband and her children. They were not used to her being gone. But they were willing to accept her absence in exchange for her sobriety. They wanted her sober more than anything else. That is the path my friend chose to get sober. I would have had a hard time with her decision. I think living in a home full of alcoholic women trying to get sober would have driven me to drink. The point is, that we must all find our own path. Each one of us is different and requires different methods for the same end result. But the end of the path must be sobriety. If we take the first step in the right direction, God will remove the rocks and the holes and all the temptations along the way. He promises never to give us more than we can handle. If your path gets bumpy, God must think you are a pretty strong person. Stand strong in that belief and God will get you to the end safely.

Thought To Meditate On:

It takes all kinds to make this world. Some are better with others and some do better alone. Sobriety works for everyone. There are no prerequisites to sobriety, only the willingness to get sober. Do whatever it takes to quit drinking. That should be an alcoholic's only goal.

Thoughts and Revelations:

by Lacy Enderson

Acceptance Without Hesitation

♥

1 Corinthians 13:4-7

Love is patient, love is kind. It does not envy, it does not boast, it is not proud. It is not rude, it is not self-seeking, it is not easily angered, it keeps no record of wrongs. Love does not delight in evil but rejoices with the truth. It always protects, always trusts, always hopes, always perseveres.

As an alcoholic I learned how to protect myself from other people, especially people I did not like. My guard was up and I was ready to fight anyone who got in my way. I didn't have time for people who did not agree with me. I shut the door on them. I shut it tight. And once that door was closed it would take nothing short of a miracle to open it up again. When I was a teenager my best friend lived next door. We did everything together. Her mother was dating a man who eventually moved into their house. He also had a daughter. I hated her. She was completely annoying. And I did not like the fact that she moved into my territory. This was my best friend's house. This was where we hung out together. I was not happy at all to have someone else hanging around, especially someone I did not like. I let her know over and over again that I did not want her around me, but she never listened. I'd hit her and yell at her to go away but she would not disappear. The more I yelled, the madder I got and one day, I really beat her up good. My best friend was forbidden to hang around me anymore. Because of my selfishness, I lost the fight. I was not willing to accept the change that was made in my life, and because of my stubborn rebellion I was left alone. Unfortunately, these kinds of irrational behaviors followed me into adulthood. I grew up hating change as much as I did as a kid. So in sobriety I have worked on this shortcoming. I have prayed and asked God to help me accept new and different situations. Of course it is not always easy and sometimes I still refuse to give in, but over time I have become much better.

Thought To Meditate On:

Sobriety is a process. It takes a long time to unlearn the behaviors we grow so accustomed to. Anytime I want my way and I don't get it I find myself frustrated and angry. Anytime I have calmly accepted a new or different person, place or thing, I find I am calmly serene. It is such a lovely and remarkable difference. One I find I can live with.

Thoughts and Revelations:

Put the Sword in the Stone

♥

Proverbs 14:29

A patient man has great understanding, but a quick-tempered man displays folly

Anger unleashes a whole different side of me. One that most people never see. I am real good at deception. Showing my kind, loving and thoughtful side has grown increasingly easy to do. I have a few different faces and as an actor I play each role well. But unfortunately I do have a dark side. Sometimes this side of me comes out when I least expect it. It can jump out of the dark and attack before I have a chance to pull it back. One evening my son got in a fight with a neighbor kid and he was pushed off his bicycle. He skinned his knee up pretty bad and came in the house crying. My husband wanted to clean up his knee but my son was hysterical. Because my son would not stop crying my husband slapped him really hard across the face. Talk about dual personalities. I saw red and that was all she wrote. If I had anything rational in me, at that moment it was gone. In anger I started yelling obscenities and told him if he was going to treat my son that way he could pack his bags and leave. So he did. He called his friends over and they cleared out everything he owned, just like that. He was gone. Our quick tempers created destruction. We should have communicated with love and understanding. I could have dealt with that situation a whole lot better if I had not had so much unresolved anger and rage within me. It's been a hard lesson to learn, but today I control my temper. Today I don't let anger and stubborn pride complicate my life. And I have learned not to say things I can't take back.

Thought To Meditate On:

We need to take the few extra minutes to really listen when someone is talking. Pride and selfish ambition doesn't want to hear what people have to say. Once we have convinced ourselves that we are right, nothing is going to change our minds. And how often do we find out in the end, we were wrong. We must lay our defenses down and learn to be responsible for our part of the problem. There is freedom in being sorry. We must put down our swords and stop fighting.

Thoughts and Revelations:

by Lacy Enderson

I Can Climb Any Mountain

♥

Habakkuk 3:19

The Sovereign LORD is my strength; he makes my feet like the feet of a deer, he enables me to go on the heights.

Recovery is a long process. It is a life-long process. Some days are tiring. Some days feel so long. During these days it feels like the weight of the world is on my shoulders. My attitude plays a big part in what my day will be like. My husband accepted a job to paint the inside of a penthouse apartment and asked me if I would help him. So the two of us set out to do something we had never done. I had no expertise in painting at all, so with all my best efforts I managed to do more damage than good. I spilled a bucket of paint all over a natural hardwood floor. I dripped paint from the ceiling onto an expensive comforter. I broke a china cup. And I tracked paint across the carpet with my shoe. It was an awful mess! When we were finished, it was obvious there was more damage than the job was worth so we went home empty handed. I felt really bad. But there was nothing I could do about it. So I apologized and let it go. Today I don't paint. I stick to the things I am good at. I have learned not to beat myself up for the mistakes I make. I learn from them and go on. In sobriety I must make right my wrongs. I must be sorry and stay sorry even if someone doesn't accept my apology. It can't be about me. I am good at defending myself. Most alcoholics are. I can justify the worst of offenses until it looks like I am right and you are wrong. But deep down inside I know the truth. Why live that way? Today I don't need the headaches. Today I would rather humble myself, be sorry and let it go. I don't have time for power games anymore. Today, I am too busy enjoying my sobriety.

Thought To Meditate On:

Some days it feels like I am climbing uphill. The weight of the world becomes heavier with each step I take. But God never gave me the job of carrying the world. He told me to lay my burdens down. When I do, I feel like I have been given the stamina to climb the tallest mountain.

Thoughts and Revelations:

He is an Overseer

♥

Micah 5:4

He will stand and shepherd his flock in the strength of the LORD, in the majesty of the name of the LORD his God. And they will live securely, for then his greatness will reach to the ends of the earth.

It is comforting to know that God sits on His throne and keeps a constant watch over me. The revelation of knowing that a power greater than myself cares more about me than anybody else ever will is the greatest joy I will ever experience. One afternoon, my best girlfriend came over and we shared a bottle of vodka and orange juice. It sounds funny to me now when I tell that story. When I was a kid my mom had girlfriend's over for coffee. Anyway, We were having a great conversation until I had too much to drink and passed out. When I woke up, I was in a nasty mood and picked a fight with my husband. He accused me of being drunk and in my rebellion left the house and walked to the park. I sat against a wall crying for two hours. I was very upset. But honestly, I didn't know exactly why. When I was finished with my pity party and had sobered up a bit, I walked back home and apologized. I felt bad for behaving so childishly, but I felt worse for allowing myself to get so drunk. I hated myself when I acted like that. And I always acted like that when I drank. It's nice to know God loved me even when I was drowning in alcoholism. And He cared enough about me even when I was drunk, to get me through it. Didn't you know that God loves alcoholics? He was sitting in heaven that day watching down on me and I am thrilled to know that today he looks down on me and smiles.

Thought To Meditate On:

I have said it before and I will say it again, alcoholism is a disease and must be treated as one. Alcoholism left untreated will damage lives, families, children and eventually the alcoholic will self-destruct. Alcoholics live in tremendous amounts of guilt. Enough guilt that we honestly believe God never will or could ever love and forgive us. This is a lie, don't believe it. In fact God loves and cares for you more because He understands that you need more.

Thoughts and Revelations:

by Lacy Enderson

Iron Wall Around Me

♥

Nahum 1:7

The LORD is good, a refuge in times of trouble. He cares for those who trust in him.

My middle son got his driver's license and his father bought him a car. Being a typical teenage driver, he had a lead foot and tended to drive a little fast. We had mentioned his speed to him on numerous occasions but to no avail. He refused to slow down. Kids have a way of thinking they are invincible. They do not believe that bad things can happen to them. So my prayers for my middle child doubled after he got his license. One day he shared with me that he was sitting at a stop light waiting for the light to turn green. He said, when the light changed he couldn't move. Something was keeping his car from going forward. Three seconds later a car came from the right and barreled through the intersection against the red light. Had my son's car gone forward when the light turned green, he would have been hit. He experienced the hand of God that day. You should have seen the look of amazement on his face as he told me that story. God saw the potential disaster and intervened to save him from the accident. God honored my prayers of safety for my son, and loved him enough to spare his life. God is definitely our refuge in times of trouble.

Thought To Meditate On:

I love to hear a praise report about something amazing God has done. I fully believe in the reality of God but some need signs and wonders in order to believe God really exists. God hovers over the earth looking to and fro in order to see what we need. There is nothing God doesn't know about in advance. Prayer changes things. If you need a miracle from God, pray.

Thoughts and Revelations:

King Eternal, the Only God

♥

Hebrews 1:8,9

But about the Son he says, "Your throne, O God, will last for ever and ever, and righteousness will be the scepter of your kingdom. You have loved righteousness and hated wickedness; therefore God, your God, has set you above your companions by anointing you with the oil of joy."

When I was in grade school we lived across the street from a very mean man. This was the type of man you wouldn't wish upon your worst enemy. He was vile and corrupt. When he was alone with his children he was a monster. He drank beer everyday and had very unrealistic expectations of his family. When they failed to live up to his high expectations, he beat them. We could hear the kids crying from across the street and my mom would become enraged. It was all she could do to keep herself from getting involved. He had a gambling problem and spent the families income on his own selfish pleasures. He had no concept of fatherly love, or husband love for that matter. He lived to please himself. One day, after many years of abuse, his wife took the children and left him. The love of God was not in this man and he was void of all spiritual help. He was spiritually sick. His wife and children went to church and knew the love of God. God honored her decision to leave and covered them with His protection. He anointed them with the oil of joy and gave them peace. Divorce is a nasty word. When two people get married and have children the last thing they want on their wedding day is a future divorce. But alcohol is destructive. A drunk damages the family. It is a sad day when the alcoholic chooses the alcohol over the family, but it is a great day when God picks the family up and moves them into a much better life.

Thought To Meditate On:

The Bible tells us that Jesus took our sins from us and gave us His righteousness. But it is a free gift we have to receive. Our sins are forgiven when we ask God to forgive us but if we choose to continue to sin then there isn't much God can do for us. By nature we are stubborn and selfish. But with God we are patient, tolerant and kind.

Thoughts and Revelations:

by Lacy Enderson

Fill Your Land With the Father's Glory

♥

Joel 2:21,22

Be not afraid, O land; be glad and rejoice. Surely the LORD has done great things. Be not afraid, O wild animals, for the open pastures are becoming green. The trees are bearing their fruit; the fig tree and the vine yield their riches.

An alcoholic who drinks lives his life under the control of the alcohol. For him the alcohol brings comfort as it flows through his body. But it is unfortunate to be an alcoholic, always needing a drink to feel better. Even when the alcohol ceases to provide that feeling of comfort it is still the only answer the alcoholic knows. My friend was sober for ten years when he married another sober alcoholic. She was a woman he met in recovery. He lived much of his sobriety alone and lonely, so when he met this woman he was elated. They had a baby and he marveled in the miracles of God. I had never seen him so excited. One day, his wife was diagnosed with cancer. By the time the Doctors found it her time remaining was very short. My friend could not live with the agonizing fact that the only woman he had ever loved was about to die. Soon after learning of the terrible news he began to drink again. He drank on and off until the sad day his wife passed away. I see him all the time trying to find the joy he once had in sobriety. He is so consumed with grief that the thought of a sober day is unbearable to him. My prayer is that God will restore the peace he once knew when God was his only focus. When God becomes bigger than the pain, God will be his comfort again and not the alcohol.

Thought To Meditate On:

It's hard to focus on God when news reports are full of crime and corruption. Bad news brings fear and doubt. And the world filled with anger and rage tends to drown out all the good God is doing. Life is not easy and we must have compassion on those who hurt. I wish I had all the answers for those who question, but I don't. But I do know that God brings comfort. He brings the greatest comfort we will ever know. Better than any alcoholic beverage, drug or even food. I know this for a fact.

Thoughts and Revelations:

You Listen When I Call

♥

Psalms 138:3

When I called, you answered me; you made me bold and stouthearted.

When I was ten I had a friend who lived around the corner. One day I was playing at her house and we were riding her bikes up and down the sidewalk. Her older brother came home with some friends and saw me on one of her bikes. Instantly these boys surrounded me, accusing me of stealing it. She was with me and they knew I hadn't stolen it, but they were having fun harassing me. They told me they were going to tie me to a tree. One boy yelled to his friend to get a rope and absolutely petrified, I took off running as fast as I could. I remember I was scared to death. Needless to say I never went back to her house again. There are times as a grown adult when people or problems are big enough to make me feel like that little girl again. I catch myself running as fast as I can to get away from the fear. But God's Word tells me not to fear. God reminds me He is bigger than any problem I will ever face. God gives me the confidence I need to stand up to any situation. He makes me bold as a lion. Fear can be as big as a house or as small as a peanut. And depending on what we are afraid of and why will determine the degree of our fear. I don't laugh at people who are afraid. I completely understand and boy can I relate. I know a lot of my drinking was done because I was afraid. So now without the alcohol I am afraid a lot. But I know with God I have nothing to be afraid of. And knowing that helps me through each fear.

Thought To Meditate On:

I suffer from the phobia of grasshoppers. I have no idea why they scare me so much, but they do. It is a very controlling fear. It has me watching every step I take in fear that I will unexpectedly walk into one. I cannot drive with my windows down because I fear one will fly into my car while I am driving. Thank God for air conditioning. Don't ever let someone make you feel bad for who you are. I would give anything to have this fear removed. And given what you fear, I bet you would too.

Thoughts and Revelations:

by Lacy Enderson

He Reigns From Heaven Above

♥

1 John 4:4

You, dear children, are from God and have overcome them, because the one who is in you is greater than the one who is in the world.

When it was time for me to get clean and sober there was no power in heaven or on earth that could have stopped me. When it was time, I was ready. God was all powerful and I had His Spirit living in me. I speculate the devil enjoyed watching me get drunk. He was my greatest fan. But when God came to my rescue, the devil was defeated. The Bible tells me if I tell the devil to flee, he must go. So I pray against his opposition and thank God for protection. When temptation comes around all I have to do is remember the party I was at where I was passed out on the living room floor in the midst of about fifty people who walked over the top of me for two hours. It is humiliating thoughts like that that keep me sober . When I'm struggling with a situation and a beer sounds like a good answer, I think back on the time I fell down in the gutter full of mud because I had too much to drink and I couldn't walk. Everyone thought that was so funny. But nothing I did was ever funny to me, especially the next day when I sobered up and realized what I had done. It is simple reminders from God of what it used to be like and what it is like now that make me so grateful for my sobriety. I wouldn't trade a sober day for any day drunk, no matter what.

Thought To Meditate On:

I feel like the luckiest person in the world to be sober; I mean blessed. There isn't one sober day that goes by that I don't thank my God for the greatest gift I have ever been given. Sobriety isn't something that can be explained. It has to be experienced. But it is definitely an experience an alcoholic will never forget.

Thoughts and Revelations:

Consider Others

♥

Lamentations 3:40

Let us examine our ways and test them, and let us return to the Lord.

I had to make amends to a man I felt had done me far more harm than I had ever done to him. In fact, I could easily have justified my resentment by the way he treated me. He was abusive and hurtful. He saw nothing wrong with calling me names and putting me down. But I was told if I wanted to be free from drinking, I would have to make amends to everyone. Even those people I did not like. I desperately needed to hear him admit his fault in our violent relationship. But I could not make amends holding onto that expectation. My apology was not to be based on what I wanted from others. It had to be about my truly being sorry for what I had done wrong. So I made a list of the things I had done wrong. Then I prayed and asked God to help me stay focused only on my part. Then one day it happened. I was truly sorry. So I called him on the phone and cleared away the wreckage of my past. A miracle happened that day. This mean, stubborn man actually apologized too. I felt a burden of resentment that I had been carrying around for years lift off of me. Our relationship has improved tremendously. Sometimes the greatest blessings are found when we trust in God and walk through the hard stuff. God's blessings come when we least expect them. And when that happens they mean so much more.

Thought To Meditate On:

We have to take an honest look at ourselves. Have we been dishonest, selfish or unkind? Have we hurt someone? Have we caused pain in those we love? Or even in those we hate. We must look at what we have done, putting aside all the wrongs that have been done to us, and we must be sorry. Only then will we be free to heal.

Thoughts and Revelations:

by Lacy Enderson

He Calms the Storm

♥

Psalm 37:8

Refrain from anger and turn from wrath; do not fret - it leads only to evil.

A few years ago two of my good friends deeply offended me. I felt completely betrayed. The more I thought about the offense the angrier I got. And because I was incapable of dealing with my feelings, I got drunk. In my drunken rage I went through my house demolishing everything I could get my hands on. I broke jars of food on my carpet and smashed beautiful ceramic dishes into the walls. I broke expensive sunglasses and items that were very special to me. I took valuable gifts received from loved ones and sent them crashing to the floor. The next morning I was horrified at what I had done. What a mess I had made. So many irreplaceable items were completely destroyed. I was overwhelmed with guilt, regret, remorse and shame. I had done something I never would have done sober, all because I was angry and drunk. Situations like this prove my need for a power greater than myself. Had I turned to God in my anger and not to alcohol, the end result could have been a whole lot more desirable. I need a God in my life who can help me during times of darkest despair. I need a God who can turn my mourning into dancing. A God who can lift my sorrow and replace it with peace. After a few years of sobriety I don't take my anger to the bottle anymore. Today, I take my anger to God.

Thought To Meditate On:

I have heard it said that worry can kill you. Worry is like a cancer and will eventually make you sick. But my experience is that anger is more destructive than worry. Not that worry is advisable, but when I worry I tend to hide under my blankets and disappear. Anger tends to lead me into violent fits of rage. It is important to control anger lest it consume us and cause us damage. Damage to ourselves, to our families, and in my experience, damage to our stuff. How many holes do you have in your walls?

Thoughts and Revelations:

The Spirit is Willing

♥

Galatians 5:16,17

So I say, live by the Spirit, and you will not gratify the desires of the sinful nature. For the sinful nature desires what is contrary to the Spirit, and the Spirit what is contrary to the sinful nature.

It has been said, "If you forget to spend time with God in the morning and you find that your day is not going very well, you can start your day over at any time." The only problem with that, in my opinion, is sometimes it is too late. I have mornings when as soon as I wake up bad thoughts are already running through my mind. It is important to combat those thoughts immediately. If I allow those thoughts to linger in my mind for even a few minutes they are almost impossible to weed out. If I spend time with God first thing when I awake, there is a good chance I can turn those thoughts around and think of brighter days. Let's not play games. There is a battle going on. It is between my sinful nature, which I was born with, and the nature God gave me when I became His child. Although God stays with me to help me always, there is an enemy who is also hanging around. He would like nothing more than to see me fall flat on my face. Therefore, first thing in the morning, before I do anything else, I close my eyes and I talk to God. If I have any troubles on my mind I immediately lay them down at God's feet. I do my best to clear my head and start my day off on the right foot. I guess I could wait and see what my day is like before I spend time with God, but I prefer to leave nothing to chance. There is no guarantee if we wait, that we will be able to dig ourselves out of the mess we find ourselves in. I find it is better to prevent a catastrophe than it is to beg God to rescue me after the fact.

Thought To Meditate On:

My first prayer in the morning is to lay my life down at the feet of Jesus, asking only for His will for my life and the power to carry it out. I am not interested in my own plans. Relying on my own judgement for the day never got me anywhere but drunk. God has taught me over the years that He is a good planner, so today I let Him make my plans.

Thoughts and Revelations:

by Lacy Enderson

Judge Not Lest You be Judged

♥

Luke 6:37,38

"Do not judge, and you will not be judged. Do not condemn, and you will not be condemned. Forgive, and you will be forgiven. Give, and it will be given to you.

The way I see it, God made us all exactly how he wanted us to be. He molded us together into unique individuals from the time we were conceived. When we criticize one of God's children we are telling God we don't approve of his handiwork. But I didn't always understand this concept. My sister was born with a long, ski slope nose. Looking back, it was actually cute and suited her. But she endured years of teasing and name calling. Children called her Pinnochio and asked if they could go skiing on her nose. By the time she graduated from high school she had no self esteem, a weight problem and no idea how beautiful she really was. She quickly got a nose job to change the one thing she believed had gotten in the way of her happiness. But people are mean. I was mean. I told my sister that her new nose didn't look right on her face. I told her it was better long than wrong. Luckily my sister didn't really care what I thought. She was quite happy with her new appearance and had become a wonderful person living a really neat life. I have learned that people who have low self esteem put other people down. I suppose maybe that is why I felt the need to criticize my sister. Confidence in my self was never a strong point. In fact, I thought very little of myself for a very long time. Examine yourself before you put others under a magnifying glass. Chances are, it is you with the problem.

Thought To Meditate On:

Hiding behind a beer or a cigarette gave me false power. They were my security blanket. I remember drinking beer and smoking cigarettes and feeling stronger and more powerful than anyone. But it was only a front. Deep inside I was weak and timid and deathly afraid of everyone. Today I still feel timid at times but I refuse to find liquid courage in a bottle. I am who I am and I have learned to be happy with that.

Thoughts and Revelations:

With Humility Comes Wisdom

♥

James 4:6,10

But he gives us more grace. That is why Scripture says: "God opposes the proud but gives grace to the humble." Humble yourselves before the Lord, and he will lift you up.

Vulnerability is hard for me. I have been burned so many times. I have been lied to, cheated on and betrayed. So I built tall, strong walls around myself that keep people out. I am very suspicious and sometimes jealous. As long as I can accuse people of doing me wrong I can justify the distance I keep. I do not allow others to take anything from me. I choose those whom I think deserve what I have to offer and it is always my choice. My wall of protection also deprives me. It deprives me of peace, serenity, friendship and opportunity. But I would rather go without than to risk being hurt. There is only so much pain a person can handle and I have had enough. In sobriety I have learned I don't have to live in a cave. I am learning how to have healthy relationships. I am also learning that not everyone is healthy. Therefore, I can still pick and choose my friends, I just don't have to be quite so careful. There are a lot of really nice people in the world. Day by day, as I grow stronger, bits and pieces of my wall break down. Brick by brick it falls. With each brick comes the potential for pain but also comes the hope of love and friendship. Being sober means I don't have anything to hide behind anymore. Today I must stand out in front and face the world. Thank you God that I don't have to stand there alone.

Thought To Meditate On:

I have had some very close friends hurt me. Still, to this day, I don't understand why. People in sobriety tell me not to take it personally, but how do I not. It is personal. I have learned that everyone has their own right to behave anyway they want. It is not up to me to tell someone how to live. So I allow others to make their own decisions about me and I live with what they decide. Even if I completely disagree.

Thoughts and Revelations:

by Lacy Enderson

With You I am Well Pleased

♥

Psalm 41: 10-12

But you, O Lord, have mercy on me; raise me up, that I may repay them. I know that you are pleased with me, for my enemy does not triumph over me. In my integrity you uphold me and set me in your presence forever.

I used to be a woman who wore many hats. I changed my hat depending upon who I was with. I was a people pleaser and pleasing people was very important to me. So I learned to look good in many different styles. I could be sexy or demure depending on the type of man I was with. I could be proper and straight laced or improper and vulgar depending upon what crowd I was hanging out with. I had no integrity. In fact, I didn't even know what the word meant. Because I wanted everyone to like me I compromised who I was continuously. I remember a group of my church friends whom I went to church camp with every year, finding out I was a frequent party attendee. I was devastated that my secret was revealed. No one was suppose to know who I really was. When it became obvious I couldn't hide myself anymore, I decided the only one I had to please was God. As soon as I became true to myself and quit hiding behind different personalities, the real me came out. And I didn't mind so much who I was. Of course there was a little work to be done. I didn't wake up one morning a perfect person. But slowly I transformed into a person I would gladly introduce my parents to. The only importance today is that I am pleasing to the one who made me. I strive to wear only one hat; the helmet of salvation. As long as I try to be loving and kind towards all, then I know I am pleasing God. And He is the only one I need to please.

Thought To Meditate On:

Sobriety is a whole new way of life. Being sober is a brand new lifestyle. Everything about us has to change. In the beginning it is hard. But don't get discouraged. It can be done. You've heard the saying you can't teach an old dog new tricks? Well you can. And the sooner you begin the process, the better.

Thoughts and Revelations:

Tossed Like a Ship at Sea

♥

Ephesians 2:1-5

As for you, you were dead in your transgressions and sins, in which you used to live when you followed the ways of this world and of the ruler of the kingdom of the air, the spirit who is now at work in those who are disobedient. All of us also lived among them at one time, gratifying the cravings of our sinful nature and following its desires and thoughts. Like the rest, we were by nature objects of wrath. But because of his great love for us, God, who is rich in mercy, made us alive with Christ even when we were dead in transgressions - it is by grace you have been saved.

Since I got sober it is extremely difficult for me to watch a loved one struggle with an addiction. Knowing what I went through and how hard it was for me to quit makes it that much harder for me to watch. I know what it is like to be driven by addictive forces. I know how it feels to want to quit and then barely make it through the evening before giving in again. The same struggle goes on with food, drugs, pornography and pills. Any addiction has a driving force behind it. That is what makes it an addiction. I am a people fixer. I want my loved ones set free...now! And yet I know there is nothing I can do about it. So I pray. I know God brings healing and deliverance. But I know it is not always as easy as it seems. Getting sober can be hard. God wants to see those demons conquered. He wants my loved ones victorious over drugs and alcohol. But where do they begin? The first step is willingness. If they are willing, God will help them. If I treat my loved ones with kindness, compassion and prayer, I am doing the best I can. The rest has to be up to them. What I want is to take them to a rehab or get them involved in a recovery program. I want them to experience the sanity I found in recovery with God. I want them set free to enjoy life or to be reasonably capable of making changes if they need to. God, see their need. Hold them tight and let them know that you are with them ready and willing to help. And then God, please help me to step back and get out of your way.

Thought To Meditate On:

God never gives up on you. God says He will love you and help you no matter what. So when you think you have failed one too many times for God to help you, think again. I must have tried more then fifty times to quit drinking. God was there to help me with each failed attempt. He never gave up on me and He will never give up on you.

Thoughts and Revelations:

by Lacy Enderson

Believe You Receive When You Pray

♥

1 John 5: 14,15

This is the confidence we have in approaching God: that if we ask anything according to his will, he hears us. And if we know that he hears us - whatever we ask - we know that we have what we asked of him.

Because of adverse circumstances my husband and I were given a thirty day notice to move out of our house. Since all things happen for a reason, I did not get too upset. I accepted the news as part of God's bigger plan and began looking for another place to live. I prayed to God everyday with the specifics I needed for my new home. I asked him for a washer/dryer hookup, and a backyard for my dog. My requests seemed simple enough. As the month quickly came to an end, I still had not found a new home. As hard as I tried to maintain my composure, the closer it got to leaving, the harder it was to do. I felt desperate and frustrated. I must have said a hundred times, " Lord, I do not understand. Why haven't I been able to find a new place to live?" That afternoon, the day we were to move, a sober friend of mine from my recovery program walked into my house and said to me, "I had you on my heart and I want you to come stay with me." She even allowed my dog to stay in her backyard. Talk about relief! And yet at the same time, I felt guilty and ashamed for doubting God. Sometimes God waits until the last minute to see if we will trust him. I call these "Last Minute Miracles." I guess I failed the test. But that situation taught me how to wait on God for the answers, no matter how long it takes. Each time God has done a miracle in my life, it has strengthened my faith and my ability to trust Him. So although it was hard to wait, the waiting proved to be a blessing in the end.

Thought To Meditate On:

I don't know why God arrives late. Maybe His watch is wrong (just kidding). I do know that God's timing is usually right and it is me with the broken watch. It isn't always obvious at first why we don't get what we ask for, but given time the reasons usually reveal themselves. How many times have we been grateful when God said no. Be careful not to judge God too quickly. We think we know what's best, but given our past, do we really?

Thoughts and Revelations:

The Joy of the Lord is My Strength

♥

1 Thessalonians 5: 16-18

Be joyful always; pray continually; give thanks in all circumstances, for this is God's will for you in Christ Jesus.

Life is easy when things are going well. Praising God and being grateful are second nature when life is going in the right direction. Life is harder when horrible circumstances show up. Especially those we are unprepared for. I have a girlfriend whose father is dying of cancer. Her mother was diagnosed with cancer about a year ago and given only a 10% chance of living past six months. She recovered beautifully and the cancer is gone. Her father wasn't so lucky. He had cancer in his lungs and after chemotherapy the lungs are fine but the cancer has spread and he has been told there is nothing more they can do. When we focus on the problem, it grows until we can see nothing else. We have to focus on God who came with healing in his wings. I don't fully understand why bad things happen to good people. I guess it wasn't intended for me to know. But what I do know is God allowed it and He is in control. When I trust that He knows what He's doing, then the problems don't seem quite so big. God doesn't tell us to give thanks for all circumstances, he tells us to give thanks in all circumstances. Problems and unexpected hardships were always easier to deal with drunk. But without the alcohol, life can get pretty painful. I hate death. I miss people very much. But today I don't have to drink in order to feel better. I have learned to trust God for comfort and He is working just fine.

Thought To Meditate On:

Dealing with the pain of death is extremely hard. I would have to say the hardest thing I have ever gone through is the death of a loved one. I didn't think that pain would ever go away, and some days I am convinced it never will. Grieving is a natural God given reaction to death, a definite path to healing. Don't run from the feelings by drowning in alcohol. Eventually, they will catch up to you. And when they do, it will be harder than if you just dealt with them in the first place.

Thoughts and Revelations:

by Lacy Enderson

Christ the Solid Rock

♥

Psalm 18: 1-3

I love you, O Lord, my strength. The Lord is my rock, my fortress and my deliverer; my God is my rock, in whom I take refuge. He is my shield and the horn of my salvation, my stronghold.

I have been divorced two times. I raised three small children on my own without child support or welfare. I earned five dollars an hour from jobs God provided me with. I always paid my bills on time and my children never went hungry. Nobody understood how I made ends meet. But I trusted in the supernatural power of God, and He's always seen me through. Don't get me wrong. There were times of doubt, and frustration. There were days when I felt desperate and afraid. But with each experience I learned a new lesson. And with each new problem I learned to trust God more. Whenever I am in doubt, I remember, if God saw me through one hard time he can see me through another. I remember when I first got sober. My greatest fear was the emotional pain. How would I make it go away? Alcohol had provided me years of comfort. I wasn't always a heavy drinker. There was a time I could drink occasionally. When alcohol was a choice, it was a good way to feel better. Now I was faced with the dilemma, what would I do now without it? Feelings are difficult for me, but nothing is too difficult for God. Remember, He formed the universe. And over the past few years in sobriety I have learned, God is better than any beer, cigarette or chocolate cake. His mercy is new every morning and great is His faithfulness. Alcohol brings a temporary relief. God's relief lasts all day and all night.

Thought To Meditate On:

After I quit drinking and realized I could go a whole day without alcohol, I then wondered how I would ever live without a cigarette. And then when I finally gave up smoking I wondered how I would ever be smoke-free without gaining weight. And then after learning to eat properly I wondered what I was now going to obsess over? I was told to make God my new addiction. Sounded strange at first, but what a great addiction He is.

Thoughts and Revelations:

Spiritual Discernment

♥

Jude 1:18-21

They said to you, "In the last times there will be scoffers who will follow their own ungodly desires." These are the men who divide you, who follow mere natural instincts and do not have the Spirit. But you, dear friends, build yourselves up in your most holy faith and pray in the Holy spirit. Keep yourselves in God's love as you wait for the mercy of our Lord Jesus Christ to bring you to eternal life.

Some people fashion a God to suit their sins. They believe in a power greater than themselves who allows them to carry out all kinds of evil and wicked schemes. They don't believe in the devil or in a hell, and they don't believe in a God who would send people there if it existed. Their lifestyle is selfishly pleasing, but an absolute abomination to God. They are so convinced in what they believe in that they have no guilt, no shame, and no conscience. They are spiritually lost and their God is the devil. I know such a man who lies, steals, and cheats freely. He sees nothing wrong with his behavior at all. He says God is good and there is only good. He believes there are different levels of good. Some good is very good and then there is the not so good, but still considered good. Sin and evil do not exist. I don't think I have ever heard of anything more absurd. And the fact that God tells us in the Bible that sin and evil exist, make Him out to be a liar. God can't lie, so someone else must be wrong. Do not be deceived by false teachers. Remember the Word says, "God cannot be mocked, a man will reap what he sows." If we sow destruction, we will reap destruction. Likewise, if we sow good things, we will reap good things. If we lie, cheat and steal there will be consequences to pay. If we abuse our bodies with alcohol, cigarettes and drugs we will suffer the bodily effects of illness. We can deny the existence of immorality all we want, but denial won't make it not so.

Thought To Meditate On:

God told us there would be a debt to pay for sin. He said there would be judgment for bad behavior. If sin didn't exist and immorality were a myth, why would God send us a Savior to forgive us? Forgive us for what? People come up with the most outlandish ideas and others believe them. Be careful. Don't believe everything you hear. God's Word says, don't get drunk on wine. I don't need an interpreter to tell me what that means.

Thoughts and Revelations:

by Lacy Enderson

I Will Celebrate

♥

3 John 1:3,4

It gave me great joy to have some brothers come and tell about your faithfulness to the truth and how you continue to walk in the truth. I have no greater joy than to hear that my children are walking in the truth.

For the first five years of my children's lives they went to church with me every Sunday. When their father left me and began having the children over to his house every other weekend, my children attended church with me twice a month. When my kids went to live with their dad and I only saw them every other weekend our church attendance dwindled down to maybe once a month. Eventually, I would go, but the kids would stay home. When they grew older and became teenagers I worried about their salvation. My boys misbehaved often, and the trouble they got in was frightening. I saw them headed quickly down a road of disaster. Unfortunately I knew what they were doing because that road was quite familiar to me. I walked that road myself for many years. I kept praying and believing that if God could rescue me from that hopeless life He could save my kids also. Through God's work in their lives my boys found a powerful youth group. They attended the Bible studies, they went to camps, they went to dances and parties and before long they had both accepted Jesus. I can't say it has been easy for them. I still see them struggle at times. But I know they believe and I know they are saved. I know God will see them through everything. The Word says it, I believe it, that settles it. Through my own experience I know just because a person is saved doesn't mean that life all of a sudden becomes perfect. I was saved and still suffered from alcoholic drinking. But having God in my life got me sober a lot quicker than if I were left on my own. Maybe my kids might have to fall a few times, but knowing God is there to pick them up sure makes me feel better.

Thought To Meditate On:

I remember having parties in my early thirties when my kids were home. I would get drunk and then turn my head while they drank. What was I thinking? I don't blame myself for their alcohol dependence but I know I am definitely not innocent. I wish I had been a better role model but unfortunately I can't go back and do it over. So I will go forward setting a better example for them now.

Thoughts and Revelations:

Be On Guard

♥

Galatians 5:1

It is for freedom that Christ has set us free. Stand firm, then, and do not let your-selves be burdened again by a yoke of slavery.

In June of 1993 I walked into a program ready and willing to quit drinking. At least I thought I was. I connected with another woman right away and the two of us became great sober friends. We were both divorced, our children were not living with us and we had plenty of time to work on our recovery. I was not drinking. but it was a daily fight. I fought anyone and anything. I had to have everything go my way. My opinion was always more important. If I listened to someone else it would-n't be very long before I interrupted with my own ideas. I worried, I was depressed and I was miserable. I was not enjoying sobriety. I did not know how to live life without alcohol. Frustration set in and I could not shake it. One day, after fighting with a boyfriend, I went to my best girl friend's house to hang out and get support. She was drinking. I needed her to pat me on the back, and tell me I was right. But she didn't. She took his side and told me I was wrong. I was really angry. And I was tired of being sober. So after two and a half years of sobriety I picked up her bottle of rum and poured myself a drink. Just like that, without any thought at all, I was drinking again. And I continued to drink for four more years. God had delivered me from alcohol. I played games with his grace and I lost. He gave me every tool I needed to stay sober and I took nothing seriously. Today it is OK to be wrong. Today I don't tell everybody what to do. Today I take my concerns about others to God and I let them go. Today, I have ceased fighting.

Thought To Meditate On:

I found out the hard way, it is as important to work out sobriety as you would a diet or a new job. It must be taken seriously. There is a plan of action that if followed can lead to lifelong sobriety, but it must be adhered to strictly. Sobriety for an alco-holic is not a game; it is a matter of life and death.

Thoughts and Revelations:

by Lacy Enderson
Greater is God Who is in You
♥

Isaiah 55:6,7

Seek the Lord while he may be found; call on him while he is near. Let the wicked forsake his way and the evil man his thoughts. Let him turn to the Lord, and he will have mercy on him, and to our God, for he will freely pardon.

Have you ever had a really great experience and then after the fact realized it was a work of God? Sometimes God's work is subtle and hard to detect. Sometimes divine intervention is so obvious it would be hard to ignore God's hand in it. Sometimes it takes getting knocked around a little and coming out all right to notice God was there all the time. I am definitely guilty of taking God for granted. I don't mean too, it just happens. God stands near waiting for me and I'm too busy doing my own thing to notice. But I have to admit, in bad situations I'm quite relieved to know that He was there, all the time. One night at a party, I had too much to drink and went into a blackout. Not aware, I drove myself home. When I woke up the next morning I did not know how I got there. I could not remember anything about driving home. Blackouts always amaze me. How could I go through an entire evening having conversations and socializing with others and not remember any of it? I should be on my knees in continuous thanks to God for every blackout He bailed me out of and got me through. That night, when I drove home drunk, I was really lucky I ever made it home. That is what I am talking about when I mention God's hand in a situation. It is only by His grace that I ever made it home, and this was not the first time. But did I wake up in the morning and thank God? No. I called my girlfriend to ask her about the evening. I called to inquire about my behavior. I called to see if someone else brought me home. It wasn't until later on when I realized what could have happened that I finally said thank you to the one deserving.

Thought To Meditate On:

Based on my attitude, I am so undeserving of all God does for me. I should be far more grateful than I am. Thank you God that you don't base your love for me on my reaction. I am so unworthy of God's grace yet He so freely gives it to me; one of many reasons why I am delighted to stay sober. For all God does for me, it is the least I can do for Him.

Thoughts and Revelations:

He Knows What You Need

♥

Psalm 29:10,11

The Lord sits enthroned over the flood; the Lord is enthroned as King forever. The Lord gives strength to his people; the Lord blesses his people with peace.

When my children were little my first husband bought me a brand new Toyota Van. With three kids and all their friends, a van was a huge necessity. I drove that van until it would no longer run. Towards the end of it's life the van developed an oil leak. I was forced to put oil in the car at least three times a week. One day I was called unexpectedly to work a job about 45 minutes away. I felt confident that my car would make it just fine. So I headed towards my destination. As I drove I heard an inward voice say, "Lacy, you need to put oil in your car." My response was, "I just put oil in my car. My car is fine." And I continued to drive. Again I heard the voice, "Lacy, you need to put oil in your car." And again I answered back, "I just put oil in my car. My car is fine." As I drove up the hill ready to pass the last gas station in town, I heard that voice a third time, so I pulled off the freeway and into the gas station. Sure enough, my oil reservoir was dry. God knew I needed oil. He knew if I continued to drive the distance I had to go my car would blow up. I can't tell you how grateful I was. And I can't tell you how bad I felt for not listening to God. Sometimes the still, small voice of the Spirit is hard to hear through the commotion of the world. Tune into the voice of God. He will speak if you will listen. Sometimes even when you won't. I tell this story because God does speak to us. We don't actually hear a voice but we do hear God. It is hard to explain. I know without a shadow of a doubt I heard God tell me to put oil in my car that day. That is all I can say. I heard Him.

Thought To Meditate On:

During my quiet time in the morning I make sure to sit silently for awhile in case God has something to say to me. I am so busy during the day talking and listening to radio and TV that if God were trying to speak to me I probably wouldn't hear Him. I value God's opinion. I look forward to His instruction. I would hate to miss out on a great opportunity because my life was too loud.

Thoughts and Revelations:

by Lacy Enderson

I Will Lack No Good Thing

♥

Philippians 4:19

And my God will meet all your needs according to his glorious riches in Christ Jesus.

I spent years worrying about finances. The more I worried the worse things got. I was so consumed with money problem worries that I thought of little else. I cried, I begged, I yelled and I carried on until I was in financial ruin. Because I failed to trust in God's provision, I had to file a bankruptcy. I had a car repossessed, I was evicted from two homes in one year and my life was a mess. I learned through it all that God could and would help me financially if I asked Him to. So I began to pray and ask God everyday to remove the financial fear and give me answers to the questions I had. I don't mean to sound mystical, but when I prayed about my finances God provided me with the money I needed. No, it didn't grow on a tree or come falling out of the sky, but I was given a great job and great ideas for a business. God isn't difficult to understand if we give Him a chance. In fact, His ways were so much easier and less tiring than mine. When I finally stopped crying and started thanking Him I was amazed at how great I felt. Another good lesson on attitude. It matters you know. I usually don't have a lot of extra money put aside but I always seem to have what I need. I have been told that God has a never-ending bank account and when I trust in Him he will provide. God must be my resource, not a man and not a job. And when I trust Him, I always have enough. Today, every need I have goes right to God. I know it is hard not to worry when the money you need is not there, but what does worry accomplish anyway? Absolutely nothing.

Thought To Meditate On:

I don't know why I ever limit God. He has never let me down and chances are He never will. I am my own worst enemy. I find myself whining and crying over seemingly small problems until they are so huge I am consumed by them. God's will is never for me to worry. His will is for me to trust in Him no matter what. And when I do, everything works out just fine. I am famous for promising myself, next time I will not worry, but lo and behold I always do. Someday, maybe I will quit wasting my time. Hopefully, someday soon.

Thoughts and Revelations:

The Lord Is My Shepherd, I Shall Not Want

♥

Hebrews 13:5,6

Keep your lives free from the love of money and be content with what you have, because God has said, "Never will I leave you; never will I forsake you. So we say with confidence," The Lord is my helper; I will not be afraid. What can man do to me?

I have never been rich. I live from paycheck to paycheck as I am sure most of you do. Sometimes the money runs out before the next check arrives. Thank God for parents who understand. I often wonder what it would be like to own a home and have a little money tucked away, but I can't miss what I've never had. Sometimes I feel blessed that way. Contentment with little is easier for me because I've never had much. My third husband hasn't been so lucky. He was very well off before I met him. He had a great business, a big house, nice cars, a boat, and plenty of money in the bank. He ate in expensive restaurants and shopped in the finest stores. Anything he wanted was his, so he never wanted for anything. And then he lost it all, just like that. I see how hard this is for him. I see how he struggles. I've tried to convince him that all will be OK, but he misses his money and his old way of life. God told us not to look at the circumstances, He told us to look only at Him. We get so fixated on the problems it is hard to focus on God. But God told us to seek Him first and everything else we need will be given to us. I believe this is true. And as time goes by it is easier for my husband to believe it too. But it has taken a long time to break the habit of spending. He gave up drugs, alcohol and cigarettes, but I think the hardest thing for him to give up was his money. My prayer today is for hope, that God will give us both a vision of what is yet to come. I pray for the ability to enjoy life whether rich or poor. And the ability to trust in God no matter what the circumstances.

Thought To Meditate On:

Some people are blessed with an abundance of wealth and some people struggle daily. I believe that God has a lesson to teach each one of us about money and finances, and each man needs to learn something different. I try not to focus on what I think God should do because I am not God and I don't know His ultimate plans, but I do know that given His track record, He has never been wrong.

Thoughts and Revelations:

by Lacy Enderson

Wholehearted Devotion

♥

Job 26:2-4

How you have helped the powerless! What advice you have offered to one without wisdom! And what great insight you have displayed! Who has helped you utter these words? And whose spirit spoke from your mouth?

When my best friend was hurting over the loss of her mother, I did not know how she felt. I had never lost a parent. And even if I had, my experience might have been completely different from hers. God gave me ears to hear. I need to learn to use them. It is hard for me to see people grieving. I want to fix everything and make it all better. But I can't. I have discovered more often than not, my job is just to listen. God is all powerful and all knowing. He knows exactly what the answer is. If I go to Him about the people in my life, He will help them. I must never think God doesn't hear my prayers. He does. Each and every one. So I will quit playing God. God does a much better job at it than I will ever do. A few years later I lost my dad. He died unexpectedly of a heart attack. It was a shock to say the least. But all of a sudden I understood what it felt like to lose a parent. I was able to relate to my friend. It's hard to know what to say in a situation we've never gone through. I guess the best we can do is just to be there for them. And even when we understand what they are going through, we still need to be good listeners. No one ever said if we quit drinking our lives would always be wonderful. We weren't told life would change for us. We were taught how to live the same life, only now we would live it sober. In sobriety we will have loss and there will be pain but we have been given a God of comfort to walk with us through it all.

Thought To Meditate On:

As a Christian I should be happier for people who pass over from this life into the next, but I am selfish. I don't think that way. I am self absorbed in my pain and I just want them back. Death is so final and sometimes I haven't said all I want to say. I need them back for even a few minutes so I can say goodbye. And when they don't come back I feel cheated. I am grateful today I don't have to drink the pain away. I can get through it sober. But I am still not good at it. I know practice makes perfect but with this problem I think I will stay an amateur.

Thoughts and Revelations:

Godly Sorrow

♥

Proverbs 14:9

Fools mock at making amends for sin, but goodwill is found among the upright.

Part of alcohol recovery was making amends to people I had harmed. But when I set out to find them I discovered some of these old friends were nowhere to be found. I was told I could find people on the internet. So I found a missing person website and began inserting the names of the people I had lost track of. But I had no luck. I tried their parents, and other family members and still had no luck. So I called my sponsor and told her of my frustrations. She said, "When God is willing, he will put these people in your life, as long as you are also willing." That night my husband and I went to our favorite restaurant for dinner and boy was I shocked to see one of these long lost friends there having dinner with her children. I hadn't seen her in years. Talk about excited and amazed all at the same time. I was willing to make amends and set things straight but I never expected God to work that fast. I made my apology to her and was able to clear away another bit of wreckage from my past. It felt good to be sorry and to be given the opportunity to tell her. And the best part is she received the apology from me. God is amazing. When I least expect Him, He shows up. Now I'm getting excited and prepared for the other women in my life I must apologize to. I am not saying it is easy, but after the amends are made there is a tremendous amount of weight lifted off my shoulders. So for a few minutes of discomfort I can look forward to a lifetime of peace. Sounds like a bargain to me.

Thought To Meditate On:

The hardest part about change is when I really don't want to change. The hardest part about being sorry is when I'm really not sorry. When I got sober I thought I had finished the job, just quit drinking. But then I found out I had a whole lot of work to do. After years of sobriety all the work has been worth it but at the time it was nothing short of bad news.

Thoughts and Revelations:

by Lacy Enderson

Ever Grateful, Ever True

♥

Jude 1: 24,25

To him who is able to keep you from falling and to present you before his glorious presence without fault and with great joy— to the only God our Savior be glory, majesty, power and authority, through Jesus Christ our Lord, before all ages, now and forevermore! Amen.

My husband remembers when he was growing up how normal he thought his family was. His mom and dad both had union jobs with good incomes. They saw to it that his sister, his brother and himself were all active in school projects and sporting events. Rarely was there an argument or disagreement. As a family they never missed church, after all, his dad sang in the choir. And other than holidays, liquor was never in the house. All the makings of a healthy middle income family. Much later he realized his mother had a problem with alcohol. She only drank on holidays and special events. However, when she drank she could not control her drinking. Of course he doesn't know everything about her life, especially before he was born and while he was young, but he doesn't remember his mother getting into enough trouble to consider her drinking a problem. But it was apparent that when she drank she could not stop. This was the disease he inherited and for thirty plus years when he drank he could not stop, either. So today, he just doesn't start.

Thought To Meditate On:

It is not unlikely that a child only remembers the good about the family. We have a tendency to block out bad memories to escape the pain. Alcoholism can cause many problems that don't exist in normal families and children from those homes probably learn to live in a make-believe world in order to survive. I have some memories of my childhood that include adult drinking. But I bet I don't remember everything. There are times in my own kids lives I pray they don't remember. When life should be but a dream, I would hate for them to have to relive so many nightmares.

Thoughts and Revelations:

Expecting too Much

♥

Philippians 1:9-11

And this is my prayer: that your love may abound more and more in knowledge and depth of insight, so that you may be able to discern what is best and may be pure and blameless until the day of Christ, filled with the fruit of righteousness that comes through Jesus Christ—to the glory and praise of God.

During my adult years, I have had four different roommates (not including my husbands.) Each time a friend moved in it started out well. I always began our adventure with good intentions. It was exciting to have someone around I could talk to and hang out with. But in no time at all, it would all go downhill. It always went the same way. Everything would be going along just fine and then all of a sudden I would start focusing on all their irritating behaviors. Soon, I was dreading the fact that I had a roommate at all. I was very controlling and I had great expectations of people. I started out with love, and tolerance, but before long I was whining about the hairballs left in the corner of the bathroom floor, and the crumbs on the counter that didn't get wiped up. I had a friend move in with me who had two small children. She was in a desperate situation and needed a place to live. I was happy I had an extra room to offer her and her children. I extended love and grace to her, but when I didn't get back from her what I felt I deserved, I kicked her out. Fighting with her for what I needed just wasn't worth it anymore. It was easier for me if she was gone. The other roommates all had similar outcomes. They were asked to leave because they were not living up to my expectations. I had unreasonable expectations of people. I demanded perfection. When I did not get what I considered respect in my home, they had to leave. When I look back on those roommate situations I am amazed I had any friends at all. It amazes me that I thought so highly of myself. Who was I to demand perfection when I was so far from it. Shame on me.

Thought To Meditate On:

I try not to beat myself up for the way I treated people in my past. I was only behaving the way I knew. I could not have expected anything better from myself because I was so lost and broken. It has taken some years to grow up and see the damage I have done. For years I convinced myself it wasn't me, it was them. But now that I see clearly, I feel so very bad. I guess the best I can do now is try harder to be a better friend. And to remember that no one is perfect, not even myself.

Thoughts and Revelations:

by Lacy Enderson

God of Every Circumstance

♥

Acts 17:24,25

"The God who made the world and everything in it is the Lord of heaven and earth and does not live in temples built by hands. And he is not served by human hands, as if he needed anything, because he himself gives all men life and breath and everything else.

The Church has been telling me for years not to put limitations on God. I have been told that He is God and He can do anything. Sometimes I doubt His power. I pray, but I am not always convinced He will answer me. It was easier when I was a new believer. There was something simple about being a child in the Lord. I had surrendered to a God I did not understand and He carried me. Today I feel more accountable. My knowledge has complicated my relationship. When I was married to my first husband I was told I could pray about his un-Godly behaviors. So I would pray each morning for my husband, believing that he would be delivered, and the crazy thing is, he was. My husband spent many evenings playing cards with his friends. I didn't mind so much except he was never home. After I had began praying, he spent more time with me and the kids. I felt this was more important than a card game. His friends became curious. There had definitely been a change in him and they wanted to know why. I told them I had been praying. It was that simple. I don't understand why I have allowed that simplicity to get away. God showed me early on in my relationship with Him that He cared enough about me to answer my simple requests. So why do I doubt Him now? Why have I complicated such a wonderful thing? I need to focus more on the power of God and not on what I think He can or cannot do. Doubt and unbelief are not attractive qualities in God's eyes. He wants us to believe He answers our prayers. So we must believe He can and He will.

Thought To Meditate On:

One of the greatest lessons I learned in sobriety was that God can be trusted. As a practicing alcoholic I didn't have as much time to spend with God as I do now, because I was too busy drinking. Now that I am sober, I have lots of time to ponder God and who He is. It didn't happen overnight, but I have learned how to trust God. He is amazing. And I am so glad I found out.

Thoughts and Revelations:

The Love of the Father

♥

Jeremiah 29:11-13 .

*"For I know the plans I have for you," declares the LORD, "plans to prosper you
and not to harm you, plans to give you hope and a future. Then you will call upon
me and come and pray to me, and I will listen to you. You will seek me and find me
when you seek me with all your heart."*

When my children were little I worked in preschools making minimum wage. My
three children were able to come with me for free, so I didn't have to pay for child
care. So despite the low pay, the free child care more than made up for it. I worked
with children for ten years. God had given me a passion for children and I enjoyed
my job. But as my own children got older I often wondered what God would have
me do next. I wouldn't be able to take them to work with me forever. They were
growing older and the preschools were for young kids. I started working with a
friend in her home child care. My kids were allowed to come with me there. But
deep down I knew I could not survive forever on minimum wage. And my children
were growing very bored and restless. One day while working, one of the child care
clients mentioned she was looking for a helper in the dental office where she
worked. Excited, I begged her to allow me the opportunity. She wasn't looking for
experience, just a helper. So I began a new career working as a dental assistant.
schooling wasn't required. I was trained on the job. I eventually earned three times
the money I made working with children. God is good. He knew what I needed. He
heard my heart cry out to Him before I ever said a word. My lesson to you is try not
to panic. God will put you in the right place at the right time also. Be patient and
rely on Him. When I got sober they told me to put one foot in front of the other
doing only what was in front of me. So I did. I went to work and did my job and
because I was faithful, God was faithful too.

Thought To Meditate On:

Trusting in God is not always easy, but if we can remember He can see the future it
will be easier to rely on Him. I am amazed at what God does for me when I least
expect it. When I make a decision not to worry because I know God is in control, I
give Him freedom to work in my life. Thanking God in advance is the first thing I
do. It opens the door for miracles. Every morning I wake up excited at what God is
going to do next.

Thoughts and Revelations:

by Lacy Enderson

Obedience of Christ

♥

2 John 1:6

And this is love: that we walk in obedience to his commands. As you have heard from the beginning, his command is that you walk in love.

I believe God puts difficult people in our lives to teach us how to love them. Each time I ran away from a difficult person there were always more waiting in line. When I realized God had a plan, I decided to quit running. I figured out I needed to learn how to deal with difficult people. Not that I wanted to, but obviously God did. I took a job in an office with a girl whom I was convinced hated me. She never had one nice word to say to me or about me. After two weeks of her awful behavior I decided I had endured enough, and I went to the boss with my complaint. He told me if I could not work with her, I could find another job. Wow, I wasn't expecting that reply. I needed that job. So I had to accept her exactly the way she was. This was no easy task. She was bound and determined to make my life miserable. But after some time and a lot of patience we did become friends. I had to quit taking her attitude personally. It wasn't about me, it was about herself. She was obviously suffering from some strong self esteem issues and my very presence threatened her. When I began to love her, no matter what she said or did, she began to loosen up and come around. Loving difficult people is not easy. It takes a lot of hard work and self determination. But God asks us to love everyone as He loves us. When you don't want to make the effort, just remember how difficult you used to be. When you were drinking, how many people still chose to love you? No matter how difficult someone might be there is probably a reason for it. Ask God for help and he will put the love that you need in your heart for these people. And never forget, God's Word says that to love is a command, not a choice.

Thought To Meditate On:

Jesus only asks one thing of you; and that is everything. Remember, He gave you everything He had. No one ever said life would be easy and comfortable. Sometimes it is uncomfortable. But it is during the hard times we grow the most. Remember the saying, no pain no gain. It is like that with most everything in life. So get ready for the discomfort and learn to go with it. Fighting will only prolong the agony, not change the circumstances. The sooner you start, the sooner you will complete, and be on your way to victory.

Thoughts and Revelations:

Hope Does Not Disappoint Us

♥

Romans 5:3-6 .

Not only so, but we also rejoice in our sufferings, because we know that suffering produces perseverance; perseverance, character; and character, hope. And hope does not disappoint us, because God has poured out his love into our hearts by the Holy Spirit, whom he has given us. You see, at just the right time, when we were still powerless, Christ died for the ungodly.

I have a friend in sobriety who has a seven year old handicapped daughter. She does not own a car and her income is limited. She rents a room from a man who continually makes her feel unwelcome and uncomfortable. It is obvious to her and everyone else that he would prefer her to leave. But where would she go? The washing machine broke and they refused to replace it so she has to take a taxi to the laundry mat with her clothes and her daughter. She has tried to find work but can't find a suitable child care trained in the care of handicapped children. Her daughter is a sweet girl but very difficult to control. Because she has no transportation she's at home most of the day alone and lonely. She has no family close by and her friends are few. I have watched her struggle daily with the obstacles in her life but I have never seen her give up hope. She continues walking forward with her head held high convinced God is watching out for her and will provide each and every need she has. Whenever I think my life is getting difficult I stop and consider what she goes through each day. Remembering her struggles reminds me that I really don't have it all that bad. Knowing people whose circumstances are much harder than mine teaches me gratitude and humility. It is important to always focus on the good of God instead of my misfortune. Given the reality of what other people have to endure, do I really have anything to complain about?

Thought To Meditate On:

No one ever said that life would be easy. In fact sometimes it is downright hard. And just because we get sober doesn't mean our lives will all of sudden become better than we ever dreamed of. Yes, eventually with some hard work and change of attitude, that can and will happen, but don't expect it right away. If you think your life will become a bed of roses immediately, you will be left frustrated. Take it in stride, be patient, and it will happen.

Thoughts and Revelations:

by Lacy Enderson

Father Knows Best

♥

Proverbs 19:21

Many are the plans in a man's heart, but it is the LORD's purpose that prevails.

I remember when my children went to live with their father, and I went to live with my parents. I was working full time in an office, but I really didn't like my job. So I answered an ad in the paper for employment. I had an interview and I was hired. But when I started that job, I discovered within hours the people there were nasty and the work was hard. In a short amount of time I was completely overwhelmed. I decided I didn't want that job so I quit. I remember I was lying on the bed crying. I had lost so much in such a short time and I felt hopeless. I didn't have my own home, a job, my kids, my husband, and I had recently quit drinking. I remember surrendering that moment to God and letting it go. This was a new principle I had learned in recovery; turning my will and my life over to the care of God and letting Him take care of my wants, my needs and my desires. The next day there was another help wanted ad in the paper. It read, no experience necessary, will train. So I had another interview and they hired me. This was a much better job. The people were nice and the job was enjoyable. Within one month I had saved enough money to afford my own place to live, and I actually felt content and alive. When I surrendered and I got out of God's way, he was able to do for me what I could not do for myself.

Thought To Meditate On:

From the time we are young we are taught to be responsible. We are told by our parents in order to learn we must follow instructions and obey. But as we get older some of us get turned around and irresponsibility creeps in and takes over. It is important when this happens to back up and ask for help. This is when God comes in and takes control. He fixes what we have broken. He makes miracles out of messes. Don't be ashamed if you can't do it for yourself. It is OK to need help. In fact, it is those who ask for help that are commended in the end. Just think of yourself as special. God does.

Thoughts and Revelations:

Change is Yet to Come

♥

Philippians 2:14,15

Do everything without complaining or arguing, so that you may become blameless and pure, children of God without fault in a crooked and depraved generation, in which you shine like stars in the universe.

I have read that anger is not a luxury alcoholics can afford to have. For an alcoholic, anger often leads to drinking and it doesn't take a lot of irritation to set us off. Sometimes anger is ignited by the need to change someone. Countless times I have been sent in an uproar because someone would not do what I wanted them to do. Sound familiar? One night, I wanted my husband to take me to a conference. It was a subject of interest to me, and I didn't want to attend alone. It was hard for me to go places by myself. My husband wasn't thrilled about going, but he said he would. An hour before we were to leave we got into an argument about something silly, and he told me he wasn't going anymore. I was furious. I started ranting and raving something fierce. I was yelling obscenities and calling him awful names. For a few insane minutes I became someone I didn't even know. One very hard lesson for me to learn was, it was OK for me to be my own person and for him to be himself. It was OK for him to say no. I always saw us together. We had always done everything together and I didn't know why this had to change. Individualism was a new concept I wasn't about to grasp without a fight. I was completely consumed by disappointment. In fact, I was convinced he probably started that argument so he wouldn't have to go with me. That thought only added fuel to my fire. Alcoholics are good at manipulating the circumstances to get what we want. We are not good with disappointment and being told no. But in order to grow and heal we must learn to walk on our own two feet and we must allow others to do the same.

Thought To Meditate On:

When we complain we are telling God we disapprove. Arguing with God is in fact telling Him He is wrong and we are right. When has God ever been wrong? Seriously? It isn't about how we feel or what we want. If we are going to succeed in this world we have to do it God's way. Nothing else will work. Believe me. I have tried it all.

Thoughts and Revelations:

by Lacy Enderson

Be of Good Courage

♥

1 Peter 5:8,9

Be self-controlled and alert. Your enemy the devil prowls around like a roaring lion looking for someone to devour. Resist him, standing firm in the faith, because you know that your brothers throughout the world are undergoing the same kind of sufferings.

I have a favorite park. I used to go there to swing on the swings. It was in the hills, surrounded by oak trees and hiking trails. It was a beautiful place to get away and meditate. One day, I decided to jog over to this park and collect my thoughts. I hadn't been drinking a lot lately and I felt pretty good. When I arrived, I noticed there was a party going on. There were lots of people obviously having a good time. I got on my swing and I began to get lost in my thoughts. A few guys came over and asked me how I was doing. They invited me to join them. I really didn't want to be bothered, and I knew they had been drinking, so I tried to be nice. I didn't want to stir up anger in a drunk. I know how we can be. I let them know I was not drinking and I thanked them for the invite. When I actually broke lose and headed for home I thought about how sneaky the devil is. He can take a perfectly good day and throw temptation right in the middle of it. It comes from absolutely nowhere. I was grateful for God's strength that day to resist. Saying no to alcohol has not always been one of my strong points, but with God's help I was able.

Thought To Meditate On:

Life is hard, and making the right decisions is not always easy. But always remember, we are not alone. Most of us found stubborn rebellion the easiest route. But in the end, it never really was. What could possibly be so easy about hangovers, headaches, arguments, lost jobs, crashed cars and for some of us jail time? The process of getting sober can be long and hard at first, but the benefits are well worth the effort.

Thoughts and Revelations:

He Rides on the Heavens to Help You

♥

Hebrews 10:24,25

*And let us consider how we may spur one another on toward love and good deeds.
Let us not give up meeting together, as some are in the habit of doing, but let us
encourage one another—and all the more as you see the Day approaching.*

I try not to discourage people who are having a hard time staying sober. I know how
hard it is. Some people get it right away but for others it takes a long time. I tried
for years to quit drinking but to no avail. I hear people speak harshly to others and I
wonder why they have to be so cynical and nasty. I was told once that we can love
an alcoholic to death if we are too nice. But I am a sensitive person. I did better
when others were kind. It was easier for me to get sober when my support group
encouraged me. When I heard, "Lacy, you're doing great. You're going to make it",
it was easier for me to say no to the drink. One day, during one of my later attempts
at sobriety, I was at a very large meeting. I only had ninety days sober. To an alcoholic this is a long time without a drink. And although I was proud of my accomplishment I had at one time been sober for over two years. An old friend who was
obviously having a bad day, thought it was OK to slander me in front of the group.
To her own glory she made the comment that no matter how bad her day ever was
she would never be like me with only 90 days. She let us all know that drinking
would never be an option. I was humiliated. I had been around those meetings for
eight years and I knew I should have had more sober time. But I didn't, and I didn't
need her comment to help me. In fact, it made me so angry I swore I would never
go back. And for two years I didn't. I know I didn't handle the situation the right
way. I should never allow people to hurt me like that. But I was ultra sensitive, like
some people are. Remember the old saying, "We can catch more flies with honey,
than we can with vinegar."

Thought To Meditate On:

When someone is rude and nasty I try to remember that hurting people, hurts other
people, and it probably has nothing to do with me at all. Some people are just
wicked. They can't help it and they have a need to bring everybody down in their
pit of misery with them. Now knowing that, why is it I still get my feelings hurt by
what some people say? Because I am sensitive. Some of us just are.

Thoughts and Revelations:

by Lacy Enderson

For the Lord is Good

♥

Psalms 145:8,9

The LORD is gracious and compassionate, slow to anger and rich in love. The LORD is good to all; he has compassion on all he has made.

One year on New Year's Eve my second husband, some friends and I went to Las Vegas for their big New Year's Eve street party. It was something we had never done before and well worth the experience. Las Vegas is my favorite place to visit. We made reservations and spent two days and nights there. My girlfriend had invited a male friend whom I had known for years. He was a nice person, but there had never been any attraction between the two of us. That night, at midnight, this guy gave me a big hug. It was all done innocently and in the name of friendship. No other intentions were meant. But my husband became very angry. I didn't see the hug as inappropriate, but I wasn't looking at it from my husband's point of view. He was definitely upset and he would not accept my apology. He left me in the casino by myself and went to the room. I know how hard it is to battle jealousy and suspicion. I do it everyday. I am the number one most jealous person I know. In the dictionary the definition of jealousy is Lacy. But the time and energy that is wasted over misunderstandings is ridiculous. I fight hard to suppress false feelings as much as possible because they are just that, false. He felt I was rude and inconsiderate of his feelings. I felt he should have received my apology. We spent New Year's Eve apart. The sad thing about arguments is they almost always come with painful consequences. No matter how badly we both felt afterwards we would never get that night back. It was ruined. Such a shame.

Thought To Meditate On:

God is patient with us. God is not mean and punishing. He is kind, understanding and forgiving. Can't we learn from Him? If we want to know how to be the best people we can be, look at God. If we want to learn how to respect and appreciate others, look to God. He should be our greatest role model. And if He isn't, than we are probably doing it wrong.

Thoughts and Revelations:

Only the Lonely

♥

1 Thessalonians 3:12,13

May the Lord make your love increase and overflow for each other and for everyone else, just as ours does for you. May he strengthen your hearts so that you will be blameless and holy in the presence of our God and Father when our Lord Jesus comes with all his holy ones.

Helen had been homeless for many years, so when she was given free housing, I thought it was strange that she was still walking the streets during the day. She still carried bags around with her like homeless people do, even when she didn't have to anymore. I met Helen in church one Sunday. She was actually quite annoying and I remember wishing I had never met her. I hesitantly gave her my address and phone number and she spent a lot of time at my house. She was extremely clingy. I was working full time, raising three children, and I didn't have a lot of time to spend with Helen. I understood her loneliness so I tried to be available. I knew she appreciated my friendship, but I felt she wasn't respecting my privacy. It was very hard to love her. She was attending co-dependents anonymous meetings which I felt were appropriate for her. I was praying she would learn their principles quickly so she would quit needing me so much. That program teaches us to rely on God and not so much on other people. One day she just stopped coming around. I don't know why but I admit I was grateful. I still see her on the streets sometimes, but that is the extent of it. As difficult as she was for me, I appreciate the opportunity God gave me to love someone who was unlovely. I've been unlovely before and people have loved me. I never really gave much thought to the homeless when I was drinking. I was too preoccupied with myself. But in sobriety I think I might look into charity work. Given life and circumstances, I could end up homeless someday. How many of us are just one paycheck away?

Thought To Meditate On:

I can't promise I will always like everyone and I don't think God expects that of me. But He does ask that I try to love people. Like and love are two different emotions. And although God loves everyone I bet there are some things about each one of us He does not like. We must pray and ask God to fill us with His love and the unlovely won't be so unlovely anymore. He gives us the ability to see people as He sees them, through His eyes of love.

Thoughts and Revelations:

by Lacy Enderson

Justified Through Faith

♥

James 1:5-8

If any of you lacks wisdom, he should ask God, who gives generously to all without finding fault, and it will be given to him. But when he asks, he must believe and not doubt, because he who doubts is like a wave of the sea, blown and tossed by the wind. That man should not think he will receive anything from the Lord; he is a double-minded man, unstable in all he does.

I do not always know what God wants me to do. Sometimes life is confusing. The Bible says I have the mind of Christ and the wisdom of God, and I believe that. But sometimes God makes me wait. He doesn't always rush to let me in on His plans just because I am impatient. I believe God tests my faith. He wants to know what I am made of. He wants to see if I can trust in Him. But even more so, He wants to see if He can trust me. Waiting is not one of my strong qualities. Most of the time I just want it now. And when God makes me wait, sometimes I start without Him. What a disaster that is. After dating a man for eight months I decided to move in with him. I knew it was wrong. I was definitely outside of God's will, but I didn't care. I was lonely and I needed a companion. We lived together for one month before my conscience started tormenting me. I could not live in sin this way. So I found an apartment, and moved out a week later. Because of my obedience to God, the landlady gave me one hundred percent of my deposit back and the second half of the month's rent that I had paid. That doesn't normally happen. When I got back on track and decided to do it God's way, God forgave me of my sin, and blessed me. It is important to stay on the path God has planned. When I step off that path and go in my direction I run head on into collision. It is hard enough staying sober when life is peaceful. Why would anyone want to stay sober in a bed of turmoil? It is important to make right choices if you ever want to stay sober for a long time. And sobriety is a life long process.

Thought To Meditate On:

One request God makes of us, if we are going to ask Him for something we must believe He will answer. If our hearts are doubtful we should not ask God for anything. If we don't believe He is going to provide, how can we expect that He will. We have to approach God with faith believing. According to the Bible, nothing less will do.

Thoughts and Revelations:

124

Love is a Decision

♥

2 Corinthians 8:8,9

I am not commanding you, but I want to test the sincerity of your love by comparing it with the earnestness of others. For you know the grace of our Lord Jesus Christ, that though he was rich, yet for your sakes he became poor, so that you through his poverty might become rich.

I can only think of one person in my life that I have truly despised. I was twelve and her family moved into a house on the corner of my street. She was an only child, and she was spoiled rotten. When she found out I was the only one on the street her age, she attached herself to me immediately. I wasn't given a choice. Had I been allowed to pick her as a friend, I never would have. She had serious emotional problems and I had no time for her games. She had pink shag carpet in her bedroom, and for some reason unknown to me, she was convinced I was jealous. I didn't care. Why would I care? I had a beautiful yellow and orange shag in my own room. She dragged me to a store one afternoon to look at clothes. She bought a bag of popcorn for a dime and said I could have some of her popcorn if I promised to pay her back when we got home. That was not the way my friends and I treated each other. And the popcorn was only a dime. One day a group of us were sitting in the gym during PE. We were passing our wallets around looking at each other's pictures. When she got her wallet back she asked me if I had seen her dollar. I had not. But I felt guilty and responsible because I was the last one with her wallet. So I began searching for it. A few minutes later she told me she was just kidding. She wanted to see what I would do. I had never met anyone more impossible in all of my twelve years. I have learned that there will be people in my life that drive me crazy. And over the years I have met a few. But the lesson I learned is, I can choose not to hang out with them but I cannot choose to treat them bad.

Thought To Meditate On:

God cannot make us love other people. That is a choice we must make for ourselves. But in sobriety it is much easier if we learn to accept other people. I know I mention other people a lot. It is a point I try to make clear. Our drinking had a lot to do with our reactions towards people. Sobriety depends on how we react to them now. Patience, tolerance, kindness and acceptance of others has to be our new way of life, whether we like it or not.

Thoughts and Revelations:

by Lacy Enderson

A Gift Opens the Way for the Giver

♥

Deuteronomy 15:10

Give generously to him and do so without a grudging heart; then because of this the LORD your God will bless you in all your work and in everything you put your hand to.

A friend from my Church was forced to sell her house, so she came to stay with me for six weeks. She had a fourteen year old daughter who came to stay also. I gave them a room even though I didn't have one to spare. My husband and I slept in a room, and that left one room for our five children and their friends to sleep in. (Thank God the kids were only with us every other weekend and Tuesday nights.) Most nights the kids camped out on the living room floor. We did our best to accommodate everyone. It was not easy, but we made it work. I have learned it isn't always necessary to have a lot to offer. Sometimes, it is when we give out of our need that the rewards are rich. I have to admit I like my quiet time. I love my husband and my kids very much but the time I can spend alone is highly valued. It is in the quiet times that God and I can communicate on a deeper level. I love singing songs to Him and praying out loud. When others are present I am forced to pray quietly. Having strangers live with me is not my first choice but because God has richly blessed me with a home I must be willing to share it with others. Sobriety has taught me how to care for others who are less fortunate. Getting sober wasn't the only thing recovery offered. I am extremely blessed by my new attitude and my new willingness to help others. God told me if I got sober He would change some things about me. Well He has, and I am glad.

Thought To Meditate On:

Sacrificial giving means we give something we don't really have to give. For example, we give the last five dollars in our wallet to a homeless person on the street. Or we allow someone to use our car when we don't have another one. It is a sacrifice on our part to give this way. But it is exactly what Jesus did for us. It is not easy but I would challenge you to extend yourself in this way just once. The rewards of sacrificial giving are personally enriching. And better yet, they are richly blessed by God.

Thoughts and Revelations:

Arise and Shine for Your Light has Come
♥

1 John 2:9-11

Anyone who claims to be in the light but hates his brother is still in the darkness. Whoever loves his brother lives in the light, and there is nothing in him to make him stumble. But whoever hates his brother is in the darkness and walks around in the darkness; he does not know where he is going, because the darkness has blinded him.

I have a brother who is eighteen months older than me, a sister who is seventeen months younger, and a brother who is seven years younger. When I was growing up, my older brother was like most older brothers. He picked on my sister and me unmercifully. He was the oldest, so he pecked on our heads. I, in turn, pecked on my sister and brother's heads. It was your basic sibling rivalry. If I was having a bad day, I took it out on them. I didn't consider their feelings at all. My own satisfaction was more important. One day, the two little girls next door wanted to ride my little brother's kick n' go, and he told them no. I thought he was being a bit selfish so I told them yes. I took his toy away from him and gave it to the neighbors. My mom was disappointed in me. She told me that when I chose to meet the needs of other children above my brother, he felt I liked them more. I felt bad when I found him playing trucks by himself in the backyard. There is a certain unity when families stick together. It is the strongest bond of love God ever created. I took my family for granted for many years. Today, they are the most important people in my life. I don't know why I remembered that story. It happened a very long time ago. Remembering that story helps me place the value on people that God places on me. The Bible tells me I should always consider other people's feelings in everything I do, so today I make a conscience effort to do so.

Thought To Meditate On:

Dark feelings of hatred never produce anything good. No matter how much we dis-like a person I bet we could find at least one good quality in them. It is important to my sobriety and my well being that I dwell on the good in a person. It makes me feel better, and for a sober alcoholic, feeling good is crucial to sobriety.

Thoughts and Revelations:

by Lacy Enderson

To Live is Christ

♥

Philippians 3:8,9

What is more, I consider everything a loss compared to the surpassing greatness of knowing Christ Jesus my Lord, for whose sake I have lost all things. I consider them rubbish, that I may gain Christ and be found in him, not having a righteousness of my own that comes from the law, but that which is through faith in Christ—the righteousness that comes from God and is by faith.

Can you remember wanting something so bad it made you feel completely irrational? I do. When I was fifteen I waited for close to a year for a mo-ped. It was illegal to ride one without a learner's permit, so I waited until I got one. It was the neatest gift I ever waited for, because I really wanted one. I can't remember ever wanting something as badly as I did that mo-ped. I remember coming home from school one day and it was in the kitchen. It was the exact mo-ped I had picked out. It was mustard colored with a brown seat. Only one other person I knew owned one. That made me feel pretty special. As an adult there are only two things I can remember wanting as badly as I wanted that mo-ped. They are alcohol and sobriety. I want alcohol so badly that my body cries out. But I also want sobriety. It all comes down to which one I want the most. Do I want to be sober more than I want to drink? Nothing satisfies like Jesus. He is really all I need. In sobriety God gives me peace, joy, and sanity. When I drink I experience heartache, grief, remorse and sorrow. I don't know why I battle over two very different outcomes. One is pleasant and the other is terrible. You would think the choice would be easy. But for an alcoholic it is not. Sobriety is a daily decision and must be made one day at a time. And each day we choose to stay sober is a great day indeed.

Thought To Meditate On:

The Bible says that the productive earnest prayer of the righteous profits much. That means if I am obedient and I do what God wants me to do I can pray and God will answer me. So, the opposite of that verse would be true, if I am willfully sinning, than God can not hear my prayer. The Bible tells me not to get drunk. So if I do I must be willing to suffer the consequences of my drinking. That would be unanswered prayer. I can't even imagine what life would be like without constant communication with my God. There isn't any amount of alcohol that would be worth that silence.

Thoughts and Revelations:

Exercise Your Faith

♥

Romans 10:17

Consequently, faith comes from hearing the message, and the message is heard through the word of Christ.

Developing faith is like going to the gym for an aerobics class. The first day I can barely get through the class but by the end of the month I am doing great. And if I continue, I get better, and the routines get easier. Practice makes perfect is a true statement. The first few times I had to believe God for something, the waiting drove me crazy. I never doubted God's existence, only His provision. I have always believed God is, I just never really trusted Him. After He provided and I realized my doubt and worry were for nothing, it was easier the next time to wait. I hear the church talk about God's speed. That's the amount of time God makes me wait. Since He knows what is best, it is usually the perfect amount of time. Although I'm sure if I had it my way, I would speed things up a bit. They say patience is a virtue. Well patience was never easy for me. But each time God provides the resources I need, my faith grows. And each blessing makes my faith stronger. I have had so many answered prayers over the years I can now trust God completely. But it took God answering me time and time again in order to develop an unconditional trust. Turning my life over to God's care took me a long time. I wasn't used to letting someone else run my life. But again, after a few tries, to see that God always did come through, and now I wonder why I ever waited. God has done such a wonderful job running my life, I think I will hire Him. And the best part is, I know He wants the job.

Thought To Meditate On:

Faith increases as we use it, just like our muscles or our minds. The Bible tells us that we have all been given the same amount of faith and it is up to us to stretch our faith by using it. Having faith in a God we cannot see is hard for some people. But if you will just give Him a try I am sure you will be satisfied with the results.

Thoughts and Revelations:

by Lacy Enderson

My Hope is in You, Lord

♥

Hebrews 10:35,36

So do not throw away your confidence; it will be richly rewarded. You need to persevere so that when you have done the will of God, you will receive what he has promised.

I had some friends take me dancing at a night club for my birthday. I had already been sober a few months so I wasn't drinking. And although my friends couldn't understand my alcoholism, they were Ok with my decision not to drink and let me be. My friends were drinking and they kept reminding me how much fun we used to have when I drank with them. We laughed at the good times. I was actually enjoying myself a great deal. When my friends began to get loud and obnoxious, it brought back old memories. I used to be the loudest of us all. In fact, I was so good at making a fool out of myself I was extremely grateful at that moment to be sober. I wouldn't trade my worst day sober for my best day drunk. I like being in control of my behavior and it feels good to wake up in the morning without a hangover. Other than special occasions, I don't go into clubs that sell liquor. I don't believe in setting myself up for the temptation. I check my motives before I go anywhere alcohol is served. If I'm honest with myself and there is not a very good reason for me to be there, then I do not go.

Thought To Meditate On:

Over the years it has grown increasingly easy to be around alcohol without the driving force to drink it. But that was not always the case. In the beginning of my sobriety, when I least expected it I would grow almost frenzied with temptation. And I never knew when it would hit me. For awhile it was best to stay out of temptation's way. Now I can't even remember the last time alcohol tempted me. One day the obsession disappeared and I just didn't want it anymore.

Thoughts and Revelations:

Listen and Obey
♥

Proverbs 23:12

Apply your heart to instruction and your ears to words of knowledge.

In one of my many attempts at getting sober I asked a good friend of mine if she had the number of someone in recovery who could help me. She gave me the phone number of a woman who had been sober for over ten years. She was also active in overcomers anonymous, which meant her God was Jesus. I liked the fact we would have the same God. One night I called her on the phone and I explained my situation. She was not very friendly. In fact, I thought she was downright rude. But I wanted to give her a chance. I really wanted to get sober and I needed her help. She told me to meet her at a meeting. So I showed up. And she ignored me the entire evening. At the end of the meeting she told me to get the phone numbers from three other women and to call all three of them each day for one week. I didn't want to talk to other women. I only wanted to talk to her. It was very difficult even calling her the first time. I had no intentions of putting myself through the difficulty of calling anyone else. I was not good at following instructions, and I thought her direction was ridiculous. Needless to say, I not only didn't ask for other phone numbers, I never talked to her again. Now that I have been sober awhile I realize her request was not unreasonable. She had been around long enough to separate the winners from the losers. She was classifying me by how willing I was to do what I was told. I rebelled and made the bottom of her losers list. Listening to those more experienced, is how I grow and God sends the perfect people to help me. It wasn't until I humbled myself and learned to take direction that I was actually able to stay sober.

Thought To Meditate On:

We try to hang around with those who have what we want, both spiritually and emotionally. That means we hang out with those who are sober, not those getting drunk. Our encouragement comes from words of wisdom as sober members share with us their experience, strength and hope.

Thoughts and Revelations:

by Lacy Enderson

Use Sober Judgement

♥

1 Peter 4:7

The end of all things is near. Therefore be clear minded and self-controlled so that you can pray.

As a teenager my friends and I would spend our summers lying around on the beach. Most of the time we were drunk acting like idiots running through the sand and splashing in the waves. I remember feeling lost as I wandered around the beach drunk. I wasn't fond of drinking during the day and being drunk in a strange place was extremely uncomfortable. So why did I drink at the beach? Your guess is as good as mine. When I was sober I could see how embarrassing my friends were. But when I was drunk I acted just like them. The Bible warns us about the second coming of Jesus. He will come when we least expect Him. We are warned to be clear minded and self controlled. I thought a lot about my behavior when I was drinking, and what God would do if He found me that way. Would He leave me here? Would He take my friends and family to heaven and make me stay here lost without Him? Even when it was hard for me to abstain from alcohol, I was very concerned about His second coming. I did not want to be left behind. But for the longest time I just could not quit drinking. I still don't know what would have happened to me if Jesus came while I was drunk, but today, I don't have to worry about that. Today, I am confident He will take me with Him when he goes. Because today I am sober. (Let me stress, I do not believe that alcoholism interferes with one's salvation. A drunk is not excluded from heaven, just from God's blessings here on earth. The Bible mentions that a drunkard will not inherit the Kingdom of God but that Kingdom mentioned is within us now. It is not the heavenly Kingdom set up for our eternal life with Jesus. Just as someone mentally sick will not lose their salvation, salvation isn't lost because of a physical sickness either.)

Thought To Meditate On:

I remember when I was a smoker, it didn't matter that people were dying of lung cancer, I wasn't going to quit smoking. And it didn't matter that I coughed for three straight months or that my dad used to pray that cigarettes would make me sick. There was no good reason as far as I was concerned to ever give up cigarettes. An alcoholic feels the same way about the alcohol. Even the fear of Jesus going home without us did not motivate us to quit drinking. We thought about it, but a powerful addiction is strong. Even stronger than our greatest desires.

Thoughts and Revelations:

Let the Weak Say I Am Strong

♥

2 Corinthians 12:9,10

But he said to me, "My grace is sufficient for you, for my power is made perfect in weakness." Therefore I will boast all the more gladly about my weaknesses, so that Christ's power may rest on me. That is why, for Christ's sake, I delight in weaknesses, in insults, in hardships, in persecutions, in difficulties. For when I am weak, then I am strong.

I remember one day awhile back being so proud of myself because I had gone all day without a drink. My husband and I were going out on a date that night and I didn't want to ruin it by getting too intoxicated before he got home. I had a habit of doing that. I knew I would be drinking that evening so I waited. When he got home from work it was obvious he had already been drinking. He had stopped off at a bar with a friend on the way home from work. I was furious. I felt betrayed. I held out for him all day and he didn't even have the decency to come straight home. How dare him. In stubborn anger I told him I didn't want to go out with him anymore. I felt disrespected and I didn't want to spend my evening with him. And if he felt the need to betray me I was equally able to retaliate. So I went to the store and bought a twelve pack of beer. I sat in the hot tub all night by myself and got drunk. What a martyr I was. And it's funny when I think about how self-righteous I acted. Here we were, two drunks, and instead of looking at my own faults, I was attacking him for his. I am so glad I don't have to live in that insanity anymore. Where I was weak, now I am strong. Thinking back over the years we have been married, it is not strange that the majority of the fights we had were either over alcohol or because of alcohol. We would fight because he was stopping at bars. Or he would find beer hidden in the bathroom cabinet and swear I was trying to hide my drinking from him. (Of course I was.) It is nothing short of amazing that we ever stayed together. But here we are eight years strong and sober.

Thought To Meditate On:

God is our strength. Without God's strength we are weak. The Bible says that God is as weak as my greatest strength which means without Him I can do nothing. It doesn't matter what our circumstances are, God is strong enough to conquer anything. The Bible says that nothing is impossible for Him and given what I know, I believe it.

Thoughts and Revelations:

by Lacy Enderson

A Circle of Friends

♥

Psalms 1:1,2

Blessed is the man who does not walk in the counsel of the wicked or stand in the way of sinners or sit in the seat of mockers. But his delight is in the law of the LORD, and on his law he meditates day and night.

I used to refer to my house as a three-ring circus, because we had a party every night of the week. My husband would get off work and he'd walk in the door with a case of beer and a friend. Before the night was over there would be another case of beer and at least one more friend. They used to hang out in the garage and play darts. Most nights I didn't mind. But sometimes it got old, and I'd tell them all to go home. I liked his friends. They were all very nice people. But they were drunks. They hated being at their own homes, so they'd come over to mine and steal my husband's attention away from me. My main concern was the amount of beer I was drinking when they were over. I was a drunk too, and I had a hard time saying no to alcohol. Once I got started, it was hard to stop. I had too many responsibilities to be partying so often. It is amazing the way friends can influence us. When I was a kid, my dad used to make me play with my friends even when I didn't want to. I think he taught me an obligation towards people. When I got sober and I started taking care of myself I learned it was OK to tell my friends to go home. Don't get me wrong, I appreciate the friends God has given me but I also have an obligation to God and my family. Sometimes it is OK to be alone, quiet before God. Or even just playing a game with the kids is a perfect way to spend the evening. I guess we need to balance our lives and put all people into proper perspective. We should always treat people with kindness and love. If a friend is monopolizing the situation, we can let them know.

Thought To Meditate On:

We need to stay away from people whose lives are filled with sin and rebellion. Even if it means getting rid of old friends. Misery loves company. They will surely do all they can to bring us down to their level. Spending time with God in prayer and meditation will give us the power we need to shut the door on the old lifestyle, and unfortunately, the old friends.

Thoughts and Revelations:

He Completes Me

♥

1 John 2:3-6

We know that we have come to know him if we obey his commands. The man who says, "I know him," but does not do what he commands is a liar, and the truth is not in him. But if anyone obeys his word, God's love is truly made complete in him. This is how we know we are in him: Whoever claims to live in him must walk as Jesus did.

If we are true and honest followers of God there are things we just won't do. They won't even be an option. The Holy Spirit becomes our conscience when we accept God into our lives. He begins to direct and lead us toward Himself. He has a greater plan for our lives and leads us onto that greater path. If we call ourselves believers but we choose to walk away from His calling, then we deceive ourselves and the truth is not in us. Before I came to know God, I stole, I lied, I was disrespectful towards adults, I drank, I smoked, and I was continually going astray. I don't remember spending any time with God at all except for church on Sunday mornings. And that is because I was forced to go. I thought nothing of drinking my father's beer in the refrigerator or smoking a cigarette butt from my mother's ash tray. My friends and I would have lunch at a local restaurant and we would walk out without paying the bill. I would sit in the restaurant and spit paper wads through my straw at the ceiling. I would laugh loud enough to offend the other customers and then laugh harder when they got upset with me. I lived a very self-absorbed life for a long time. It's nice to be Holy Spirit led today. It feels good to consider other people's feelings. I have actually learned to get pleasure from seeing others smile, and to know that I have contributed to their happiness.

Thought To Meditate On:

I hate to think of how much pain and discomfort I caused others. It embarrasses me to think of the way I used to treat people. I don't spend a lot of time dwelling on my past mistakes, but remembering clearly helps me with my relationships today. I was told to treat others the way I expect others to treat me. This is a good rule to follow and one I highly recommend.

Thoughts and Revelations:

by Lacy Enderson

He Will Swallow Up Death Forever

♥

James 1:13-15

When tempted, no one should say, "God is tempting me." For God cannot be tempted by evil, nor does he tempt anyone; but each one is tempted when, by his own evil desire, he is dragged away and enticed. Then, after desire has conceived, it gives birth to sin; and sin, when it is full-grown, gives birth to death.

I met a young man in alcohol recovery who didn't have much time sober but he had developed what appeared to be an incredible amount of peace. He wasn't very old. I enjoyed talking to him at meetings because he seemed humble and sincere. I was impressed at the amount of knowledge he had acquired in such a short amount of time. Shortly after meeting him I was told he had walked out in front of a train and killed himself. I was completely shocked. That was the last person I ever guessed would have killed himself. Another guy I knew locked himself in the garage with the car running until he suffocated. When I asked why these two young men would take their own lives, I was told, "They could not take the pain any more."
Alcoholics are not used to feeling the uncomfortable feelings. We numbed our feelings with drugs and alcohol for a long time. Drinking the pain away was a habit we grew to know and love. Some of us couldn't bear the painful feelings. So when we got sober and the emotional pain overwhelmed us we were left tormented and confused. For many alcoholics mental torment was too much to bear and drinking became the familiar comfort again. For others, the thought of drinking again was detestable so the feelings were ended once and for all. I have learned to take the uneasy feelings to God. He comforts me when I can't find the relief I need anyplace else. God is a much better option than suicide. If my friends were still alive I am certain they would agree with me.

Thought To Meditate On:

Just because we were delivered from drugs and alcohol does not mean we won't fight the temptation to return to them. Everyday the temptation grows smaller as long as we maintain a close relationship with God. Remember, the enemy would like nothing more than to see us fail. We need to continue growing in the knowledge of God and His will for our lives in order to secure our success.

Thoughts and Revelations:

No More Getting Even

♥

1 Thessalonians 5:14,15

And we urge you, brothers, warn those who are idle, encourage the timid, help the weak, be patient with everyone. Make sure that nobody pays back wrong for wrong, but always try to be kind to each other and to everyone else.

My husband hired a plumber to do some work for him on a job site. This man did a few things wrong and then disappeared. They waited for him to return to the job, but he never did. So we wrote him a dismissal letter. We asked him to send us a bill for the work he had completed. We received the bill thirty days later. We put it in our bill file with the other bills we could not pay because of funding issues. Fifty days after sending his bill, the plumber became impatient and called the homeowner threatening to lien the property if he wasn't paid immediately. The homeowner called my husband who then called the plumber right away. The plumber didn't want to negotiate. He was angry and called my husband a few obscene words in an attempt to show just how upset he was. When the plumber got off the phone he went up to the job site and broke two windows. A few days later he made harassing phone calls to our house. He called some of my husbands clients to let them know how incompetent he was. My husband's first response was retaliation. He wanted to get even. But he didn't. He let the matter go. It takes a strong person to turn his back on an offense. It is not an easy thing to do, but God will bless the man who does. As a sober believer, we try to do what God wants us to do. But sometimes we can't. Financial problems are very real and sometimes the bills can't be paid. We are taught in recovery to keep our side of the street clean. So even though the plumber hadn't finished his job our responsibility was to pay him for the job he had done. It really wasn't our fault that we couldn't pay him. When he became angry and retaliated, we could have fought back, but instead we treated the situation with love and in the end we came out the winners.

Thought To Meditate On:

An eye for an eye, and a tooth for a tooth. That is the motto we use to stand by. Today we turn the other cheek. Revenge is something most of us turned to when we were offended and hurt. Today we turn to God. The Bible says it is God who will get vengeance for us. It is not to be taken into our own hands. Nothing good ever comes from retaliation.

Thoughts and Revelations:

by Lacy Enderson

The Enemy is Under My Feet

♥

Isaiah 54:17

no weapon forged against you will prevail, and you will refute every tongue that accuses you. This is the heritage of the servants of the LORD, and this is their vindication from me," declares the LORD.

When I was in jr. high school I had the entire gang of Mexican girls after me. I hadn't done anything to them that I was aware of, but for some reason they did not like me. My dad was a coach for youth sports and he had a few of the Mexican boys from school on his team. At school, these boys would say hi to me, but that was the extent of any friendship. I thought maybe the girls were jealous that their male friends were acknowledging me. To this day I still don't know what the real reason was. All I know was, I was the target of their hatred and they were out to get me. I was at a winter formal in the eighth grade with my friends when the whole gang of girls circled around me and told me to go outside. I knew what that meant. They wanted to beat me up, so I refused. I stood there, immobile, until a teacher came to my rescue. For months I ran home from school to avoid any confrontation with these girls. It seemed everyday when school let out they would be waiting for me near my locker. Eventually after some time they left me alone. But it definitely scarred me. I was very frightened by that situation and the fear of people stayed with me long into my adult years. Today I try not to allow others to frighten me. I know I can't be friends with everyone and sometimes I might rub a person the wrong way. But instead of running from confrontation, I try to face it. Facing my fears means I might not have to be afraid anymore and that would be a perfect end result. There is no situation or circumstance that my God cannot handle for me. His Word tells me He will make me bold as a lion.

Thought To Meditate On:

God says He will protect me from all harm. He also says His perfect love casts out all fear. The Bible tells me I can sit under God's shelter of protection and not even a vicious word spoken against me will harm me in any way. I used to gain courage from drinking, now I get my confidence from God.

Thoughts and Revelations:

He Longs To Be Gracious

♥

Deuteronomy 11:13-15

So if you faithfully obey the commands I am giving you today—to love the LORD your God and to serve him with all your heart and with all your soul— then I will send rain on your land in its season, both autumn and spring rains, so that you may gather in your grain. I will provide grass in the fields for your cattle, and you will eat and be satisfied.

My mother used to sew my clothes. She made me beautiful wardrobes every year. I had the prettiest outfits of any girl at school. My mom and I would go shopping to see what the latest fashions were and then we'd copy them on mom's sewing machine. She was very talented and I was very proud to wear her creations. It was important, as a teenager, to fit in and to feel good about my appearance. We didn't have a lot of money, so we couldn't afford to buy the designer originals. But my mother had the answer. God is also in the business of creating. He sees what we need and provides His own special solutions. God knew we would fall on our face, so He came to pick us up. He knew addictions would consume and entangle us, so he inspired support groups. He knew all about emotional pain, sorrow and grief, so He sent us a comforter. He has an answer to every one of our questions, and a solution to every one of our problems. He gave us a manual for life, full of guidelines and instructions. The Bible. Read it! With everything that goes on in the world there is no way we could figure it all out. God never expected us to. He created us, therefore He knows us. He knows that we need Him. So He has given us Himself.

Thought To Meditate On:

Our purpose in life is to know God and make Him known. In my opinion, that is the only reason we are here. Unfortunately man sinned, and when he did the devil's door opened up and all God's original plans broke into a million pieces. Sin and destruction became our normal lot in life and God has been trying ever since to turn our hearts back towards Him. God desires to know everything about us as well as for us to know everything about Him. When we give God our hearts, souls, and minds, He gives us all we need for life. If you're looking for the easy way out, look no farther. It is God, and He has been ready and waiting for a very long time.

Thoughts and Revelations:

by Lacy Enderson

I Am Not My Own

♥

1 Corinthians 6:19,20

Do you not know that your body is a temple of the Holy Spirit, who is in you, whom you have received from God? You are not your own; you were bought at a price. Therefore honor God with your body.

My friend Jim had a number of extra-marital affairs. He blamed his lack of self control on his rock cocaine addiction and his alcoholism. He told me when he drank and used drugs, he looked for sex. He craved it. He said he wasn't proud of what he did, but was glad today to be sober and self-controlled. God had delivered him and the urge was gone. My friend Bob also committed adultery. He could not find the strength he needed to be faithful to his wife. No matter how hard he tried, he always gave in to the desires of his flesh and allowed women to lure him into their rooms. Although he was in therapy for his problem he still fought the battle daily. Both men suffered from a sex addiction. It was just as hard of an addiction to break as drugs or alcohol. I read a book called Bondage Breaker where they discussed sexual urges. It helped me to understand the sickness behind the behaviors. Fortunately there is a program to help people with this problem, just as there is one for alcohol and drugs. Nobody has to remain in the grips of the sin. God can and will break the chains. I believe the devil uses our weaknesses to keep us down, under his control. He discovers what we are driven by and dangles it in front of our face until we give in to the desire. The Bible says the devil is the god of this world and so he does have the power to destroy us. But we have to let him. For every force against us God makes a way of escape. The Bible also says, if God is for us, nothing can be against us. That means no power in hell can keep us down.

Thought To Meditate On:

When we gave our life to Jesus He took up residence in our hearts. That means we have given Him control of our bodies as well as our minds and spirits. We have an obligation to God to refrain from sin that destroys us since we no longer belong to ourselves. God bought us with a price when He sent Jesus to save us and it is our duty to properly care for His property. And it also never hurt to have a little self respect and dignity. Don't you think you deserve it? I do.

Thoughts and Revelations:

Choice Morsels
♥

Psalms 119:11

I have hidden your word in my heart that I might not sin against you.

When I was in grade school we had a scripture memorization contest in my Sunday school class. The winners got to go to Mexico to visit an orphanage and I really wanted to go. We had a list of verses we were required to learn each week for three months. I learned them all and I won the contest. The trip was a blessing. But I had no idea just how much more a blessing it was to have those scripture verses hidden in my heart. When life was difficult, it was quoting these scriptures that gave me comfort and strength. God knew even as a kid what I would need as an adult, so he prepared me for what was yet to come. God sees into our future, and knows the trials we will face. He loves us too much to watch us walk through the fire on our own. He goes with us. When I was consumed by alcoholism, I remembered the verse, "I will never leave you, nor forsake you". And when I couldn't pay my rent I quoted the scripture, "God will provide all of my needs according to His riches in glory". When my children were driving around past midnight it comforted me to know the Word said, "And God will keep you from all harm". God's word brings the peace I need no matter what the circumstances. There is power in the Word of God. God sent His Word to perform it, so when we quote scripture back to Him it sets the wheels in motion and the scripture comes to life. Now that I am sober I have lots of time to memorize scripture. It is the Word of God in my heart that keeps me alive and well, not alcohol in my stomach.

Thought To Meditate On:

I wasn't always close to God. I did grow up in a church, and attending Sunday school and summer camp was my norm, but a personal relationship with a real God didn't happen until I was twenty four. Even after I discovered who God was and He became real to me, I still couldn't quite believe He could take care of me the way I needed Him too. Once you determine to get sober and start believing in a power greater than yourself, don't get discouraged if God doesn't become real to you right away. If you don't give up He will not let you down. They say it takes what it takes and it is different for everyone. So whatever it takes for you, is when it will happen.

Thoughts and Revelations:

by Lacy Enderson

Jesus is the Way

♥

John 12:26

Whoever serves me must follow me; and where I am, my servant also will be. My Father will honor the one who serves me.

I will follow where Jesus leads me, and I will be who He wants me to be. I will do what He wants me to do because I am tired of wandering aimlessly knowing not where I am going, having no hope at all. I have tried to do it my way and nothing ever works out, so I'm ready to give God a chance. What more can I lose? I remember needing to be in control of everything. I went to church a minimum of three times a week in an attempt to hear how God wanted me to live. I was afraid if I wasn't in a service I would miss the important message God had planned for me. And that message was going to be attached to a miracle I felt I needed more than anything. I was desperate and miserable. After church I would return home and continue to do things my way. God wasn't quick enough for me. I was impatient and imperfect. I wanted a change now, not tomorrow, and God was taking too long. One year I bought my younger son a bike for Christmas. This was a special present because not only did my son want a bike really bad, in normal circumstances I could not have afforded that bike. Only God knew how I was able to afford it. My son loved his bike, but one night he left it outside and it was stolen. I was furious. I cried and prayed up and down my street convinced if I did this long enough his bike would show up. It never did. I somehow thought if I cried and begged loud enough God would deliver that bike back to me, but I was wrong. I lived my life worried and frantic. I never trusted God to provide anything, and so He never did. It wasn't until I got tired and gave up that God arrived. Be careful that your attitude and behavior doesn't tie God's hands. I believe He wants to do great things for us but sometimes, we in our own selfish determination, hinder Him from working.

Thought To Meditate On:

Get out of the way. Stop trying to fix everything. Relax and take it easy. God doesn't put stipulations on His grace. He doesn't require you to write fifty times, I will believe, in order to help you. Just believe. Stop trying to do everything yourself and let God help you. Stop. Right now. Just stop doing everything. Bow your head and ask God to help you. And then quit; quit crying, quit begging, quit worrying. He will help you when you get out of His way.

Thoughts and Revelations:

Take a Deep Breath

♥

Proverbs 19:11

A man's wisdom gives him patience; it is to his glory to overlook an offense.

One year when I attended church camp I had laryngitis. I could not speak at all. There wasn't much I needed to say, but one night we were all standing in a group waiting to enter the cafeteria for dinner when a daddy long leg spider crawled by me. I never killed spiders or bugs of any sort. We were outside. We were in their territory. But one of the girls threatened to step on it. I kept trying to tell her to leave it alone but my words wouldn't come out. I kept trying to get her attention but she couldn't hear me. When she stepped on the spider I was so completely frustrated, without thinking, I hit her across the head. Those standing around me were in shock. They couldn't believe I had hit her. I couldn't believe it myself. It happened so quickly. It was an impulsive reaction to my anger. When I tried to explain and tell her I was sorry, there was still no sound coming from my voice, so I gave up and ate dinner alone. Sometimes human reactions are not quite what God would intend. And sometimes it isn't our intentions either. But we don't always have the time to think about our reaction when we are responding to a bad situation. It is a good idea to be prepared within to handle all situations, so when they do come up, we will react appropriately. Today I try not to react in anger. The impulsive behaviors of anger, rage and violence have to be smashed. I don't want to be that kind of person anymore. Deep internal rage surfaces when we least expect it. So it is wise to get rid of such anger so it can't respond at all. When my voice came back a few days later, I did apologize.

Thought To Meditate On:

The Bible tells us that our battles here on earth are against the wickedness in a person rather than the actual person we are battling with. It doesn't mean that the battle is easier because we know this, but it does influence how we respond to it. Not everyone has a good purpose, some people are full of evil intentions. Today I choose not to hang around with agitated people but I do keep them in my prayers. I have replaced hatred with compassion.

Thoughts and Revelations:

by Lacy Enderson

Be My Rock of Refuge

♥

1 John 5:18

We know that anyone born of God does not continue to sin; the one who was born of God keeps him safe, and the evil one cannot harm him.

I had been drinking a lot one afternoon and decided it would be fun to take my daughter to a church carnival across the street from where I lived. Being intoxicated did not matter because we were close enough to walk. I did not have to drive her anywhere and the fact that this particular church was selling beer meant I wasn't going to be the only drunk at the carnival. While walking around the carnival carrying my daughter I tripped over a big wide extension cord and fell. I landed on top of her and she hit her head really hard. As though it wasn't humiliating enough to fall, a sober friend of mine from my recovery program walked by just as I was falling. She told me, I never had to drink again if I didn't want to. I was completely embarrassed. I think God was trying to get my attention. It was unfortunate that my daughter was caught in the middle of God and myself but her head was fine and there was no damage. I was suppose to be sober. I had already attended a few months of alcohol recovery meetings and met some very nice people who promised to help me whenever I wanted to drink. But instead of calling one of them, I drank instead. Running into a sober friend was just what I needed to shake my world a little. It wasn't long after my fall that I got sober again. Even when we fail to meet God's expectations, He provides a way. I needed to quit drinking and God gave me a nudge.

Thought To Meditate On:

I bet if we paid closer attention we would see more of God in our lives. But because we are self absorbed and too busy to notice Him, we don't see Him at all. Alcoholics have the disease of alcoholism. It is a fatal disease if left untreated, and so far there is no cure. God said He would heal all of our diseases but His healing can't begin until we allow it. Because we are in a life or death situation, God is busily trying to get our attention. So when we finally do notice Him and quit drinking, the healing then begins.

Thoughts and Revelations:

Our Heavenly Mediator

♥

Hebrews 7:24-26

...but because Jesus lives forever, he has a permanent priesthood. Therefore he is able to save completely those who come to God through him, because he always lives to intercede for them. Such a high priest meets our need—one who is holy, blameless, pure, set apart from sinners, exalted above the heavens.

My son had a friend who spent time at my house after school. He was a good kid, but he had problems. His parents didn't get along well with each other and they separated shortly after we met. He became quite rebellious over the situation. He began having problems in school and developed a bad habit of smoking pot. He seemed troubled and angry most of the time. I felt sorry for him. One day, my son went to visit the boy at his house. His friend was playing with a BB gun and shot a bird to the ground. My son is ultra sensitive towards animals, and this bothered him tremendously. He picked the bird up and held it gently in his hand. He silently prayed that God would heal the bird. Miraculously, the bird stood up and flew away. This had an incredible impact on the boy. He came to me and asked about Jesus. The boy came to the saving knowledge of Jesus that day. He needed a loving father and Jesus met him with a miracle. Don't think for one minute that God does not want to take care of you. That is exactly why you were created. Wait and watch. Miracles happen everyday.

Thought To Meditate On:

Have you ever had a divine appointment? That is a meeting God sets up to lead a person to Jesus. God uses people, places and circumstances to accomplish His missionary work on earth. It amazes me to watch and see just what God will do next. I don't think of myself as a minister or evangelist but if God sets up a divine appointment in my life to lead someone to Him, I am all for it. Bring it on.

Thoughts and Revelations:

by Lacy Enderson

Fear Not For I am With You

♥

Psalms 118:6-8

The LORD is with me; I will not be afraid. What can man do to me? The LORD is with me; he is my helper. I will look in triumph on my enemies. It is better to take refuge in the LORD than to trust in man.

I was introduced to a man who worked in a small office as an insurance agent. He seemed like a respectable businessman and we began to date. It wasn't long before I realized looks can be deceiving. I had never met a more perverted and corrupt man than he was. He had more pornographic movies hiding in his office than a video shop. He kept pornographic magazines in the top drawer of his desk, and he had a photo album with pictures of past girlfriend's in the nude. He hid this behind a tile in the ceiling. His office was a den of sin and evil. This man had mental problems, so his Doctor put him on lithium. His temper was wild, and when he was angry, he was out of control. He kept a list on his computer of all the girls he had dated. He had their names, and descriptions of each one in the database. After just a short time with this man I became completely disgusted. Had I not been a heavy drinker, that relationship would have ended after one date. It's funny what I tolerated while under the influence of alcohol. They say not to judge a book by it's cover, but they also say looks can be deceiving. I never would have guessed this man to be wrapped up in so much sin. And to justify his behaviors he had the nerve to say, he was forgiven. How dare he take my God's grace for granted. People are not always who they appear to be. Be careful. Get to know someone before you make a commitment to spend any amount of time together. As an alcoholic, I was quick to jump in. As a sober member of society I have learned to be cautious. With the stories I hear about the corruption in the world, you should be too.

Thought To Meditate On:

God is all powerful and all knowing. He will never fail us. He can do for us what nobody else can. Trust Him to reveal the evil so you are aware of it's presence. Don't let sin take you by surprise. Sin hides in the dark but the light that Jesus brings sends sin scurrying back to it's hiding place. Don't rely on your own senses. When it comes to sin and deception, let Jesus light the way.

Thoughts and Revelations:

He Pardons Sin

♥

Isaiah 43:25

"I, even I, am he who blots out your transgressions, for my own sake, and remembers your sins no more.

There was a family at my church I was acquainted with. We were not close friends but we talked. On a few occasions I had joined them for group prayer. I loved when this man prayed for me. He was quiet and gentle and I could sense the love of God flowing from him to his family. He was the perfect representation of a true man of God. One day he walked into a recovery meeting and I was completely shocked to see him there. He said he hadn't had alcohol in fifteen years but he had never been able to get rid of the rage. He said he went in cycles. He could be calm for long periods, and then for no reason at all, he would blow up. He was controlling, and a perfectionist, and no one could meet his high expectations. No matter how hard his family tried they just couldn't measure up. He was a dry drunk. He had never dug down to the deep issues of his past and his personality was suffering. He had not cleared away the wreckage of his past and those earlier mistakes continued to haunt him. Sobriety doesn't just mean freedom from alcohol, it means a complete transformation of our lives, starting from the secret places within us. When my friend got rid of the alcohol, he was still left with himself. Nothing had changed as far as who he was. God wants to cleanse and deliver us from every obstacle that stands in the way of our serenity. He wants complete control of our lives. We must allow Him to take away all of our defects of character if we ever want to experience perfect peace within.

Thought To Meditate On:

Sin has consequences. You cannot do something wrong without punishment. If that were the case, crime would run rampant, even more than it already does. But God says He forgives us if we are sorry and repent. And not only will He forgive us, He will blot out the transgression and remember the sin no more. So when you are wrong, apologize. It is when you are sorry that God forgives.

Thoughts and Revelations:

by Lacy Enderson

A Stronghold in Times of Trouble

♥

James 5:13-15

Is any one of you in trouble? He should pray. Is anyone happy? Let him sing songs of praise. Is any one of you sick? He should call the elders of the church to pray over him and anoint him with oil in the name of the Lord. And the prayer offered in faith will make the sick person well; the Lord will raise him up. If he has sinned, he will be forgiven.

I struggled for years with bulimia. No matter how hard I tried I just could not stop making myself throw-up. Anytime I felt uncomfortable feelings I would eat large quantities of food. I used food especially to numb feelings of anxiety or impatience. Food fed my hungry heart and for the moment it made me feel better. But always just for the moment, never longer. Inevitably the fear of gaining weight would take over my thoughts and I would throw everything up. Sometimes I would go days without eating. I would get so tired of vomiting I welcomed starvation. I mean, what was the worst of the two evils? I hated them both. I was so addicted to purging that anything I ate had to come out. It was an addictive mental behavior I could not control. I had lost the power of choice over eating. One day, God saw my pain. He extended His mercy to me and I was delivered. Outside of His help, I would probably still be bulimic. It is a deliverance that is hard to explain, and one that I know could only have come from God. I have an alcoholic girlfriend who suffers from bulimia. I feel very bad for her. I know the torment in her mind. Sharing with her my own story of binging and purging gives her hope that one day she too can be set free from such an awful obsession. I wish I could snap my fingers and make it all go away for her. But I can't. So I pray, and listen. That's all I can do.

Thought To Meditate On:

Eating disorders can be just as debilitating for the overeater as alcohol is for the alcoholic. No one's addiction is worse than another's, especially to the one suffering. I wish I had all the answers for those who still struggle but I don't. I cannot even fully explain how I was able to quit throwing-up. So how can I really help someone else going through similar circumstances? By prayer and listening.

Thoughts and Revelations:

Love is a Many Splendid Thing

♥

1 John 4:7,8

Dear friends, let us love one another, for love comes from God. Everyone who loves has been born of God and knows God. Whoever does not love does not know God, because God is love.

I began dating my third husband when we both had two years sober. We met in alcohol recovery meetings and became good friends. In fact, it was more of an infatuation. There weren't many things wrong with him physically. He was easy on the eyes. But he had a lot of emotional problems. His wife had recently left him, and he lost everything he owned. He was angry, resentful and drowning in self-pity. My nurturing tendencies took over and I began to coddle him. I didn't like seeing him in pain. So I voluntarily suffered his emotional abuse, and enabled him to feel sorry for himself. He was a victim and I was the martyr. What an unhealthy combination we were. I thought God had put me in his life to take care of him. But I was wrong. God had greater plans for his life and I was only getting in the way. I was a hindrance to the fulfillment of God's plan and healing was impossible with me constantly clinging to his side. I was so focused on him it was actually destroying us. I had to allow him to take care of himself and yet I didn't know how. I had to quit playing the roll of mother and allow him to stand on his own two feet. I began attending meetings on my own to learn how to take care of myself. I was so used to taking care of everyone else that I neglected myself. By putting myself first, and giving him space, our relationship actually grew stronger. The fact that I loved him gave me the strength to back off. It helped knowing God was with him. And God was with me also.

Thought To Meditate On:

I believe co-dependent behavior is nothing more than a distraction from ourselves. In fact, anything we obsessively focus on becomes just another delay in our own growth. Self-pity and feeling sorry for myself were part of who I was. I wanted everyone feeling sorry for me, so I made sure everyone knew how miserable I was. Alcohol, cigarettes, food and people were great distractions, but when I got rid of them, I was left with me. What I found was a person I didn't like very much. I better understood why no one else seemed to like me either.

Thoughts and Revelations:

God's Enabling Power

♥

Philippians 2:13

For it is God who works in you to will and to act according to his good purpose.

One Sunday while attending church, an old friend of mine came in with her family. We were very surprised to see each other. She shared with me that she had suffered a battle with drugs and alcohol, but had been clean and sober for a year. After the service we spent some time together sharing stories but we did not keep in touch like we promised. Almost seven years later I ran into her at an alcohol recovery meeting. I was so excited to see her there and I ran over to say hi. She was belligerent and offensive. I had never seen her like that before and it frightened me. I know I'm supposed to help other alcoholics, and she was a long time friend of mine, but I actually ran from her. She was not herself. She was definitely not clean. She was under the influence of some kind of drug that was controlling who she was. It saddened me to see her that way. I felt very badly afterwards for running out on her like I did. It's amazing the impact addictions have on our lives. They had changed her from a level-headed, intelligent woman to a violent, angry addict. I guess it was good she was at a meeting. Maybe it won't be long before she gets the help she needs. It wasn't that I judged her, but people on drugs are unpredictable. I don't recommend hanging around them no matter who they are.

Thought To Meditate On:

I was a completely different person when I was drinking. Nobody ever knew how I would behave after that first drink. Sometimes I was sweet and sappy, and other times I was nasty and mean. But no one could predict which person I would become, not even myself.

Thoughts and Revelations:

My Father's House

♥

1 Thessalonians 2:11,12

For you know that we dealt with each of you as a father deals with his own children, encouraging, comforting and urging you to live lives worthy of God, who calls you into his kingdom and glory.

When I was a kid my parents encouraged me to do whatever I was interested in. They were active in my development and wanted to see me excel in my God-given gifts. Throughout my childhood I was involved in several activities, but my greatest passion was playing the piano. My dad had a friend who stored an antique piano in our garage and I would spend hours plucking away at the keys. I had an ear for music, so even without lessons I could play songs. My parents were very proud of my ability. We didn't have the money to purchase a piano until I was fifteen and then my parents bought me one and I took piano lessons. But this was at the age when boys and parties were far more important than practicing scales on a keyboard. I just could not dedicate the time necessary to be a great piano player. Of course, now that I am older, I wish I had taken it a little more seriously. I hear some of the most beautiful piano music and I wish I could play. As an adult I try to tune into the voice of God. I want to know what His plan is for me so I don't waste anymore time. I don't want to look back in five years and regret that I didn't listen to Him. I've let too many opportunities slip through my fingers already. It's time to develop my talents.

Thought To Meditate On:

God gives distinct abilities to a variety of people so we have a wide range of talents across the world. But many talents go unnoticed because of drug and alcohol abuse. When you get sober take some time to figure out what gifts God gave to you and then set out to develop those skills. You might discover a rainbow waiting for you. One that was there all the time.

Thoughts and Revelations:

by Lacy Enderson

Broken and Contrite

♥

Isaiah 57:15

For this is what the high and lofty One says—he who lives forever, whose name is holy: "I live in a high and holy place, but also with him who is contrite and lowly in spirit, to revive the spirit of the lowly and to revive the heart of the contrite.

One Sunday morning when I was ten my dad came home from the swap meet with an old, antique doll. This doll had a hard, cracked face and body, and she was dressed in a dirty, red, satin dress. She barely had any hair left on her head and she had a far off look in her eyes. I hated that doll. It frightened me. It didn't say ma-ma, and it wasn't soft and cuddly like my baby dolls. It was cold and gloomy and I didn't like looking at her. The other day while I was shopping at the mall I saw a doll that looked almost identical to that doll, so I went in to take a closer look. While I stood staring, the saleswoman walked over and wound the doll up. She began to play beautiful music. I was shocked at my instant change of attitude towards her. All of a sudden, the doll changed. She was capable of making beautiful music and I didn't perceive her as ugly anymore. I relate this memory to first impressions of some people. They seem so broken and my first reaction is to run. But then they speak, and I see the hidden beauty. From the place in their hearts where God lives, comes a sweet spirit. I have to remember never to judge a book by it's cover. There could be an awesome story inside.

Thought To Meditate On:

Years of alcohol abuse can weather the look on one's face. Our bodies weren't made to tolerate the dehydrating effects of alcohol, so over time we start looking older than we are. Getting sober and learning how to be a better person might change who we are on the inside, but not usually our looks. So even when we change from nasty to sweet, people's first impressions of us can be all wrong.

Thoughts and Revelations:

Your Word Have I Hid in My Heart
♥

Deuteronomy 6:5-8

These commandments that I give you today are to be upon your hearts. Impress them on your children. Talk about them when you sit at home and when you walk along the road, when you lie down and when you get up.

Growing up, I went to fifteen different summer and winter church camps in nine years. They usually took place in the mountains somewhere by a lake. I remember by the end of each week I was so hungry for God that He was all I thought about for weeks. There was something powerful about being away from peer pressure, up in the mountains, surrounded by nature. If I could have stayed on the mountain forever, I would have. Oh, the years of misery I could have alleviated. But as soon as I'd get back into the old crowd, and the old lifestyle, God was pushed to the side and my life was falling down hill all over again. It wasn't that I didn't want to live right. I just didn't know how to. I had friends from church who sat in a circle on the lawn at lunch time. They ate and had fellowship. I was so jealous of their relationships. They actually socialized with each other outside of church. I really wanted to join them but I could not pull myself away from the corrupt crowd I hung around with. I always felt so guilty sitting with them. I felt like a hypocrite. They heard the stories about me at the parties I attended. Everybody did. I felt unworthy of their friendships so I stayed far away from them. I try not to beat myself up because of my mistakes. Nobody is perfect. Even they have failed over the years. But at least they gave themselves a chance. I was always too afraid.

Thought To Meditate On:

My church friends never judged me. I was the one who judged myself. It was my own guilt that kept me separated from some very nice people. At camp we got along great, but at school I just couldn't join them. Personal guilt and self condemnation stood in my way. Drugs and alcohol were my god when I was down off that mountain, and unfortunately would remain my central focus for a very long time.

Thoughts and Revelations:

by Lacy Enderson
My Redeemer Lives

♥

1 John 2:1,2

My dear children, I write this to you so that you will not sin. But if anybody does sin, we have one who speaks to the Father in our defense—Jesus Christ, the Righteous One. He is the atoning sacrifice for our sins, and not only for ours but also for the sins of the whole world.

One Saturday, a girlfriend I worked with invited me and my children to her daughter's birthday party. The party was held at a park an hour away from my home. There was lots of beer, but my son had a baseball game that afternoon and I knew I could not drink. I fought the urge to drink for more than three hours. I did everything I could to stay away from that beer. But the temptation soon grew too big and my resistance wasn't strong enough. Before I knew it, I was drunk. There was no way I could drive my son to his baseball game. I was completely intoxicated and unable to drive anywhere. So I called my family and told them he wasn't feeling well and would not be playing in the game. I continued to drink the rest of the day and we ended up staying the night at her house. I wasn't feeling like a very good mom by the end of that day. It wasn't that I meant to be irresponsible. My intentions were always good, but alcohol had such a hold on me. To deny it was pure hell. Since I got sober and God removed the obsession, I don't play those alcoholic mind games with myself. Today, drinking is not an option. I don't have to fear going anywhere that I won't be able to get myself home from because I'm drunk. I hate to think about all the times I told my kids no because I was drinking. I feel bad that alcohol was more important than my family. But that is what the disease of alcohol does. It destroys.

Thought To Meditate On:

Guilt played a huge role in my life for a long time. Even after God forgave me, I still found it hard to forgive myself. After we accept Jesus into our lives, there is not suppose to be anymore self-condemnation. That means guilt is a lie. Forgiveness is vital to our sobriety. We drank because we wallowed in self-pity over all our past mistakes. We drank because we felt guilty. Being sober means there is no more reasons or excuses. It is time to forgive ourselves and let them go.

Thoughts and Revelations:

No Weapon Formed Against Me Will Prosper

♥

Psalms 18:16-19

He reached down from on high and took hold of me; he drew me out of deep waters. He rescued me from my powerful enemy, from my foes, who were too strong for me. They confronted me in the day of my disaster, but the LORD was my support. He brought me out into a spacious place; he rescued me because he delighted in me.

I heard Xanax pills worked great for tension and stress. So I called my Doctor for a prescription. He told me they were highly addictive, but wrote me the script anyway. But it was only ten pills for ten days. For those ten days nothing bothered me. It was like a miracle drug had landed in my lap. Although I wanted more, it embarrassed me to ask my Doctor for drugs. I didn't want him to think I was an addict. So I fought the desire to acquire more. Thirteen years later I was working in the medical field and was able to get my hands on any drug I wanted. So I ordered two bottles of a hundred each of Xanax. The side effects were different than I remembered. When I took them I became very tired, and my memory was effected. After taking a few pills one day, I had a very long conversation with my mother on the phone. We made plans to go shopping the next day, but when she showed up at my house, I couldn't even remember that I had talked with her. She was very upset with me, but not as upset as I was at myself. After a few more horrible episodes like that one, I reluctantly flushed the pills down the toilet. Taking those pills was like putting a band-aid on top of a splinter. Until the splinter was taken out, the wound could not heal. Instead of a temporary solution, God wanted me permanently healed. Stress and anxiety can be treated, but continuous taking of narcotics is not the best solution. I have found it much more liberating learning to deal with problems rather than medicating them.

Thought To Meditate On:

Working through emotional pain can sometimes hurt more than the original wound. We get so used to the pain it seems to become a part of who we are. Healing takes effort and sometimes that energy is exhausting. But please don't let the pain stop you from seeking the healing you need. Remember, once you are delivered and set free, there is now no more problem. And a problem free life is better than any drug or medication.

Thoughts and Revelations:

by Lacy Enderson
Love is Not Self Seeking
♥

1 Corinthians 10:23,24

"Everything is permissible"—but not everything is beneficial. "Everything is permissible"—but not everything is constructive. Nobody should seek his own good, but the good of others.

I have a girlfriend I went to school with who has had a very hard life. Her mom spent most of her childhood in a mental institution. Her brother died when he was a teenager, and her sister's emotional problems caused her to cut off their relationship in their early twenties. One night my friend went dancing at a club. Her good friend was driving home very intoxicated and ran into the back of a car. My girlfriend was not wearing her seat belt and the impact threw her forward into the dashboard. She broke every bone in her face. She told me that in the hospital when they were taking her to the room a child screamed in fright at the sight of her face. When I saw her a few days later I understood what she meant. My friend was not the same person I grew up with. Her voice was still hers, but her face had become someone unfamiliar to me. She had gone from being stunning to being shocking. Years and numerous surgeries later, she is very beautiful again. She still does not look like my old high school friend but I have learned to accept her new look. It didn't seem fair that my friend had to suffer at the hand of someone else's careless mistake. But I am just as guilty. I have driven my friends around drunk more times than I care to remember. It scares me to think of the damage I could have caused and it fills me with gratitude at the same time for God's grace. God had mercy on carloads of innocent people when I didn't care enough to let someone else drive.

Thought To Meditate On:

Alcoholics are self-centered egotistical spoiled-rotten brats. I know it is the effect of the alcohol that makes us that way, but none the less, we do choose to drink rather than live sober. Defending myself was common. I'd say, I am an alcoholic and I have a disease therefore it is not my fault. But it was. Now that I am sober I see I had a choice. If I have diabetes, I take my medicine. If I am an alcoholic, I quit drinking. I chose to drink, therefore the lives I endangered was a choice, nothing less, and I should be ashamed of myself.

Thoughts and Revelations:

Reap With Songs of Joy
♥

Galatians 6:7,8

Do not be deceived: God cannot be mocked. A man reaps what he sows. The one who sows to please his sinful nature, from that nature will reap destruction; the one who sows to please the Spirit, from the Spirit will reap eternal life.

Next door to my apartment at college was a stereo store. The manager was a twenty three year old married man. He was friendly and attractive. I was only eighteen so I enjoyed hanging out with this older man. He bought my roommate and me bottles of wine and we would sit in our apartment and talk for hours. One day he invited my roommate and I to go to the mountains with him. I was delighted. We stopped off at a corner cafe for pie a-la-mode. Then, we proceeded to hike two hours through the trees and down by an old river. The weather was beautiful. The sun was hidden behind the clouds and there was a cold breeze in the air. At the young warped age of eighteen, I thought it was nice hanging out with a married man. I didn't feel uncomfortable. I didn't have to worry about what I looked like, or what I said because he was married. It was a good feeling. As far as I was concerned it was a great way to spend an afternoon. I was the type who fell in love with every guy I met. I was constantly on the lookout for the man of my dreams. I was obsessed with men. But not this one. He was unavailable and that made everything OK. At least I thought. But when he took us home and tried to kiss me I realized what a fool I had been. I had to question my intelligence. I knew God did not make me an idiot. Maybe just young, stupid and naive. Today I'm older and wiser, thank God. And one thing I was always grateful for; even when I was drinking I knew a married man belonged at home with his wife. It was a deep conviction planted in me at the young age of eighteen.

Thought To Meditate On:

You've heard the saying, if you play with fire, you will get burned? Are we that stupid to think we can hang out with drunks and not get caught up in the destruction of their lifestyle? I know I dated a few men who drank after I got sober. What was I thinking? I know what it taught me; I really dislike people who are drunk. In sobriety I stay as far away from the flame as I can. Remember, even a small flame can destroy acres.

Thoughts and Revelations:

by Lacy Enderson

Actions Speak Louder Than Words

♥

James 1:27

Religion that God our Father accepts as pure and faultless is this: to look after orphans and widows in their distress and to keep oneself from being polluted by the world.

I used to work with children in a childcare center. I was hired to work in the infant room with a very nice lady named May. She was a happy woman with a lot of happy stories about her family. She was proud of her kids and grandkids. In my opinion, May had it all. Only two weeks after I began my job May's husband died of a stroke. I was horrified. I felt so sad for her. She said there wasn't any sign that he was sick and he died so suddenly she never got to say goodbye. May continued to come to work each day, but her disposition changed. She was not happy anymore. She was so grieved she became anxious and short tempered. She began to yell at the kids and also at me. She was not herself. When it was obvious the stress of her personal life was interfering with her job, the director asked her to leave. So now she not only had no husband, she also had no job. I began visiting with her at her house. It was hard for me at first because her personality was so unpredictable, but when I was able to quit caring so much about myself and start caring more for her, I was able to deal with her mood swings better. I saw her need for a friend and I took time from my busy schedule to help her. She really was a kind woman. The circumstances of life robbed her of her joy, but not forever. I ran into May three years later, and she had a new life. She appeared to be happy again. I was blessed to have known her during the hard time in her life. It taught me how to take my eyes off of myself and care more about someone else. Not something I was used to.

Thought To Meditate On:

Depression changes people. It's hard watching the pain of grief and sorrow turn my loved ones inward. Depression and hopelessness consume them and they become someone else. Over time depression lifts and the emotional wounds heal. It is important not to focus too much on the difficulty of the moment but to rejoice at what God can and will do through the hard situations of life. And remember, someone else's sorrow is not about you. Don't make it about you.

Thoughts and Revelations:

Light the Fire in my Soul

♥

1 Peter 2:9,10

But you are a chosen people, a royal priesthood, a holy nation, a people belonging to God, that you may declare the praises of him who called you out of darkness into his wonderful light. Once you were not a people, but now you are the people of God; once you had not received mercy, but now you have received mercy.

I once saw a movie called Private Benjamin. It was about a girl who enlists in the army and then decides she doesn't want to be there anymore. This movie brought light to the fact that there are some things in life I don't want to do, but dropping out is not always the answer. I know that everything I decide to do isn't always going to work out exactly as I thought it would. I will make mistakes and fail, but that does not make me a failure. I had a job for nine months with a company I really liked. I did very well. In fact, the boss praised me continually. I asked him once if after knowing me and my performance, would he still hire me. He said yes. I needed that kind of praise and recognition. I had very low self esteem and I hungered for continual affirmation. One day, I made a mistake. I did something upsetting to my boss and for the first time in nine months he became angry with me. I was so horrified, without even thinking, I gave my two week notice. I quit my job. Something about my personality could not handle rejection. Quitting gave me back the power he took from me when he got angry. It felt like revenge, and I have to admit it felt good. Unfortunately, that is not the only job I left because my feelings got hurt. Back to the movie, I thank God I never enlisted in the military. Quitting would not have been an option. I am working on this character flaw of mine. I know it is important to overcome my need to be perfect. Life means eventually I will fail, but today I need to know, occasional failure is OK. Rejection is hard for everyone but there is a positive way to deal with it, and running away isn't the solution.

Thought To Meditate On:

The reason I got sober was I hated getting drunk. Alcohol became detestable to me. I hated the fights and the hangovers. I couldn't stand the headaches and the lack of sleep. But after I got sober I had no comfort from anxiety. People made me anxious and I could no longer drink away those fears. I had a lot of personal growth to do in sobriety and although difficult, it has all been good. People still make me nervous, but I have learned to deal with the anxiety, sober.

Thoughts and Revelations:

by Lacy Enderson

Lead me Not into Temptation

♥

Matthew 26:41

"Watch and pray so that you will not fall into temptation. The spirit is willing, but the body is weak."

When I was a single mother raising my three children, I had a single male neighbor who used to compliment me on my eyebrows. I know it seems silly, but I would glow with flattery because he thought my eyebrows were attractive. This guy lived with his girlfriend, and although I felt guilty for accepting his compliments, I was desperately in need of them. This couple had a lot of parties at their house. Since I lived across the street, I was able to leave the kids in front of the TV and join their fun. I drank entirely too much beer when I was there and always ended up feeling ashamed the next day because of my behavior. I was flirtatious and extremely too friendly. One night after I had left to go home, my neighbor followed me over to my house and kissed me in my hallway. I melted at his touch and gloried in his attention. Yet deep down inside I knew he was wrong. In the morning I felt incredibly guilty. He had no business kissing me and I had no business letting him. I never went back to their house again. I could hardly look at his girlfriend in the face. I hated the person I became when I drank. It wasn't the real me. I never flirted with other women's men when I was sober. Fortunately, that was a great lesson learned and I never behaved that way again. If I could take it back I would, but just like all the other awful things I did, I can't.

Thought To Meditate On:

I knew how it felt to have a woman steal my man from me. I had gone through two divorces and hated the feeling of losing a man. The last thing I would ever want to do is break up a couple, but when I was drunk, I didn't seem to care. In all of my drinking I can only remember this one engagement with an unavailable man, but that was one too many. It wasn't OK. Not drunk, not ever.

Thoughts and Revelations:

160

A Fragrant Offering and Sacrifice to God

♥

2 Corinthians 8:7

But just as you excel in everything—in faith, in speech, in knowledge, in complete earnestness and in your love for us—see that you also excel in this grace of giving.

For Christmas one year my parents gave me and my children season passes to an amusement park. We must have gone twenty times over the year. We never had a lot of money, so it was great being able to go someplace special for free. The drive would take less than thirty minutes and we'd bring sandwiches in a back pack. Sometimes we splurged and bought sodas. When we were really broke we'd drink from the water fountain. My kids never cared, they were just happy to be given the opportunity to run and play. It was nice for my children to have a sober mom during this time who could sacrifice an afternoon to spend with them. When I was drinking, I didn't have the time. Or I should say, I wouldn't make the time. I can draw strength from these memories. It is my goal to make more happy memories with my children. I want the scales to tip to the happy side so that the bad memories can be trampled in their minds. It is never too late to change the future. Now that my children are grown I am pouring out all my love and attention on my granddaughter. I am grateful to God to be sober during her young life so I can participate in her upbringing. I can't imagine the nightmare of being told by her parents that they didn't want her around her drunk grandma. I don't think I could bare the thought. But today I don't have that fear. Because today I am the sober grandma. The level headed, clear minded, full of grace and love grandma Lacy.

Thought To Meditate On:

Unfortunately for an alcoholic we can't take back those days we chose to drink and mess everything up. We can't go back and do it different. We chose to drink and spoil the day and there isn't anything we can do about that now. But we can change the future. We can choose to get sober and start today making happy memories. It is never too late to stop drinking. But if you don't stop soon, it might be too late.

Thoughts and Revelations:

by Lacy Enderson

Your Love is Like the Morning Mist

♥

Romans 13:8-10

Let no debt remain outstanding, except the continuing debt to love one another, for he who loves his fellowman has fulfilled the law. The commandments, "Do not commit adultery," "Do not murder," "Do not steal," "Do not covet," and whatever other commandment there may be, are summed up in this one rule: "Love your neighbor as yourself."

My third husband worked with a man who enjoyed drinking. He always smelled of liquor and I wasn't fond of him. I didn't hate this guy, but I did blame him for my husband's behavior. He was a bad influence and often led my husband astray. He and his wife spent a lot of time at our house in the evenings having dinner and drinks. I wasn't one for lots of company and I thought they completely overstayed their welcome. I liked my quiet times in the evening and I was losing them rapidly to this couple. The friendship seemed to go well especially because I was good at keeping my mouth shut but when my husband and I would get into an argument he would run with them to their house and leave me stranded at home alone. It bothered me that these two were so quick to jump in the middle. This woman called herself my friend yet she never took my side. She was the first to grab my husband and drag him home with her. She said it was for my own good because she didn't want us fighting. But before we met this couple we had no problem straightening out the messes on our own. It didn't take long to discover this couple was like a virus eating through our marriage. They were up to no good and I wanted them gone. Convincing my husband that they were destructive was not as easy. In fact, it took me quite a few years. But one day he was able to see what I had seen all along. And since they have been gone it is like we have a whole new marriage.

Thought To Meditate On:

My husband and I don't have many friends. We find it easier to get along this way. I know it sounds unhealthy to be friendless but finding friends that enhance a marriage and not tear one apart is hard. These days, the first criteria is sobriety. Don't even think about coming into my house with alcohol. You will not be welcomed. The second criteria is loyalty. If you are not for my marriage than you are against it and I have no place for you in my life.

Thoughts and Revelations:

Lover of My Soul

♥

3 John 1:2

Dear friend, I pray that you may enjoy good health and that all may go well with you, even as your soul is getting along well.

I realized a long time ago my blessings were directly related to my behavior. It wasn't that God stopped loving me when I misbehaved, but He did withdraw His blessings when I sinned. Why would God or anyone for that matter, reward me for misbehaving? Getting sober was one of the greatest blessings in my life. I actually had time to live. I wasn't laid up miserably suffering a hangover, incapable of leaving my house. I was able to visit friends and go shopping. I had time for my kids I never seemed to have while I was drinking. The life God had blessed me with was incredible. It was better than my wildest dreams. God blessed me with a relationship with Him I never thought possible and it was truly the greatest blessing of all. A sober friend of mine in alcohol recovery introduced me to a guy, also in recovery. The three of us used to go out for hot fudge sundaes and coffee. We would sit and talk for hours. He was a very unhappily married man and spent a lot of time away from home. One day his wife found my jacket in his truck and became suspicious of me. I knew the friendship I had with her husband was innocent but she didn't. She felt threatened by me and I was uncomfortable with that. So I broke off the friendship. I said it wasn't worth her pain. My relationship with God was far more important to me than interfering in another woman's marriage. It wasn't an easy thing to do because I really enjoyed his company. The problem was, his company wasn't for me to enjoy.

Thought To Meditate On:

The blessings of obedience are peace, joy and serenity. If you have never experienced God's blessings, you are truly missing out. Some people want God's blessings of wealth and prosperity, and although these are not bad desires, peace in my mind is absolutely God's greatest gift to me. I could have all the money in the world but without God's peace I would lose my will to live. What's money without peace of mind and joy in my heart?

Thoughts and Revelations:

by Lacy Enderson

Sits Enthroned

♥

Ephesians 2:6,7

And God raised us up with Christ and seated us with him in the heavenly realms in Christ Jesus, in order that in the coming ages he might show the incomparable riches of his grace, expressed in his kindness to us in Christ Jesus.

I've read a lot of novels. I started reading them when I was a teenager and continued until my children were grown. I would get a really good book and sit for hours until it was finished. And then I'd buy another one. I loved the way the stories made me feel. They took me far away to unknown places. I could live anywhere in the world I wanted through these books. I escaped into the lives of the characters and I could be them as long as I was reading. I remember the disappointment I felt when the books would end. I would be back in my own reality, back at home with all my problems. I was the fifteen year old whose New Year's resolution was to quit drinking, stop smoking pot, and give up cigarettes. The only New Year's resolution a fifteen year old should have is how to talk nicer to mom. Drugs and alcohol are not suppose to be a problem for a child that age. It was hard to be me. Even as an adult I welcomed the escape from my reality. Anywhere I could escape to was far better than being home. My world was painful and my reality was hard. I don't find it necessary to read novels anymore. Not only do I not have the time, I no longer have the need to live in a fantasyland. God has made me comfortable with who I am and he has given me the ability to find pleasure in my own surroundings. Life is not always perfect, but it is far better today than it ever was before.

Thought To Meditate On:

God has given to us everything we need for life and happiness. It is up to us to choose the road we will travel on. The one road leads towards God and His blessings. The other road leads to destruction. It is up to us what life we want. Maybe you are controlled by drugs or alcohol and feel helpless. Don't ever think you have to stay that way. You can seek help, get sober and find the happiness that God provides. I did.

Thoughts and Revelations:

164

My Reward is With Me

♥

2 Timothy 4:7,8

I have fought the good fight, I have finished the race, I have kept the faith. Now there is in store for me the crown of righteousness, which the Lord, the righteous Judge, will award to me on that day—and not only to me, but also to all who have longed for his appearing.

I went to a movie called Frequency with my seventeen-year-old son Shaun. It was a time travel movie about what could happen if the past were altered. Each event that was changed caused a chain reaction. Sometimes the changes were for the better and sometimes they were for the worse. In fact, some of the changes caused catastrophic events to happen. I have heard people say if they had the knowledge years ago that they have now, they would go back in time and do things differently. But watching this movie opened my eyes to all the life events that would be different had I made different choices. I wasn't happy with the outcome in my mind. I looked at my son and I was grateful I married his father. No, the marriage didn't last and a divorce was necessary but if I had not married his dad I wouldn't have my wonderful Shaun, my sweet Joshua and my beautiful Brittany. When I look back over my life and the mistakes I have made, my first reaction is to wish I had done things differently. But I have come to the conclusion that things are exactly the way they are supposed to be. I am right where God wants me. And if he wants me somewhere else, he will take me there. For every wrong decision I made I have one hope, that what I experienced can help someone else. By sharing my life with others I would hope to spare even one person from making the same mistakes I made.

Thought To Meditate On:

I am grateful for my family just the way they are. I am grateful for my kids, each one of them heavenly made. I am grateful for my life just the way it is because I know it is exactly as it ought to be. But I can't say I always felt that way. When I first got sober all I wanted to do was die. I saw no good reason for living anymore. My life was a mess and without alcohol I had no way to alleviate the pain. It took awhile to get over the depression but here I am more grateful than ever to be alive.

Thoughts and Revelations:

by Lacy Enderson

Kingdom Authority

♥

Luke 10:18,19

He replied, "I saw Satan fall like lightning from heaven. I have given you authority to trample on snakes and scorpions and to overcome all the power of the enemy; nothing will harm you."

When I was a teenager, I met a guy who worked with my next door neighbor. He was just my type. He had long hair, no personality, and he drank too much. Everyday, I made sure I was home at four when I knew they would return from work. My day was not complete if I couldn't lay my eyes on him. After a few weeks of staring, I finally introduced myself. He was friendly but a little older and not very interested in me. But that didn't stop my pursuit. I kept right on staring. Finally, one day, he asked me out on a date. My parents reluctantly said I could go, but he had to take me to the roller rink where all my friends would be. They didn't want me alone with this guy. Much to my surprise, but not to my parents, his intentions were bad, and he was up to no good. I should have known a boy his age would have only one thing on his mind, but a girl my age is naive to such things. The whole evening was a disaster. Of course, not at the time, but years later I can see the humor in it. He wanted a serious moment with a young girl and I was definitely not the girl to give it to him. So when all he tried failed, he took me home. After that day, I could barely get him to look at me. I was heartbroken. I wanted a romantic relationship with this boy and all I got was let down. I don't know why I ever thought I would get anything more from him. His looks were not deceiving. I got exactly what I bargained for. It reminds me of the saying, you can't squeeze mustard from a ketchup bottle. So why did I try?

Thought To Meditate On:

Life brings many disappointments and we wonder how we ever lived through them. Don't you remember swearing to yourself you would never get over it? And then you did. That's life. No need living in denial looking for drugs and alcohol to escape the reality you are in. You might as well learn to live it. Who knows, it might be better than you expected. And if it's not, we will refund your misery at no charge.

Thoughts and Revelations:

What a Friend We Have in Jesus

♥

Proverbs 13:20

He who walks with the wise grows wise, but a companion of fools suffers harm.

I suffered terribly from peer pressure when I was a teenager. My brother had a group of friends and I wanted them to include me in their plans, so I did what they did. I admit I was hyperactive and it was hard for me to calm down, but didn't that mean I was fun? The kids in his group were heavy pot smokers. They spent their lunch money on marijuana they bought from people selling it right on the school campus. Just to fit in, I began buying it too. I went to the swap meet with a friend and bought a marijuana pipe and a baby bong. I was set. I had everything I thought I needed to fit in with the so-called "in crowd." The group was going to an Aerosmith concert and I talked my brother into allowing me to go with them. When we got there, I sat down and took out my stash. I was so proud. I was going to share my weed with my new friends, and let them use my baby bong. But before I knew it, I was wasted badly. And this was not fun. I had to hide in the bathroom because I was afraid the security guards were going to take me to jail. I did not function well on marijuana and this time was the worst. I tried to be cool. But everyone laughed at me for weeks. My friendships with this crowd ended abruptly. I guess I didn't fit in as well as I had hoped. It took a while for me to develop my own identity. I wanted to be like everyone else because I didn't much like being myself. If I could be like the others I felt important. But today, after many years of self-help, it's OK to be me. God instilled in me qualities unlike anyone else's, and I have grown to find importance in exactly who He made me to be. Looking back to that time in my life and those people, God only knows what I ever saw in them.

Thought To Meditate On:

It wasn't that I thought people were better than me, I wanted them to like me. I was friendly, I was helpful, I would do anything you wanted me to, so why couldn't I be your friend? I think it was because God didn't want me hanging out with that group. I couldn't get accepted by them no matter how hard I tried because God didn't want them to accept me. It took me years to figure that out.

Thoughts and Revelations:

by Lacy Enderson

A Hand to Guide Me

♥

1 Peter 2:25

For you were like sheep going astray, but now you have returned to the Shepherd and Overseer of your souls.

I only had cocaine offered to me one time. A friend offered it to me, so I gave it a try. Being a good friend of mine I trusted her to make the right decision. I had no reason not to. But since then I have learned I don't need to trust everyone, not even a good friend. I didn't notice the effect of the cocaine until the next morning when I reflected back on the night before. I had gone to a party by myself, something I never did. It was a group of people I did not know. My friend was going to take me and decided she really wanted to stay home, so I got directions and went by myself. I talked to quite a few strangers as if I had known them for years. I had a quiet confidence about me I had never experienced before. I had no problem interacting and mingling. The next day I realized what I had done and I was shocked. I never went anywhere by myself, especially to a stranger's house. I suffered from mild social anxiety and seldom went anywhere alone. Instantly, I recognized the effect of the drug. I was in an altered state of mind and was not even aware of it. That day I had a whole new awareness and understanding of the cocaine addict. I developed a greater compassion for those who were addicted. Never again was cocaine offered to me. It was as if God knew I would want it, so He made sure it was unavailable. I would definitely have taken the drug again if it were around. I am grateful for God's mercy and protection. I have had enough trouble quitting the things I am addicted to. I can't imagine one more stronghold to overcome.

Thought To Meditate On:

Without God's guidance we are like sheep who have gone astray. The Bible says we are in need of a Shepherd to lead us. Jesus was sent to be our guide leading us towards the path He has prepared. While I was drinking, I was headed down the wrong path full of sin and destruction. Since I have quit drinking, I walk a path full of life and blessings. Don't be deceived. You don't need drugs and alcohol to have a good time. That is a lie from the devil used to destroy you. Be bold and be strong. Turn from evil and do good.

Thoughts and Revelations:

Sincerity of Heart
♥

Hebrews 10:22,23

Let us draw near to God with a sincere heart in full assurance of faith, having our hearts sprinkled to cleanse us from a guilty conscience and having our bodies washed with pure water. Let us hold unswervingly to the hope we profess, for he who promised is faithful.

My ten year high school reunion was held in a fancy hotel. I'm not quite sure where it was because I do not remember most of the evening. It was a great big blur. I was very drunk. I wouldn't say I was in a blackout because I remember enough to put the evening together, but not enough to say I was completely coherent. I do know I was extremely embarrassing to my husband, my friends and myself. I heard that I called an old friend's husband an ugly dork. I flirted with some of my old class-mates in front of my husband and in front of their wives. It is a wonder some other woman didn't knock me to the ground. I know I talked a lot and I was very loud. I remember I had recently quit smoking and I was walking around the room asking everyone for cigarettes. But every cigarette came with an explanation about how I was trying to quit smoking. How pathetic is that? I have often wondered what those few sober ones thought about me when they got home. Probably not any different than they remembered me from high school. I can hear it now, "Poor Lacy, she's still a drunk." I have my twenty-year reunion coming up shortly. It'll be nice to attend sober. It'll give me the chance to redeem myself. At least I won't be giving them something new to talk about.

Thought To Meditate On:

With an undivided allegiance towards God, and a faith that does not doubt, we can trust in God completely in all He says He will do. No matter what we have done in the past we know we are forgiven, because He told us we were. Loving God and trusting Him are hard at times, especially when we don't feel worthy. But God says you are worthy no matter what you've done, so just believe it. If God says it, it is true. Because God cannot lie.

Thoughts and Revelations:

by Lacy Enderson

His Name is Wonderful

♥

Philippians 2:9,10

Therefore God exalted him to the highest place and gave him the name that is above every name, that at the name of Jesus every knee should bow, in heaven and on earth and under the earth.

When I was in high school I entered a speech contest sponsored by the Lion's Club. The topic of the speech had to be "Who Am I?" My father and I worked on it together. My dad was always very proud of my involvement in extra school activities and loved to help me. We were a great team. The contest was held in the banquet room at a local restaurant where we were served a very nice dinner. One at a time, the four contestants gave their speeches in front of twenty men. It was scary to say the least. I had spoken at many school speech tournaments but this was different. It was professional. I was up against one of our school's greatest speakers. She won almost every contest she entered. But this night, I was the winner, and I got to go to the finals against three other schools. At the finals I read my speech just like before, but I accidentally left out the entire section about God. Being a religious organization, I was sure this would hurt my chances. I was even more certain when the last speaker got up and most of her speech was about God. I didn't win. She did. My father was convinced I would have won had I included the God part. God is an important part of many people's lives, as He should be. To some of us, He is everything. We have a greater chance for victory if we remember not to leave Him out.

Thought To Meditate On:

Remember when you are spending time with God to keep your mind off of you. Try not to think about yourself. Say to the Lord when you pray, none of me, all of you. Let God know how much you love Him and ask Him what His will for your life is for that day. Ask Him to make it plain so you can hear and understand. Develop a relationship with God as if He were your very best friend sitting in the chair across from you. If you do this, you will be amazed at how real God is. Seek this day to find Him. He can be found.

Thoughts and Revelations:

His Crown of Love and Compassion
♥

John 14:12-14

I tell you the truth, anyone who has faith in me will do what I have been doing. He will do even greater things than these, because I am going to the Father. And I will do whatever you ask in my name, so that the Son may bring glory to the Father. You may ask me for anything in my name, and I will do it.

When my son was little he had quite a few problems with his ears. He had lots of ear infections which eventually began to effect his hearing. I had him prayed over several times while he was growing up, and although his ears got better he still had problems. One night, when he was nine, he was laying in bed trying to fall asleep, but his ear was bothering him. I felt bad for him. I didn't have medical insurance and I didn't have the money for a Doctor bill. So I took out my Bible and opened it up to John 14:12-14 and prayed the Word over him. I told God I couldn't afford to take him to a Doctor, so I was turning to Him as my only hope. The scripture in John told me to ask the Father anything in Jesus' name and it would be done for me. So I asked God to heal my son's ear, and He did. If you don't believe that is what the Bible says, read the scripture above. That is exactly what it says and it is exactly what it means. The pain in my son's ear disappeared and he was able to fall asleep. The next morning the infection was gone and to this day my son has never had another problem with his ears. God heard my heart cry out for my son. He knew the sincerity of my concern. God isn't cold and unresponsive, God is gentle and compassionate. And His word works.

Thought To Meditate On:

A coincidence is a miracle from God in which He chooses to remain anonymous. When we experience something wonderful, although we cannot see God, we know He is there. When we are faithful to God, sticking with God and His word no matter what, He is faithful to us. When you are faithful, quitting is not an option. You will flourish and thrive becoming extremely successful in whatever you endeavor. Faithfulness is a choice. Don't let pressure weaken you. Don't look back, stand your ground, do not compromise, and you will reap the benefits.

Thoughts and Revelations:

by *Lacy Enderson*

Cleanse Me Oh Lord

♥

John 15:3,4

You are already clean because of the word I have spoken to you. Remain in me, and I will remain in you. No branch can bear fruit by itself; it must remain in the vine. Neither can you bear fruit unless you remain in me.

My husband was sixteen in 1968 and worked in a supermarket as a box boy. On Christmas Eve the market had an open buffet dinner in the stock room along with an open bar. The employees could eat and drink as much as they wanted, provided their work was getting done and they were not getting drunk. As for my husband, he thought Christmas had come a day early! He would bag a couple of orders and go to the stock room and make a drink. After a few trips back and forth, he was drunk. He really tried drinking responsibly, but just like every other time, he drank until he was drunk. His extremely sociable personality surfaced and before long he was telling dirty jokes to the customers. He loved the feeling he had achieved. He lived for drinking. He felt as though he could have run for president. At some point that evening he experienced what he believes to be his first black out. His family was called to come down and pick him up for he had gotten sick all over the back store room and was acting violently towards his fellow employees. On the way home he repeatedly beat his head against the car window screaming, "Take me to the hospital, I'm dying!" But when he woke up the next morning he couldn't remember any of it. It took my husband many years of pure misery to come to the belief that only God could help him. As much as he loved the effect alcohol had on him, he equally hated the person he became, so after many years, he quit drinking. I mean, what other choice did he have? Sobriety for him was not easy but has since proven to be his greatest blessing.

Thought To Meditate On:

The Holy Spirit has been shouting at us for years, but we choose not to listen. God has an answer to every question we have but we choose to ask everyone else but Him for the solution. It isn't that God doesn't do anything for us, it is that we won't receive from Him. Gods' grace, love and mercy is for every believer, but only when we accept them for ourselves.

Thoughts and Revelations:

172

To Obey is Better Than Sacrifice

♥

Jeremiah 7:5-7

If you really change your ways and your actions and deal with each other justly, if you do not oppress the alien, the fatherless or the widow and do not shed innocent blood in this place, and if you do not follow other gods to your own harm, then I will let you live in this place, in the land I gave your forefathers for ever and ever.

I have a friend who is pushing fifty years old and has been an active alcoholic for most of his life. He is verbally abusive, he lies, and he manipulates people into doing what he wants them to do. He is angry, mean-tempered, deceptive and immoral. The all around perfect enemy. But these are not traits he asked for. These came along with the uninvited alcoholism. Drinking opened the door to all kinds of nasty behaviors. People who knew him were convinced he had a dual personality. One person sober and another person drunk. If my friend could have remembered the next day after the chaos he caused he would have agreed with our assumptions of him, but given most of the drinking episodes ended up in a blackout it was hard for him to understand what we were accusing him of. Unfortunately, this disease does not have a cure. Alcoholics are given remission one day at a time. Reluctantly, my friend decided he needed to quit drinking. He had lived through one too many episodes he couldn't remember and it started to scare him. By staying sober and working through a program of recovery, my friend has allowed God to change him from the inside out. He is not proud of what he's done, but there is no shame in who he has become. With a little willingness and a God in his life he has found God's peace and has become a much better person. God never fills a cup, He overflows it. When we are willing, God is ready to fill us up with more than enough of everything we need.

Thought To Meditate On:

Living right is not always easy, but the blessings are endless. We cannot compare the life of righteousness we now live to the disobedience that once controlled our lives. Our lifestyles were as different as night and day. Obeying God is definitely the easier way to go. And God is good all the time, not just some of time like we once believed. Remember, if you don't stand for something, you will fall for anything. So stand for holiness, righteousness, obedience, and of course, your sobriety.

Thoughts and Revelations:

by Lacy Enderson

Remain In Me

♥

Revelation 14:12

This calls for patient endurance on the part of the saints who obey God's commandments and remain faithful to Jesus.

We all know hardships are an unwelcome part of life. Tough times are unfortunately familiar to everyone. They are impossible to avoid and hard to ignore. The Bible tells me that Jesus came to be my help through all of them. I know a lot of what I go through is used to teach me important lessons that will help me in my future. I don't believe God creates the hardship but His word says He will walk through them with me and use them for my good. Many times I have wanted to tell God, "Enough is enough! I'm tired of learning." When life throws a disturbing situation my way I find myself pleading with God for salvation; save me from sin, save me from sickness, and please dear God save me from myself. Growth is not usually very pleasant but change and character development is essential to our health and well being. We cannot continue on the same path we are on and expect to live very long. The odds are against us. I have given up on myself many times. Each time God has had to start all over again. But the great thing about God is He never complains. The process of sobriety seems never-ending. If I am drinking I wish I was sober, when I am sober I fight the fact I never want to drink again, but might. I know drinking was never God's best for me, but I actually learned more about myself than if I had never had a problem. God used alcoholism to bring me closer to Him and closer to myself. The Bible says that God works everything out for good, even alcoholism.

Thought To Meditate On:

Tests and trials are not fun. The emotional pain can be so extreme all we want to do is crawl under our beds and hide. God lives to help us. He gives us a vision of hope that keeps us moving forward. He gives us great expectations to look forward to. Don't let life get you down and rob you of the dream God has for you. Always remember, God is a dream-maker and wants to birth a dream in everyone. Live expecting and you will receive.

Thoughts and Revelations:

A Heart Full of Compassion

♥

Lamentations 3:22,23

Because of the LORD's great love we are not consumed, for his compassions never fail. They are new every morning; great is your faithfulness.

Kevin's alcoholism had worked so hard against him by the time high school had ended he decided to do a geographical and join the military. He wanted to right his wrongs and please his family and he thought getting away would help him quit drinking. His parents had experienced so much disappointment over the years they actually saw hope in his decision. Kevin had been lazy and rebellious for so long they were excited to finally see some ambition and motivation. They prayed this was the decision that was going to turn his life around. The only problem was that his hometown wasn't the reason for his drinking. Relocating solved nothing. He joined the Navy, traveled around the world and learned to drink in six other languages. His disrespectful, unruly behavior while under the influence of alcohol escalated, and in three years he had twelve captain's masses, one court marshal, he was in and out of seven different jails, had two felonies, and five years felony probation under special supervision. Yet with all of the trouble he got into he still denied having a problem with alcohol and absolutely refused to quit drinking. God extended his love by keeping a constant watch over His child until he was able to see the problem within himself. Kevin was completely protected from all physical harm. During circumstances where Kevin should have died, not a single hair on his head was harmed. God is an awesome God. He is faithful even when his children are not.

Thoughts to meditate on:

Circumstances can be extremely overwhelming. Some are so big we couldn't possibly handle them on our own. But we have a God who is bigger than all of life's troubles. He is faithful to handle any situation we encounter if we let it go and trust in Him. Remember, God is not an absentee Father but one who promises never to leave you.

Thoughts and Revelations:

by Lacy Enderson

Worthy of Grace

♥

Isaiah 61:7

Instead of their shame my people will receive a double portion, and instead of disgrace they will rejoice in their inheritance; and so they will inherit a double portion in their land, and everlasting joy will be theirs.

I know a man whose parents helped him buy his first car when he turned sixteen. He was so excited and so proud of his accomplishments: sixteen, working a respectable job, and now the proud owner of a car. It was actually a boat on wheels, a 1967 Galaxy 500, four-door sedan. He hadn't owned the car for very long when he was invited to a party. Feeling deserving he decided to have a little fun. The worst he imagined happening was maybe breaking curfew and coming home late, so he went to the party. The evening started off innocently enough with a few beers but escalated quickly into drinking all kinds of hard liquor. He was pretty intoxicated when a girl asked to be driven to the market for cigarettes. Any normal person would have admitted being too drunk to drive and said no, but not an alcoholic. Especially not a drunk in a blackout. On the way, instead of pulling into the store, his car climbed a traffic light. Completely in shock and realizing what he had done he backed off the pole and went back to the party. The next morning he woke up at his house with no recollection of the night before. He went outside to discover his car was completely totaled and he couldn't remember anything. The girl in his car had been hurt pretty badly, and it was only by the grace of God they both had not been killed. It took a few more of these daring, destructive adventures to not only realize he was an alcoholic, but to see his definite need to quit drinking and get a God in his life.

Thought To Meditate On:

God is merciful and he will overlook an offense, but never forget, there are personal consequences for every wrongdoing. When we deserved punishment God loved us instead. But don't play around with the law of nature too long. There are only so many car accidents and fights one can get into before some real damage is done. Even believers are not invincible. If God does you a favor, don't take advantage of His grace. God will carry you for a long time, but someday He will require you to stand on your own two feet.

Thoughts and Revelations:

Signs and Wonders
♥

Acts 4:30

"Stretch out your hand to heal and perform miraculous signs and wonders through the name of your holy servant Jesus."

The greatest miracle next to the saving grace of Jesus, is an alcoholic who quits drinking. If you have ever lived with an alcoholic who becomes sober, you can attest to that. Each day an alcoholic lives without a drink is a true miracle from God. Everything within us cries out for a drink, and yet by God's great strength and mercy we discover we can say no. I wish I had stumbled onto this secret years ago, but I guess I got sober when I was supposed to get sober. The Bible says there is an appointed time and a place for everything. So when it was God's time for me to quit drinking He motivated and encouraged me towards sobriety. I believe that. (I had the same experience when I quit smoking. When it was God's time, I quit and I have not smoked since.) I guess if I had been pulled over for drunken driving I might have sobered up sooner. I suppose if I had been caught at a party for drinking underage, a recovery program might have been a mandatory sentence. But I was never pulled over or even confronted by a cop. In all my years of drinking, I never got into trouble with the law. There are people who have been around recovery for more than a decade, and they are not even thirty yet. Their time came sooner than mine. But mine came. And eventually, given what I know about God's time, your's will too.

Thought To Meditate On:

Jesus was enabled by the power of the Holy Spirit to do great works and miracles. The Bible says when Jesus ascended into heaven He gave us that same great power so we too could do the same works Jesus did. The Holy Spirit empowers alcoholics to quit drinking, and in my book, this is classified as a miracle from God. We must never underestimate the power of God. That power changes lives forever.

Thoughts and Revelations:

by Lacy Enderson

The Truth Shall Set You Free

♥

James 5:16

Therefore confess your sins to each other and pray for each other so that you may be healed. The prayer of a righteous man is powerful and effective.

The Bible tells us there is never any condemnation for those who believe in Jesus. That means we are forgiven and God wants to rid us of our guilt and shame. When I was younger I had very low self-esteem. I never saw myself as pretty or smart or even interesting. I needed the validation from other people to feel good about myself, so I was constantly flirting to gain approval. It didn't matter to me who they were. I didn't need an attraction because I wasn't looking for a relationship. I needed a boost in my self esteem. As soon as their heads were turned my way their attention was mine and I had accomplished my goal. But that behavior to get what I needed was not always fair. My intentions were not honest and I felt terrible inside. I'm not quite sure how I was healed, but one day God actually gave me a sense of self-worth. He lifted my head and I no longer needed the approval of others. Today, I see flirtatious women and I am reminded of the goodness of God's grace. I am saddened when I see a women desperately trying to get a man's attention. But then I stop and pray for her because I am reminded that deep down inside she is hurting and insecure.

Thought To Meditate On:

Sharing our faults with God and another person brings a powerful sense of healing and freedom. We carry hidden secrets around in fear of what people would think if they really knew who we were. The funny thing is, most people have their own secret sins, and if you knew what they were hiding, you would soon find out you are no worse off then they are. Share yourself with someone and open the door for them to share with you.

Thoughts and Revelations:

He Rolls the Stone From the Grave

♥

Hebrews 2:14,15

Since the children have flesh and blood, he too shared in their humanity so that by his death he might destroy him who holds the power of death—that is, the devil—and free those who all their lives were held in slavery by their fear of death.

I had a friend who was dying both physically and spiritually. He had lost about fifty pounds, six inches from his waist, and lost complete control over his bodily functions. He would get sick from both ends at the same time; vomiting and diarrhea. And he had no control over when and where this would happen. He believed in God, but he never listened to Him. God had a different agenda, one my friend did not approve of nor did he agree with. He was a man who lived on self-will alone. We could compare him to a man in intensive care, on life support. He had little, if any, chance of surviving. He admitted it was time to call for the priest because the odds for life were against him. He was dying and he knew it. Even though he was near death, he still could not see his cocaine addiction as a problem, and he adamantly denied being an alcoholic. Or maybe like most addicts, he was unwilling to admit defeat. So he continued to drink and use cocaine until it was obvious he could no longer do so. He enrolled himself in a 30-day lockup recovery home. Here, he actually saw a small glimmer of hope for recovery, but it still took him three more years to draw a sober breath. Only by God's loving hand upon his life did he live to see sobriety. There was absolutely no human power who could have delivered him from such bondage. Even when it seemed his life was over, God had other plans. And now that my friend is living sober and listening to God, God's great plans are manifested in his life; plans that were there all the time.

Thought To Meditate On:

We spend years trying to free ourselves from drugs and alcohol. Each time we try and fail, we fall a little harder. And each time we fall it is harder getting up. But with God's help and our determination we do get up and try again. Jesus came to destroy the works of the devil and his power over us. Jesus came to give us life. The Bible says that Jesus came to give us exceedingly and abundantly more than we could ever ask or think. All we have to do is receive it. God's plan is good, He is good, and He will take care of us.

Thoughts and Revelations:

by Lacy Enderson

I Will Catch You

♥

1 Corinthians 10:12,13

So, if you think you are standing firm, be careful that you don't fall! No temptation has seized you except what is common to man. And God is faithful; he will not let you be tempted beyond what you can bear. But when you are tempted, he will also provide a way out so that you can stand up under it.

A lady I know once told me a story about a night she knew she would never forget. She had been out with a group of people and she was drinking a little more than she was used to. Because her body hadn't developed much resistance towards alcohol she found herself in an unexpected blackout rather quickly. Being in an unconscious state of mind she continued drinking until she lost her balance, fell off her chair and hit her head. An ambulance came and took her to the hospital where she spent the night recovering. In the morning she was told, had she gone to bed that night, she would have died in her sleep from alcohol poisoning. It was actually a blessing from God that she fell. She did not have an alcohol problem and was able to stop drinking after her accident. It saddens me to think as an alcoholic I probably would have continued drinking even after such a frightening episode. The temptation for me to drink was too great to resist, and I continually gave into the cravings. Today I don't put myself in such compromising situations, but I will always remember those times when I did. And for each and every one of them, I thank God for catching me when I fell.

Thought To Meditate On:

God warns us to be careful. There is temptation all around us. Relying on God's help to resist the temptation is mandatory. Remember, the sin is not the temptation, the sin is in the yielding to it. God gives us the strength, the resistance and the ability to say no.

Thoughts and Revelations:

Slaves Set Free

♥

Romans 6:20-22

When you were slaves to sin, you were free from the control of righteousness. What benefit did you reap at that time from the things you are now ashamed of? Those things result in death! But now that you have been set free from sin and have become slaves to God, the benefit you reap leads to holiness, and the result is eternal life.

When I was drinking I acted in ways I am not proud of. I caused a lot of damage not only in my life but also in the lives of those around me. My drinking got in the way of making good decisions. Drinking was always my priority. Errands would go undone and my children's plans would have to change if I wanted to drink. My daughter used to take dance lessons every Friday afternoon. She would beg me to stay and watch her. But I always chose to drop her off so I could go home and drink. It was Friday and the start of the weekend! How could I possibly sit in a dance lesson for an hour and let the weekend start without me? Needless to say, I always picked her up slightly intoxicated. I would like to say that I never drove my children around under the influence of alcohol, but that would make me a liar. I have numerous stories of the way I allowed alcohol to interfere with the safety of people I cared about. I have so many awful stories to tell there would not be room enough in this book to contain them all. It shames me to think of the decisions I made that could have caused some serious harm to me and my children. There really is no excuse, and I thank God everyday that no one was hurt because of my drinking. I pray that I would never be under the control of alcohol again. The freedom I have in sobriety today is a freedom I never want to give up. Thank you God for my freedom.

Thought To Meditate On:

Sin is destructive no matter what angle you view it at. There is never any good in it, not ever. I don't know why it took me so long to figure out my life was completely out of control. Why did I view my life as so unimportant that I would continuously engage in sinful behavior? I know once we get sober we must focus our sites forward on the things ahead, but every now and then I remember some vile thing I did and I feel so ashamed. Memories are good and can serve a good purpose if used properly, but try not to fixate on them. God has forgiven the sin and wiped the slate clean.

Thoughts and Revelations:

by Lacy Enderson

Whom the Son Sets Free is Free Indeed

♥

1 John 3:7,8

Dear children, do not let anyone lead you astray. He who does what is right is righteous, just as he is righteous. He who does what is sinful is of the devil, because the devil has been sinning from the beginning. The reason the Son of God appeared was to destroy the devil's work.

Sin brings pleasure. If it were not true then nobody would be doing it. It amazes me to think about the pleasure I got from sin. I knew better. I was raised in church and knew right from wrong. Problem is, the knowledge never stopped me. My husband and I had two years of sobriety when we started dating. We actually met in Alcoholics Anonymous. Within five months of our relationship I was drinking again. I hadn't yet been in a relationship sober and this one was far too difficult for me to handle without alcohol. My husband watched me drink for four years without participating. I can't say he was happy about it but what was he going to do? Tell me to quit? As if that ever worked before. But what fun is drinking alone? Subconsciously, I hoped that he would start drinking again. I thought if he would drink with me we could go dancing. We could sit in bars and listen to music. We could carry on like two young lovebirds. I just knew we would have the time of our lives. The deception of the alcohol was lying to me. My husband did start drinking again after six years sober. I actually encouraged him to and soon found out there wasn't anything fun about it. His kind of alcoholism didn't include a wife. He was a bar drinker and I wasn't invited to join him. We fought everyday, until one day we had a domestic quarrel that landed him in jail and left me with a warrant out for my arrest. It only took two months for me to see the dead-end road we were on. So we both got sober and started over again. Sin is deceptive. It always appears to be more fun and attractive than it really is. If you don't believe me, try it for yourself. And when you come back with your tail between your legs, don't say I didn't warn you.

Thought To Meditate On:

Sin is always fun for a time but never for very long. It is like a cancer that will eat through you after awhile and leave you as good as dead. Sin is from the devil himself and we all know he never had any good intentions. If it seems wrong, it probably is, and you don't have to try it to find out. Just say no and walk the other way. It might be hard to do at first, but keep trying, you'll get the hang of it.

Thoughts and Revelations:

Thy Great Power

♥

Deuteronomy 3:24

"O Sovereign LORD, you have begun to show to your servant your greatness and your strong hand. For what god is there in heaven or on earth who can do the deeds and mighty works you do?

A few years back I attended a women's retreat with a friend of mine from church. It was at a conference center in Big Bear, California, up in the mountains. It was such a beautiful place. I could have stayed there forever. I was driving up the mountain road listening to Christian music and enjoying the scenery. On the way, I turned on the heater and something blew into my eye. I could not find it and it would not come out. For the rest of the day I was miserable. When I awoke the next morning my eye was so irritated and swollen I could hardly open it. As I was standing in the breakfast line completely hopeless, I opened my Bible to a passage of scripture on healing. With a humble heart I read the verse to God and instantly my eye was healed. There was no more swelling or irritation. I hit my girlfriend on the arm, and said, "Look at my eye!" She was amazed and asked what I had done. I told her I prayed God's Word over my situation and He answered me immediately. She could hardly believe it. It was a true miracle indeed. I try to remember that story when I feel frustrated over my circumstances. I relate that story to people who are beaten down and have no hope. It is a story of God's power and His love. It is also a reminder of the awesome power of God's Word. He told us to pray His Word to Him. He said it would not return to Him without accomplishing the purpose in which it was sent. It is so true. God will honor His Word. He is no respecter of persons. What He has done for one of his children, He will do for all of them.

Thought To Meditate On:

God's power is never ending. He has all the power you will ever need. His radiant beauty shines brighter than the brightest star. His glory is magnificent and his grace is beyond measure. Stop for a second and really think about what God has done for you, and then thank him. If you can't think of anything, ask Him to do something for you so He can prove to you His great power is all you need.

Thoughts and Revelations:

by Lacy Enderson

Abounding in Love

♥

Romans 12:9-14

Love must be sincere. Hate what is evil; cling to what is good. Be devoted to one another in brotherly love. Honor one another above yourselves. Never be lacking in zeal, but keep your spiritual fervor, serving the Lord. Be joyful in hope, patient in affliction, faithful in prayer. Share with God's people who are in need. Practice hospitality.

I had a friend who was married to a practicing alcoholic and drug addict. She was the strongest person emotionally I've ever known. She read her Bible daily and memorized scripture because it strengthened her. The Word of God gave her the power and confidence she needed to get through each day. Many evenings her husband would be at a bar and she would call me just to talk. Sometimes she would cry, but not very often. She lived in a two bedroom, one bath apartment with her husband, two little boys, a dog and two cats. Her husband made enough money to afford a bigger place but he used his money to feed his addictions. Drugs and alcohol were far more important to him than having two bathrooms. And he was rarely home anyways, so what did he care about the size of their home? The one passion my friend had was gardening. The whole front of her apartment was adorned with every color flower imaginable. It was truly splendid. The garden was her serenity. I couldn't understand why God would give such a wonderful lady such a horrible life. But then I was reminded, God didn't give it to her, she chose it. Then one day her husband left her for a neighbor lady he'd been having an affair with. She moved in with her parents and began a new life. God honored every moment she had spent in obedience to Him. As much as she missed her husband, she was grateful he had left. And when he left, he took every bit of his alcoholic misery with him. A few years later she met and married a wonderful man who loved Jesus as much as she did. This man was everything and more she had always wanted in a husband. Even in adversity my friend honored God. She was obedient to his commands and in the end God rewarded her for her faith.

Thought To Meditate On:

Even when your life seems hopeless, read God's word, pray and believe that He has your best interest in mind. It might seem hard for awhile but a miracle blessing is waiting just on the other side. It is hard for the family of an alcoholic because they just don't understand, but God understands and will see you through. Your faithfulness will not go unrewarded.

Thoughts and Revelations:

Carry One Another's Burdens

♥

1 Corinthians 9:19,22

Though I am free and belong to no man, I make myself a slave to everyone, to win as many as possible. . To the weak I became weak, to win the weak. I have become all things to all men so that by all possible means I might save some.

I was sitting in an alcohol recovery meeting one afternoon when I noticed a girl sitting across from me who looked distressed and anguished. She was crying and obviously disturbed. When it came time for the coffee break she gathered up her things and got ready to leave. Feeling led by God to confront her, I walked over and asked her if she was leaving the meeting. When she said, "Yes", I asked her if she wanted to talk. She hesitated, but went outside with me. That's when I noticed she could barely walk because she was stoned on Vicodin pills. She proceeded to tell me her story. Her mother had kicked her out of the house and her boyfriend broke up with her. She was living in her car. Her biggest problem, as far as she was concerned, was that the pills were gone. I could relate and I knew immediately that I would have to share my story with this girl. My success would make her's possible. That's why Paul said, "I have become all things to all men so that by all possible means I might save some." I believe I went through what I did for a reason. God had a purpose for saving me and getting me sober. I had struggled with narcotic pills myself, so I had a great story of deliverance to share with this girl. That is why God led me to talk with her. He knew beforehand that I could help. Always be willing to share your successes and your failures with others. Be willing to humble yourself and God will use you in a powerful way. Don't let your testimony die with you. Pass it on.

Thought To Meditate On:

The best gift you can give people is hope. Never be too proud to lower yourself in order to lift them up. God has a purpose for every person and a reason behind every plan. If God thinks He can use you to help someone He will lead you to them. Your job is to listen and follow so you know where to go. God has an amazing way of getting His work done here on the earth and you should feel honored that He chooses to use you.

Thoughts and Revelations:

Make a list of people whom you need to reach out to.

by Lacy Enderson

Shield of Faith

♥

1 Peter 1:5-9

Who through faith are shielded by God's power until the coming of the salvation that is ready to be revealed in the last time. In this you greatly rejoice, though now for a little while you may have had to suffer grief in all kinds of trials. These have come so that your faith—of greater worth than gold, which perishes even though refined by fire—may be proved genuine and may result in praise, glory and honor when Jesus Christ is revealed. Though you have not seen him, you love him; and even though you do not see him now, you believe in him and are filled with an inexpressible and glorious joy, for you are receiving the goal of your faith, the salvation of your souls.

Some people need to see God with their eyes in order to believe in Him. Others need signs and miracles. I have never been like that. I have never been one who had to see God in order to believe in him. I cannot remember a time when I didn't believe. I went to church every Sunday until I was seventeen, and if the church told me there was a God, then there was a God. I know not everyone has this same experience. Some people are raised in religious homes but walk away never to believe again. I guess I had a little bit of spiritual help from my family's prayers. I had grandparents and other relatives who were pastors and preachers. I would assume they included me in their talks with God. Now, believing in God and knowing Him as a personal Savior are two very different experiences. I saw God as a higher power. But I didn't understand that Jesus came to Earth as 100% human and 100% God to be my personal Savior. God was way up there. He was untouchable. I didn't understand when Jesus said, "…you will receive power when the Holy Spirit comes on you..." Acts 1:8. He also said, "For John baptized with water, but in a few days you will be baptized with the Holy Spirit" Acts 1:5. But then one day I had a revelation. The whole concept of the trinity made complete sense to me and I was on fire for the Lord. I finally understood who God was. The Holy Spirit walks with me minute by minute. If you are struggling with a higher power who seems "out there," pray that the Father, Son and Holy Spirit will reveal Themselves to you in a real and powerful way. Our God wants to meet you, so introduce yourself to Him.

Thought To Meditate On:

Remember, it is only for a little while that we will be on this Earth. Then we will spend all eternity in Heaven with our Savior Jesus Christ. In a little while we will be with the Father. So get ready.

Thoughts and Revelations:

186

Do Unto the Least of These

♥

James 2:14-17

What good is it, my brothers, if a man claims to have faith but has no deeds? Can such faith save him? Suppose a brother or sister is without clothes and daily food. If one of you says to him, "Go, I wish you well; keep warm and well fed," but does nothing about his physical needs, what good is it? In the same way, faith by itself, if it is not accompanied by action, is dead.

I am amazed at how many people resent the homeless. They walk past these dirty, broken, tattered people and offer nothing more than rude comments. I have been one paycheck away from the street many times. It could happen to any one of us. Wouldn't it be better if we treated the homeless the way we would hope to be treated if we fell into their position? One Christmas I was especially poor and was having a hard time affording presents for my children. But when I passed by the Christmas wish tree at the department store I felt a tugging at my heart. The Salvation Army was sponsoring children whose parents couldn't afford presents. The children whose names hung on that tree were even worse off than my own. Some of them didn't have homes. They probably went hungry many nights. And I knew they would not have a Christmas without my help. I instantly felt like I had gone from a position of having nothing to having so much more than I thought. I picked a name from that tree and bought a present for a little boy who would have nothing except for my meager gift. And I must say that I walked away from that tree feeling rather good inside. I was excited to be able to help out a child. That Christmas an amazing thing happened. I opened my door on Christmas Eve and found a box full of food. There was a present for each of my children and even one for me. It was definitely unexpected. I stepped out of my fears to bless someone else, and God blessed me. God says that if we give, it will be given back to us. Believe that. It's a promise.

Thought To Meditate On:

When we accept Jesus into our hearts we begin to experience the many benefits he has promised us. We will automatically want to do good for others. It is an outward manifestation of an inside transformation. Once you get your mind off yourself, others will start becoming more important to you and you will want to do nice things for them. It is like a domino effect.

Thoughts and Revelations:

by Lacy Enderson

Do Unto Others

♥

Galatians 5:13-15

You, my brothers, were called to be free. But do not use your freedom to indulge the sinful nature; rather, serve one another in love. The entire law is summed up in a single command: "Love your neighbor as yourself." If you keep on biting and devouring each other, watch out or you will be destroyed by each other.

When my children were young I took classes in child development. I was working in a preschool and the classes were a requirement. I learned things in these classes that changed the way I parented. I learned that there is something called the labeling theory. If you call a child names, he will live up to your expectations. If you tell him he is good for nothing, he will probably be just that. You know the kids. They rebel against authority. They have no manners or respect. They drop out of school. They turn to the only means of comfort they can find. They use drugs and alcohol to quiet their pain. But the pain of hurtful words never goes away. I tell you this because even though this theory exists, and most people know about it, parents do call their children names. They let their frustration turn into insults that are hurled at their children like bombs. Good for nothing! Stupid punk! Failure! Idiot! Hopefully these parents get help before it is too late. Although it is never too late to right the wrongs, so often the damage done is so deep the pain seldom ever fully goes away. self-esteems suffer and these children rarely grow up with proper self-confidence. If you feel convicted right now, get help. Hurtful words penetrate a child's soul. It's not too late to change. I have heard it said before, it is better to spank a child because the physical pain will leave. The emotional pain of name calling never does. The emotional wounds are forever and the damage can be long lasting. If you find you are one of these parents who are afraid to extend love because you yourself never received love, please get help for yourself. If you are an alcoholic, you might consider recovery, not only for yourself but for your children also. You can stop the vicious cycle. You can learn to love.

Thought to meditate on:

Even though God gave us a new attitude when we got sober, He still allows us our own free will. It becomes easier for us to live like we should, but this is not always what we choose to do. We must ask God each morning to give us the ability to be better parents and better people. He will transform our lives if we ask Him to, but we have to be willing to do as He says. And from now on, name calling is not an option.

Thoughts and Revelations:

God Gives Grace to the Humble

♥

Ephesians 2:8-10

For it is by grace you have been saved, through faith—and this not from yourselves, it is the gift of God— not by works, so that no one can boast. For we are God's workmanship, created in Christ Jesus to do good works, which God prepared in advance for us to do.

God's grace is awesome. To love and accept me with all my inadequacies, is truly remarkable. My behaviors over the years have been less than acceptable, yet God has accepted me anyways. God's grace given to me teaches me how to extend grace to others. If God can love me even when I'm drunk I can love my husband even when he's drunk. If I want God's grace in my life I must extend it to others. I had a friend who was completely disgusted by her husband's addiction to chewing tobacco. She was bound and determined to get him to quit. She would call me frantic because she saw tobacco in his teeth when he had sworn he would never chew again. His habit didn't affect his behavior towards her. He loved her and treated her good. He simply had an unhealthy addiction. She convinced herself that if he loved her he would stop this nasty habit. But it wasn't about love. She was intolerant. If we are going to be completely honest with ourselves, we must admit that we all have secret sins. We all have fleshly cravings. Whether we crave food, or sex, or a substance, most of us are guilty. We all must learn the grace of God. We must learn to extend grace, if we expect to receive it from God.

Thought To Meditate On:

Choose your battles wisely. There is a fine line between love and control. We must learn to be tolerant of those we love and pray for them daily. Your nagging will not change a person but your prayers can work wonders. Don't try to be another person's God. You will do a lousy job and mess everything up.

My thoughts and revelations

by Lacy Enderson

Ever Present Help

♥

Proverbs 25:28

Like a city whose walls are broken down is a man who lacks self-control.

The success rate for those trying to quit a bad habit is low. The enemy attacks our minds and bodies with such force we fail before we ever begin. He encourages filthy habits to fester within us. He is good at using temptation to lure us back again. Some addictions are mental and some are physical, but regardless, the withdrawal symptoms are tremendous. I have quit smoking many times. After a couple of days clean, I always start smoking again. I was miserable without my Nicotine. I instigate fights. I argue. I cry. I can't function. All because my body is crying out for the substance it craves. If I could go back in time, I would never have started smoking in the first place. I tell teenagers, "The easiest way to quit, is to never start." I'm not saying that bad habits can't be broken. I am saying that without God's help it is very difficult. Why do you think the twelve step programs are based on a power greater than we are? Left relying on our own power we are failures, to weak to succeed. Abstinence has to come from within. It is an inside job that comes from God's Spirit. If you face a battle of self-will, and the lack of self-control, turn it over to God. He wants to and will deliver you. When I finally quit smoking for the very last time I was told to give myself permission to feel the feelings. Many times I tried to quit but I could not stand myself. I was moody and nasty and people couldn't stand to be around me. I would convince myself that smoking was the easier, softer way and I would be back to smoking again in days. I think the longest I went without a cigarette was nine days. And then one day I knew it was time, so I called Nicotine Anonymous and they walked me through the first two months. They told me it was all right to have mood swings and if the people in my life loved me they would tolerate me through them. Well, with great endurance they did, and I quit. I haven't had a cigarette since and I don't want one.

Thought To Meditate On:

The Bible talks about being lost in sin. That means we are controlled by Satan. He keeps us blinded to God's power of freedom. A man who is covered by the protection of God has a barrier of God's love surrounding him. This wall keeps evil out. The Devil wants to discourage you by making you believe you don't deserve Gods's wall of love, but He is a liar. You are invited to rest in the shadow of the almighty, for He is your refuge and your strength.

Thoughts and Revelations:

Shout to the Lord All the Earth Let Us Sing

♥

Psalms 100:1-5

Shout for joy to the LORD, all the earth. Worship the LORD with gladness; come before him with joyful songs. Know that the LORD is God. It is He who made us, and we are His; we are His people, the sheep of His pasture. Enter His gates with thanksgiving and His courts with praise; give thanks to Him and praise His name. For the LORD is good and His love endures forever; His faithfulness continues through all generations.

The most serenity I've ever known was on a family vacation at a hotel on the beach in Santa Barbara. I had only been sober two months and I wasn't smoking. I had a fabulous conscience contact with God in my life. This certain hotel had a train track that ran through the middle of it. The kids liked putting pennies on the track for the train to smash. My three children were still young enough to think smashed pennies were neat. One night my son Shaun placed his coins on the track and sat down to wait for the train. He asked me if I would wait with him. I said yes, and I sat down next to my middle child. We must have sat there for over an hour. It was absolutely the most peaceful time I can remember. I sat there with not a care in the world. I wasn't drinking, so I didn't need to get a drink. I wasn't smoking, so I didn't need a cigarette. I wasn't even obsessing over food, so I wasn't distracted by thoughts of eating. I was at perfect peace and I was completely content. I am not one who can sit still for very long. I have a hard time sitting in front of the TV for more than ten minutes. I am very active and very busy. When I'm not physically busy, I'm mentally busy. I seldom ever stop. So for me to sit and enjoy the smell of the air, and the sound of the waves, and my son's company, was an absolute gift of God.

Thought To Meditate On:

I wish I could tell you I've had similar experiences. But I can't. That is why this particular trip stands out so prevalent in my mind. It was a once in a lifetime moment of utter peace. The kind of peace that only comes from God. It was the greatest sense of God's serenity that I had ever known. And since my life has only just begun, I pray for more of this awesome peace.

Thoughts and Revelations:

by Lacy Enderson

Seek Peace and Pursue It

♥

2 Timothy 2:23,24

Don't have anything to do with foolish and stupid arguments, because you know they produce quarrels. And the Lord's servant must not quarrel; instead, he must be kind to everyone, able to teach, not resentful.

There is a certain tone of voice I use only with my husband. I never use it with anyone else. It is not a very nice tone of voice. In fact, it is a sound that cuts right through him. The tone of a person's voice can say a lot about their feelings. I've used it when I was angry. I've used it when I was hurt. I've used it when I was afraid. My defenses go up and I prepare for battle. He would tell me, "It's not what you say, it's how you say it." I can start a fight that lasts for days just by the way I say something. So I try really hard to calm down before I started confrontational conversations. But emotions have a way of taking over. I try to remember to count to ten and breathe. If that doesn't work then I try prayer. Sometimes a long walk does the trick. Boy! With so many character defects to work on, this one will probably surface now and then. But with God's help it will be less and less often. The one time I really notice my emotions taking over is when my husband does something I don't like or agree with. I get angry with him if I've told him my wishes and he doesn't listen to me. I find it completely frustrating when my wants, feelings and desires are discounted. I think anger is a natural human reaction to our hurt feelings. But, if I take it to God and not my husband, it has a way of working itself out. And the fight doesn't last for days, maybe only hours. Sometimes just minutes. It's called tolerance, and we must learn to possess it.

Thought To Meditate On:

Sometimes people just don't agree with us. We must allow others the right to their own opinions. God gave us each our own minds and the free will to use them. We have to allow others the right to use theirs also. Just because we think we are right and have all the right answers, doesn't mean we always do. How many times did you think you knew it all only to find out you were wrong? Let it go. It's not important who wins. What is important is to stay calm, stay connected, and stay sober.

Thoughts and Revelations:

Life Abundantly

♥

John 10:10

The thief comes only to steal and kill and destroy; I have come that they may have life, and have it to the full.

The Bible speaks of the devil as an angel of light. He is also referred to as a wolf in sheep's clothing. The enemy has a way of making the darkest sin appear irresistible. His lies sound so real and appealing, before I know it I'm caught up in his deception. It's not always the depressed, difficult days that I find myself tempted by alcohol. When all is well and I feel good, the devil tells me that it might be a good day to celebrate. A new job is a good reason for a beer. A meeting with an old and dear friend might seem like the perfect reason for a mixed drink. It is the times when I'm feeling really good that I can forget where I came from. I have learned that I must not take any day for granted. Every day can present a problem if I am not careful. God needs to be my first and foremost thought, everyday all day long. Developing my spiritual defenses will enable me to resist the temptation when I am hit with it right between the eyes. The devil doesn't care what kind of day it is. He is ready and waiting to attack. And he knows when I'm the weakest. Please, God. Make me strong. I remember one day specifically. I had about a year sober. It was a Friday and I had taken the day off of work. I lived in a condo complex. There was a community pool. I decided I would take my country music CD and lay out by the pool. But no sooner had I laid down, but the thought of a beer hit me so hard I was blindsided. The whole situation reminded me of the past when I would lay on the beach with my music and my beer. So I got up, got dressed and went to the movies. I kicked that thought out of my mind just as quickly as it entered. But thank God I was spiritually prepared.

Thought To Meditate On:

One vital truth when I got sober was that I would need to change most everything about my life. I was told to get rid of the reminders. In some cases that meant people and places. As an alcoholic it is important to remember that the ultimate goal is sobriety and it takes what it takes. Don't feel bad for taking care of yourself. Your family has screamed at you forever to get sober. Don't let them be the ones to sabotage your effort. Stay true to yourself and eventually people and places will fall in line.

Thoughts and Revelations:

by Lacy Enderson

The Just Shall Live by Faith

♥

Mark 11:22,23

"Have faith in God," Jesus answered. "I tell you the truth, if anyone says to this mountain, Go, throw yourself into the sea, and does not doubt in his heart but believes that what he says will happen, it will be done for him."

I define an obstacle as something that is standing in the way of my happiness, joy and freedom. Whether it is an addiction, debt, a bad marriage or a problem with other people, it gets in the way. It is an obstacle that must be removed. Every now and then I become overwhelmed with a friend's troubles. I carry her weight on my shoulders and sometimes she gets real heavy. I want my friend to be happy. I can see the mess she is creating in her life and I want to fix it. She becomes an obstacle to my happiness in the process. Eventually I realize that I do not have the power to fix anybody. God never told me to be responsible for the world, but he did give me an overly sensitive heart. I used to think that meant I was supposed to carry the world's burdens on my shoulders. Now I realize that I simply have to remember them in my prayers. You see, my friend has something to learn from her situation. Just like I have something to learn from mine. I pray and God fixes. It's not supposed to be the other way around. Another friend, because of careless mistakes, received three traffic tickets in one week. He was not employed and had no money to pay these fines. I wanted to bail him out by paying his tickets for him. But I knew that was not the right thing to do. I have to allow others to learn the hard way, to pay for their own mistakes. If I step in, the lesson might go overlooked and the crime could be repeated. I have to step back and mind my own business, allowing others, even my children, to mind theirs. It's not always an easy thing to do, but not impossible either.

Thought To Meditate On:

People are constantly making mistakes that I just don't understand. My father raised me to be smart and practical. He taught me responsibility and how to be conservative. People who over extend their bank accounts or can't pay the bills are foolish, as far as I am concerned, and it irritates me to see them behave that way. Thank God I am not suppose to fix them. It is not my job. It is their job. And it is between them and God, not them and me.

Thoughts and Revelations:

194

Do All in the Name of Christ

♥

1 Thessalonians 4:11,12

Make it your ambition to lead a quiet life, to mind your own business and to work with your hands, just as we told you, so that your daily life may win the respect of outsiders and so that you will not be dependent on anybody.

I often wonder what my purpose is here on this earth. I am told God has a plan for me, a plan that was established before I was ever born. That sounds encouraging. When I got out of high school I wanted to get married and have children. My father wanted me to attend college and become somebody important. I tried college for one semester and then quit to get married. At eighteen, I thought I knew it all. I was far wiser than my parents. But I look at my son who is eighteen and I could never imagine him married with children at his age. He is just a baby himself. I guess that is how my parents thought about me. Over the years I have tried several different careers, so far none to my liking. I get a job and if I'm lucky, I last about three months before I quit. Work to me is a distraction and a waste of time. My passion is staying home and being a housewife. I actually enjoy cleaning my house. I enjoy running errands for my kids. I have friends with small children who hate being home. They would go crazy if they were at home all day with their kids. I consider myself blessed that my children aren't that much of an inconvenience. I'm twenty years out of high school and I still don't know what my purpose is, and that's OK today. God will reveal that to me when it is his time. Just a quick update since this story was written. I have since gone back to college. I received my Associate's Degree in Behavioral Science. I will start my Bachelor's Degree this semester. My studies will be in Religious Psychology. I am very excited! I still don't know what God's plan is, but at least I am on my way.

Thought To Meditate On:

I feel sorry for kids right out of high school. They turn eighteen, become an adult and they are suppose to have it all figured out. I didn't have much figured out until I was forty and I am still not 100% sure of everything. I don't think we should assign responsibility to people based on age. We should be more patient with people and pay more attention to ability. Some kids should go to college, but others should do something else. God designed us all to be different and we need to respect His decisions.

Thoughts and Revelations:

by Lacy Enderson

Double Edged Sword

♥

James 1:19,20

My dear brothers, take note of this: Everyone should be quick to listen, slow to speak and slow to become angry, for man's anger does not bring about the righteous life that God desires.

Keeping secrets is hard for me. I am ashamed to admit that I am a gossip. I was asked by a friend not to share with anyone what she had told me about her relationship. So I told my husband. Unfortunately, my husband is a gossip, so he told his best friend. It didn't take long for the hurtful words to make their circle back to my friend. I can no longer be trusted in her eyes. I lost a good friend. The urge to gossip is pure weakness on my part. It is a character defect that I am not proud of. You would think I would know better. I have been the subject of gossip many times and it hurts. Now, I would rather not know secrets about people than to be tormented by them. So now I tell people that I cannot be trusted. I urge them not to confide in me. Proverbs 10:19 says, "When words are many, sin is not absent, but he who holds his tongue is wise." Proverbs 11:22 says, "Like a gold ring in a pig's snout is a beautiful woman who shows no discretion." And Proverbs 12:18 says, "Reckless words pierce like a sword, but the tongue of the wise brings healing." I am not a bad person and I do care deeply for others, but I have a flaw in my personality that I am working on. I have left destruction behind me that cannot be repaired. But with God's help, my character will be strengthened. And hopefully in the future I can keep the secrets I hear.

Thought To Meditate On:

Have you ever found out that a secret you told someone in confidence had been spread around like a forest fire? How did it feel? I told a secret to a friend once that got back to the person I was talking about and she refuses to forgive me to this day. Gossip is like a cancer. It will eat you alive and destroy really good relationships. But if you pray and ask God to help you keep your mouth shut, He will.

Thoughts and Revelations:

Hedge of Protection

♥

Isaiah 43:1,2

But now, this is what the LORD says—he who created you, O Jacob, "Fear not, for I have redeemed you; I have summoned you by name; you are mine. When you pass through the waters, I will be with you; and when you pass through the rivers, they will not sweep over you. When you walk through the fire, you will not be burned; the flames will not set you ablaze."

My second husband used to drive his truck up in the mountains. One night we went out with friends for some drinks and then he decided we'd go four wheel driving up in the hills. Not feeling very well, I thought bed sounded better, but I lost. We drove up to a hillside and began driving around, up and down the sides of these mountains. All the while I'm getting sicker, begging him to take me home. We were not going home. So I opened up the door of the truck and I jumped out. I began running. It was very dark and I had no idea where I was. My husband was not considering my feelings and I was offended. He wouldn't do what I wanted so I set out to get his attention. Like a two year old, negative attention was better than no attention at all. He followed me as I ran. I feared stepping on snakes or falling down the mountain, but it didn't matter. I wanted him to care. If I had gotten hurt maybe he would feel bad. That's what I wanted. Alcoholic behaviors can be so ugly. We are the most self-centered and selfish people alive when we are drinking. We think we are important, and we feel you should think so too. But in reality, we are pathetic. It took getting sober to see this. Thank you God for opening up my eyes. When I woke up the next morning after this pathetic episode, I felt like a complete loser. I couldn't believe I had acted so childishly. It always amazed me how different I was drunk compared to being sober. I would never have ran around a mountain side in the dark had I not been drinking. I am lucky I wasn't hurt. I mean blessed.

Thought To Meditate On:

It thrills my soul to be sober after remembering so many pathetic things I did drunk. It scares me to think I am only one drink away from that insanity. I am pretty convinced I will never drink again and by the grace of God, I won't, but I can't help but wonder if my sobriety will last a lifetime. I am told to live one day at a time and not look into the future, but sometimes I can't help it. I want to stay sober so badly I go into preventative mode. What can I do today to ensure I won't drink tomorrow? It can't hurt to be prepared.

Thoughts and Revelations:

by Lacy Enderson

Honesty is the Best Policy

♥

1 John 1:8-10

If we claim to be without sin, we deceive ourselves and the truth is not in us. If we confess our sins, he is faithful and just and will forgive us our sins and purify us from all unrighteousness. If we claim we have not sinned, we make him out to be a liar and his word has no place in our lives.

I protected myself from others so I wouldn't get hurt. Friends were OK until they got too close to me. Sharing intimate secrets with others made me feel naked and exposed. I felt like I was sitting on a judgement seat. I knew everyone was talking about me even though they weren't. I guess I was superficial. I could be your best friend, as long as you needed a good listener, but I couldn't be expected to share with you personal things about myself. I hated feeling vulnerable. I thrived on getting phone calls from people, but I found it hard to make calls myself. I was afraid I would be bothering someone. I heard a girl share once that when she came home from work she had three messages on her machine. She didn't feel like returning any of them, so she didn't. That only confirmed in me my fear to call. It made me wonder how many messages I left that were nothing more than an annoyance. God told me I didn't have to be afraid. He told me even if the whole world turned against me, He never would. So I'm learning how to lift my head high and have more confidence in myself. There will be people in my life who do not accept me for who I am. There will even be people who pretend to care, but really don't. They might even be kind to my face and talk bad about me behind my back. God has taught me today, that is OK. I have learned that there are those who are more afraid of intimacy than I am. I know I drank to cover these fears, and now that I am sober I can't hide from them. But over time I have grown less fearful and people are becoming easier for me to deal with.

Thought To Meditate On:

Although people are hard for me face to face, I really hate the telephone. I have a problem when I can't see the face of the one I am talking to. My mind has a funny way of convincing me that people on the other end of the phone really don't want to be there and if I could see their face I could confirm whether or not this was true. I sure hate the way my mind thinks sometimes. It keeps me preoccupied with nothing but wasteful thoughts.

Thoughts and Revelations:

Trust and Obey

♥

Hebrews 3:12,13

See to it, brothers, that none of you has a sinful, unbelieving heart that turns away from the living God. But encourage one another daily, as long as it is called today, so that none of you may be hardened by sin's deceitfulness.

The serenity prayer is my favorite. "God grant me the serenity to accept the things I cannot change, the courage to change the things I can, and the wisdom to know the difference." I pray this prayer when I am in a bad place emotionally. But I do not always know how to apply it to my life. I understand the part about accepting what I cannot change. And I understand the part that says I should ask God for the courage to change the things I can. It is the "Wisdom to know the difference" part that baffles me. The Bible tells me if I pray and ask for wisdom, God will give it to me. But when I am faced with a difficult decision, I don't always find the wisdom I seek right away. I am often quick to act and slow to wait. If I knew I could change a situation, I would change it. If I knew there was a situation that was completely out of my control, I would step back and leave it alone. But I do not always know the difference. I need to remember the saying, "Let go, let God." I must admit, sometimes this is easier said than done. Waiting can be frustrating. Human nature wants things now. But I am learning how to let things progress. Just as a seed planted doesn't become a plant in a day, some things take time. And each day I wait gets me another day closer to my destination, no matter how long it takes. So whether something needs changing or not, today I practice wisdom and patience. These two go together like a hand in a glove.

Thought To Meditate On:

There have been times I have asked God for wisdom but he gave me an answer I didn't like. So I asked again, over and over thinking He might change His mind and give me what I wanted. I found it important to be careful in asking. It is important to know what God's will is first. If you ask for something believing you will receive it, you will probably get what you ask for. It would be a good idea if it was what God originally had in mind. You know the saying, be careful what you ask for, you might just get it? Ask God first what His will is for you, and then after He tells you what it is, then ask for that. It is safer that way.

Thoughts and Revelations:

199

by Lacy Enderson

Renew Your Mind

♥

1 Peter 1:13-16

Therefore, prepare your minds for action; be self-controlled; set your hope fully on the grace to be given you when Jesus Christ is revealed. As obedient children, do not conform to the evil desires you had when you lived in ignorance. But just as he who called you is holy, so be holy in all you do; for it is written: "Be holy, because I am holy."

There was a time when I was extremely vindictive. I loved to get revenge. The sick part was, it made me feel better. It was an ugly behavior I can honestly say has since been removed. Many evenings my second husband came home late from work. He always had a good reason, but it was never good enough for me. I waited for him at the door when he arrived home so I could make sure he knew exactly how I felt. I had myself convinced he was out doing something wrong and I was going to make him pay. He was a very quiet individual. It took a lot to get him upset. I was not used to mild mannered men. I was used to men who yelled and screamed back. So I would viciously attack him in an attempt to get a reaction. But I never got one. When he had enough of me, he would go to sleep. That is how he dealt with my uncontrollable behavior. He chose not to deal with it at all. This aggravated me more and I would set out to hurt him. Let me mention that by the time he arrived home I was already intoxicated. I started drinking as soon as he was late and probably had five or six beers in me by now. We all know what an angry drunk woman look like. The worst episode in a list of many was the night I took a car key and scratched up the side of his brand new truck. I have thrown water on him while he was sleeping and physically attacked him when he wouldn't fight back. He had a black eye for a week and scratches all over his body many times. It shames me to think of the ways I reacted. It's hard to imagine I was ever that person. But I was. I have since been delivered from getting pleasure from other people's pain. And thank God I don't drink anymore.

My Thought To Meditate On:

I wish couples who drink could get sober for even a week to see how much better their relationships could be. I know personally, the majority of arguments I had with my husbands were alcohol induced. Fights were as common as the daylight when I was drinking. But sobriety has ended all that. It is hard to tell drinkers how much better their lives would be sober. It is an experience they must live for themselves.

Thoughts and Revelations:

He Commands His Angels
♥

Daniel 3:28

Then Nebuchadnezzar said, "Praise be to the God of Shadrach, Meshach and Abednego, who has sent his angel and rescued his servants! They trusted in him and defied the king's command and were willing to give up their lives rather than serve or worship any god except their own God.

I don't believe I have ever suffered at the hand of God. Most of my suffering has been self-induced. I have made choices in my life that even I couldn't believe I made. I believe in a miracle working God, but there comes a time when I must be held responsible for my choices. I like living in a make believe fantasy world where nothing can go wrong, but that's just ridiculous. I have walked on the road of righteousness. I have tasted the sweetness of God's grace. I have been under His care and protection. I have lived worry and stress free. And then one day I get a bright idea. I make my own plans. And before I know it, I am drunk. I am headed down the path of self destruction, misery and hopelessness. There have been many times when the storms I created gave me a good reason to drink. Alcoholics need excuses. I do appreciate the quiet, and boredom can be a blessing, but maybe in some way I am comfortable with chaos. Problems keep me busy. They give me something to focus on. As I become healthier I'm beginning to realize that chaos isn't comfortable at all. Since the first step to any healing is awareness, I think I am ready for the deliverance to begin. God, if I am on the wrong road and your blessings cannot be attained here, I ask you to please reroute me. I am not strong enough to turn back on my own, but I give you full permission to pick me up and plant me where you want me to grow.

Thought To Meditate On:

Some people do not feel comfortable unless they are in the midst of a fight. I think it is sad they don't like peace and quiet. I bet if they ever experienced a peaceful day they might want more like them, but a person doesn't miss what they have never had. In sobriety we slowly learn to accept quiet in our lives. It happens slowly but then becomes our everyday norm. Today I am so grateful for peace.

Thoughts and Revelations:

by Lacy Enderson

Healing in His Wings

♥

Luke 5:12,13

While Jesus was in one of the towns, a man came along who was covered with leprosy. When he saw Jesus, he fell with his face to the ground and begged him, "Lord, if you are willing, you can make me clean. "Jesus reached out his hand and touched the man. "I am willing," he said. "Be clean!" And immediately the leprosy left him.

I have never had a change take place in my life that I wasn't first willing to make. God will not impose His will on my life without my permission. If I hate something bad enough, I will make changes. If I am willing, God will help me. Until I get to that point, God sits back and waits. Changes are decisions that I have to make first. I can desire to quit eating sugar, but God isn't going to take the candy bar out of my mouth. I can get tired of looking at my dirty kitchen floor, but God is not going to put a mop in my hand. When I grew tired of getting drunk, God didn't shut down the bars and pour my beer down the drain. What He did do, was take the obsession away. He made it easy for me to say no. He instilled the desire in me to be happy and healthy. Willingness is the key to deliverance. When I am struggling for freedom from addictive behaviors, I know what my solution is. If I find I am not willing, I ask God to make me willing. I don't have to tolerate the intolerable anymore. God offers me a way out.

Thought To Meditate On:

I tolerate what I don't hate. If I hate something bad enough, I make changes. If I am willing, God will help me. Until I get to that point, God sits back and waits. When my life becomes unmanageable and my choices are weighing me down, God is there to rescue me, but I have to ask Him first.

Thoughts and Revelations:

202

King Jesus is All

♥

1 Timothy 6:17

Command those who are rich in this present world not to be arrogant nor to put their hope in wealth, which is so uncertain, but to put their hope in God, who richly provides us with everything for our enjoyment.

Unspeakable joy comes from the inside. It starts with hope. If I am hoping for something, I feel better. When the circumstances of life are crazy but I focus on the solution, I'm happier. When I have nothing to look forward to, I become stagnate. Looking forward to something gives me the hope I need for tomorrow. The Word says without hope I would die. I believe it means a spiritual and emotional death. When I get up in the morning and focus on what I have, I develop a reason for living and I strengthen my resolve. When there isn't enough money in the bank to cover my expenses, I have learned to thank God for His provision in advance. I take my focus off the financial insecurity and place it on God's ability to provide. When my husband and I are fighting and anger and fear want to ruin my day, I think of a quiet cabin in the desert. I must keep my thoughts and my attentions on the hope and not on the circumstances. I am renting a house. I have never owned a home of my own. But in my morning prayers I thank God for the house He is preparing for me. I tell God how I would like for my house to look. We talk about the wallpaper, and how many rooms I need. I center my thinking on the things I hope for. It has done wonders for my attitude. It is exciting when I hope for something I don't yet have and it gives me purpose when I am expecting a wonderful move from God.

Thought To Meditate On:

I am tired of living in despair, always worried about my future. Worry and depression are a thing of the past. God has wonderful plans for me and someday I will know what they are. I will not allow the way life looks today to rob me of my joy. And remember, never put your hope or trust in money. When it is gone, then what will you do?

Thoughts and Revelations:

by Lacy Enderson

Listen Carefully

♥

Proverbs 3:5

Trust in the Lord with all your heart and lean not on your own understanding; in all your ways acknowledge him, and he will make your paths straight.

Believing in God was always easy for me. I was raised in a home where we attended church on a regular basis and the God I grew up with was a kind and loving God easy for me to believe in. I believe God works in our hearts to give us the desires He would like for us to have. So I never rebelled against the church as so many forced attendees had. I knew God only wanted the best for me, so I tried to pay attention and stay true to myself. Trusting in God was an entirely different issue. I was told to get out of the way, that the best was yet to come. They said God didn't need my help. He was entirely capable of running my life for me without my input. But I was a chronic worrier. I just knew that if I didn't spend countless hours sitting at my kitchen table trying to figure everything out, nothing was ever going to happen. Well, in this way nothing ever did happen and I wasted many hours and many days worried about my life. I have since learned by the grace of God that when I do turn my cares over to Him he really does take care of everything. I have since quit trying to figure it all out and I have given that job to God. And the amazing thing is to see all the really great things God has done in my life, and I didn't have to worry about any of it. Imagine that.

Thought To Meditate On:

Trust in God and not in yourself. Haven't you learned by now? Worry will keep you really busy and you might even feel like you are accomplishing something, but in the end of the day, as you will find out, nothing is ever done. Only God knows the beginning and the end and everything in between. And since He has this great knowledge, don't you agree, He will do a much better job with your life than you will?

Thoughts and Revelations:

Be Quick to Listen, Slow to Speak

♥

Ecclesiastes 5:2,3

Do not be quick with your mouth, do not be hasty in your heart to utter anything before God. God is in heaven and you are on earth, so let your words be few. As a dream comes when there are many cares, so the speech of a fool when there are many words.

Emotional pain is hard to get rid of especially when you are emotionally weak. I have been called names that I wouldn't repeat to my worst enemy. I have been criticized and put down. I have been slandered and ridiculed. I discovered that if I could transfer the emotional pain I was feeling to my body then my heart wouldn't hurt so bad. So I began hurting myself. I scratched my arms with my fingernails and I beat my head with my fists. I have even experienced such moments of insanity when I tore up my face like a desperate animal. Self-abuse is a lot like alcohol. They both numbed the pain. When my body was hurting, I couldn't feel the pain in my heart as intensely. The focus of my pain switched from one I could not control, to one I was responsible for. I was in control of self-inflicted pain. I have since learned that nobody has the right to hurt me with words. I realize people can be hurtful, but more often than not it is because they are hurting also. It is not always about me. Sometimes it is about them and if I practice compassion, I would be less offended. God has given me an imaginary shield. It blocks the fiery darts of attack and the words don't penetrate my heart like they used to. I feel sorry for people who hurt others with their words. Only a monster could spit out such slander with no regret. The Bible tells us; "Out of the abundance of the heart, a man speaks." If our hearts are not right, then our words will not be right either.

Thought To Meditate On:

Be careful what you say. God spoke the world into existence. We give more power to the devil by the words of our mouths than in any other way. Let the words of your mouth be holy and acceptable, pleasing unto God. Quit speaking death and destruction over your circumstances and start speaking life. For example; let us say you get sober and you are very happy about it but you share with your friend how you don't think you will be able to stay sober long. That is speaking destruction over your life. If that is the way you truly feel than you might as well drink again. Learn to think positive and before long you'll be speaking it too.

Thoughts and Revelations:

by Lacy Enderson

He Will Supply All of Your Needs

♥

Philippians 4:12,13

I know what it is to be in need, and I know what it is to have plenty. I have learned the secret of being content in any and every situation, whether well fed or hungry, whether living in plenty or in want. I can do everything through him who gives me strength.

Alcoholic, drug addicts will do anything to fund their disease. They steal, they rob, they cheat, and they lie. Teenagers steal from their own parents. Desperate people vandalize cars and sell the contents to pawn shops. Drunks lose their homes, their cars and their families. Respectable businessmen lose their jobs and become unemployable. Women prostitute themselves for a fix. They dance for drugs. They give up their dignity for a drink. Non-alcoholics don't understand. They call us weak. We are told that we simply need to quit. Well, It's not that simple. We know what we should do and we want to. But we can't. Drinking is only a symptom of underlying issues. Our pain and our fears are sometimes too much to deal with sober. We have to escape. Our realities hurt too badly. When we do sober up we are faced with financial insecurity. We are alone. We have no food. We are hopeless. But there is good news, God came to set the hopeless free. He has a solution to every problem we face. He will provide one day at a time if we will trust in Him. There is nothing the drink is going to fix. When I awaken from my drunken stupor, every problem I drank over will still be there. I must rely on God.

Thought To Meditate On:

Fear of the unknown is one of our biggest problems. We allow ourselves to believe that everything bad we think is eventually going to happen. The thought gets bigger and bigger until it seems like an overwhelming reality. People with obsessive compulsive disorder are my best examples. They get a thought in their head based on a past fear. The fear usually comes from something they heard on the news. (Turn it off.) This fear goes around and around in their minds until they are convinced it is going to happen just the way they fear it will. It is sad, because none of it is based on facts. It is all a big lie, full of deception. The Bible tells us we can take those thoughts captive. I suggest you do before they drive you crazy.

Thoughts and Revelations:

Diligent Hands

♥

Matthew 6:33

But seek first the kingdom of God and all his righteousness, and all these things will be given unto you.

I have never been a materialistic person. In fact, I was always content in having just my immediate needs met. As long as I was able to stay home and daydream, I felt I had the perfect life. I had so many things to think about all the time. I hated going to work because it took too many precious hours out of my day. I think maybe I came from another planet. I have since come to realize all this daydreaming just meant I was lazy. God desires more for my life than just sitting around wasting time. He wants to give me the land overflowing with milk and honey. He wants to develop my talents and teach me how to use my God given gifts. But I need to do my part. So I wake up in the morning and I give my day to Him. I ask Him to lead me where I will be of maximum service. I ask for the strength to accomplish His will for my life each day, one day at a time. It is amazing just how much God has for me to do each day when I allow Him to lead me. Now, I barely have enough time to think, let alone daydream. Today, you can call me many things, but lazy isn't one of them. Thank God.

Thought To Meditate On:

Materialism isn't always bad. God never said we shouldn't have nice things. What is bad about it is when you never have enough. Some people have been afflicted with a shopping addiction. It seems they are never happy unless they are buying something new. That is one aspect of life I don't understand. I hate spending money. I guess greed is just another distraction from life like drugs and alcohol. It is considered an instant gratification for those who are not comfortable with life. It is sad, and I feel sorry for these people. But just like with any other addiction, there is a program that can help.

Thoughts and Revelations:

by Lacy Enderson

A Sure Thing

♥

Psalms 27:13,14

I am still confident of this: I will see the goodness of the Lord in the land of the living. Wait for the Lord; be strong and take heart and wait for the Lord.

I have heard many sermons and I have visited many churches that have different interpretations of scripture. Some preach that the good God has for us begins in heaven. Some preach that God wants us to experience the good things today while we are still living on this Earth. Through my sobriety and by practicing the principles of my recovery program and scripture I am convinced that God's blessings are for us today. Each and every day, as I turn my will and my life over to God, He has another adventure waiting for me better that my wildest imagination. So I patiently wait on God, expecting, today.

Thought To Meditate On:

The blessings I have experienced since I got sober completely convince me that God blesses my life today. I don't have to wait until I die and go to heaven to experience God's best. He has it right here waiting for anyone who wants to enjoy His better life now. Heaven will be beyond anything we could ever imagine, but with God working in our lives we can experience a touch of heaven here on earth.

Thoughts and Revelations:

The Lifter of My Head
♥

1 Peter 5:6

Humble yourselves, therefore, under Gods mighty hand, that he may lift you up in due time.

The hardest time for me to be truly humble is when somebody has hurt or offended me. I have been taught that I should always have an attitude of forgiveness toward my enemies and turn the other cheek. But sometimes anger gets in the way and I want retaliation. When I choose to hold onto the offense, I can think of nothing else. "Look what that person did to me," I say, "I want an apology and I won't let it go until I get one!" I become obsessed. Anger separates us from God and prevents Him from working in our lives. Anger robs us of peace, joy and serenity. When I humbly forgive, and trust in God, more times than not, these people come to me truly humbled as well. I continually pray that God will help me to always be humble. The Bible asks me to humbly treat others better than I treat myself, and to love my neighbor as myself. So although I have my work cut out for me, I will do my best to practice these principles. God wouldn't ask us to do something we couldn't handle, and almost everything He requires comes with an added reward.

Thought to meditate on

In humility, consider others as greater than yourselves. Not because you always feel like it, but because God asks you to. There is something powerful about loving other people. Love has a way of opening doors of blessings and overflow in our lives. Love will cancel out hate, resentment, hurt feelings and control. It makes a way for peace, joy and freedom. When we humbly rely on God, and completely trust in Him, he will never fail us.

Thoughts and Revelations:

At Ease

♥

Philippians 4:6

Do not be anxious about anything but in everything, by prayer and petition. With thanksgiving, present your requests to God. And the Peace of God, which passes all understanding, will guard your hearts and your minds in Christ Jesus.

I have had situations in my life when I thought I needed an immediate answer from God. Those panic situations are agonizing. I run around in circles, calling out to God. "Don't you hear me, Lord?" I groan. "Can't you see I need your help?" I picture God on His throne just shaking His head and saying, "Lacy, I have it all under control. Cast your cares on me because I care for you." I have literally wasted days in worry and fear only to have everything work out on it's own, in God's time. Why do I waste so much time worrying? I have a tendency to pray a prayer expecting to see the answer immediately. I know God hears me because He says He does, so why does He not give me what I want now? I hate waiting only to see my prayer answered days later when I have forgotten all about it. I think God has a sense of humor. I guess that is a good thing.

Thought To Meditate On:

There is great power in being thankful. God asks us to come to Him in prayer with thanksgiving. We are told to thank Him even before we see Him move in our lives. God blesses the prayer of faith. How much more can we prove our faith in Him, than to thank Him in advance for His blessing? It is not manipulating God because you think He might do what you ask. He wants you to ask and then thank Him. He says so in His Word, so it must be OK. Pray with a grateful heart, and believe that God hears you. He will flood you with an all consuming sense of peace and everything will be all right.

Thoughts and Revelations:

Window to My Soul

♥

Ephesians 1:18

I pray also that the eyes of your heart may be enlightened in order that you may know the hope to which he has called you, and his incomparably great power for us who believe. That power is like the working of his mighty strength.

Decisions are not always easy for me to make. When I was drinking, the only decision before me each morning was when I would take that first drink. Or would I drink at all? Alcohol related decisions took up most of my day. Now that I am sober I live in the fear that if I make a wrong decision I will have to suffer uncomfortable consequences. Because fear has a way of growing, it can spill over into decisions that should be simple to make. I actually have a difficult time deciding whether or not I should clean my bathroom or go to my computer class. I find it very hard to prioritize my daily tasks. I am always so afraid of making the wrong decision, that sometimes I won't make any decision at all, even in the little things. But I have found a solution to this problem. If I go to God with my list of things to do and ask Him to direct my path, everything seems to get done. God has a way of directing us to do exactly what He knows is best. God wants me to bring my simple, ordinary concerns to Him. No request is too small a task for God. He always has time for me.

Thought To Meditate On:

I am a planner. I am not the type of person who jumps up and goes somewhere on the spur of the moment. I guess that means I am not spontaneous. I don't call this a character defect. I think my mom and my husband would because they both love last minute planning, but for me it is just who I am. Because I know this about myself, I do try to be flexible for those in my life who need me to be. I can and will make exceptions to my plans if someone needs me to. I can't say I am always happy when my plans get changed but at least today I can better accept it. I don't get too frustrated and I don't let it ruin my day. I used to, but not so much anymore.

Thoughts and Revelations:

by Lacy Enderson

Your Loving Kindness is Everlasting

♥

1 Peter 4:8

Love each other deeply, because love covers over a multitude of sins. Offer hospitality to one another without grumbling. Each one should use whatever gift he has received to serve others; if any one serves, he should do it with the strength God provides, so that in all things God may be praised through Christ Jesus.

Serving others has not always come easy. Prior to my recovery, my good deeds always had strings firmly attached to them. If I did something nice for you, I expected something nice in return. I always made sure that those around me knew about all of the great and wonderful things I did so that I could receive praise and recognition. But the praise and recognition was never lofty enough and sometimes I waited in vain for returned favors. Most of the time, I ended up frustrated and full of resentment. I have since learned that I receive the greatest joy when I expect nothing in return. And then I am not left disappointed. To know that I have helped someone else simply because God enables me to has become a powerful reward in itself.

Thought To Meditate On:

The commandment God gives us to "love thy neighbor as thyself" means we should do unto others as we would have them do unto us, not treat others the way we are treated. Resentment and retaliation used to be our motto, but since we got sober we have had to change all that. If I made a list of all the birthdays that someone ruined for me you would cry me a bucket full of tears. And how many times did I want to make sure I ruined their's. "I will show you how it feels", I would say. But I had to change that way of thinking. I had to make sure I made their day better than any other day. That is what God asks of me. And the funny thing is, even though they hurt me, it felt really good to make their day special. Who would have thought I would get more pleasure out of being kind than vindictive?

Thoughts and Revelations:

Never Failing Compassion

♥

Joel 2:12-14

Return to me with all your heart...Rend your heart and not your garments. Return to the Lord your God, for he is gracious and compassionate, slow to anger and abounding in love, and he yields from calamity. Who knows? He may turn and have pity and leave behind a blessing.

When I was knee deep in my alcoholism, "compassionate" was not a word that you could have used to describe me. I simply did not have the time to worry about those people around me. I had so much junk in my life that my own problems cluttered my mind and I didn't have room for anymore. I fooled people into thinking I cared about them. They would call and I would listen, but if I could get a word in edgewise, the conversation would always change and become all about me. In alcohol recovery I prayed for compassion. My sister used to tell me I needed more compassion and I think she probably prayed for me too. Because our God is faithful and our God knows just what we need to serve Him he gave me a lot more compassion than I asked for. Now I have so much compassion that my heart aches for all those around me. I cannot watch the news or read the paper because I care too much for hurting people. If the compassion I feel for hurting people is even a touch of what God feels for you and me, we are truly loved. He has opened the eyes of my heart and I am blessed.

Thought To Meditate On:

If you compare the love that God has for us, to the love an earthly parent has for his/her child and add to it a thousand times more, it is easier to understand just how much God does love us, no matter what. Pray for God to replace your inward eyes with eyes of compassion. Look outward towards others and learn to place other people's needs above your own. They told me in recovery I would have a much better chance of staying sober if I worked with another alcoholic. They said if I took my eyes off of myself and put them on someone else my problems wouldn't seem as big and drinking wouldn't seem so important. If I drank to drown my problems and all of a sudden my problems seemed small, then the likelihood of drinking would lesson also. What a great concept.

Thoughts and Revelations:

by Lacy Enderson

Refiner's Fire

♥

1 Peter 5:10,11

And the God of all Grace, who called you to his eternal glory in Christ, after you have suffered a little while, will himself restore you and make you strong, firm and steadfast. To him be the power forever and ever.

"Help me God!" I remember begging Him time and time again. I couldn't figure out what was wrong with my life. I was convinced it couldn't be the drinking. You see, a true alcoholic is supposed to drink. It is our nature to drink. For so long, everything became O.K. with that first drink. So the drinking couldn't possibly be the problem. It had to be something else. Boy was I wrong. It is amazing how so many of those problems I was having seemed to go away when I gave up the alcohol. I was powerless over alcohol, but God had all the power. And if all the pain and suffering I went through has gotten me to this wonderful place I am in today, then to God be the glory. Never throw the baby out with the bath water. Take the good and leave the rest. Use what you can if it is useable. If your alcoholism brings you closer to God and gives you a better life then thank God for the alcoholism. God just wants to have you in His kingdom. Whatever He uses to get you there is part of His divine plan. Don't argue with God's plans. He is smarter than you think. No one ever looked towards alcoholism as a blessing. But God uses what He can. Learn to be grateful in all things.

Thought To Meditate On:

Just as gold goes through the fire to become stronger and more refined, we go through the hard times in life so God can accomplish this same purpose in us. I don't believe the hard times come from God, they come from the devil, but God can use them for our good. We go through the fire kicking and screaming all the way, but when we come out on the other side, we are shiny and beautiful.

Thoughts and Revelations:

He Will Council and Watch Over You

♥

Psalm 25:4-7

Show me your ways, O Lord, teach me your path; guide me in your truth and teach me, for you are God my Savior, and my hope is in you all day long. Remember, O Lord, your great mercy and love, for they are from of old.

My road to recovery has been a long and painful process. It did not happen overnight. I hear so many wonderful stories of people walking through the doors of recovery and never drinking again. That did not happen for me. I have relapsed three times. Each time I failed to really work hard on my recovery. I relied on my own power and when life got really hard I turned to a friendly bottle. I'm told we're not ready until we're ready. Maybe it just wasn't my time. But what I do know is that God has been with me every step of the way. Each time I relapsed, I learned more about why I drink. This time, I am immersing myself in the Word of God. When my life gets hard I turn to a friendly God who wants me to succeed. If you're having a hard time, hold on. Be patient and trust God. He is walking with you every step of the way.

Thought To Meditate On:

God has said in His Word that He will neither leave you nor forsake you. It doesn't matter to Him how many times you fall as long as you get up and try again. God has a never ending flow of patience. He has a very deep well of endurance. He can wait as long as you need Him too. Just wake up each morning and give it your best. Whatever you can't do, God will do for you.

Thoughts and Revelations:

by Lacy Enderson

You Light Up My Life
♥

2 Samuel 22:29

You are my lamp, O Lord; the Lord turns my darkness into light.

I am not a visual person. I do not notice beautiful sunsets or gardens blooming with color. I do not stand in awe of the city lights from atop a high cliff. I have spent a lifetime defending myself. I say, "I am not a visual person. It's not my fault that I didn't notice your new haircut. It's not my fault that I didn't compliment your decorating." I just don't notice things that other people see. One day I was sitting in a meeting and the speaker said that alcoholics see the world through a mirror. Boy did that make sense. For the first time I was able to recognize a character flaw in myself I hadn't seen before. It is not that I am not visual, it is that I spent so much time looking at myself and all of my problems, that I became blind to anything else. God's beauty and your wallpaper never caught my eye because I was looking inward. I have to wake up each morning and ask God to deliver me from self. I ask him to open my eyes and to direct them outward. I don't want to miss another thing.

Thought To Meditate On:

When I am doing God's will and not my own, I see things in a brand new light. God doesn't make mistakes. His ways are perfect. He made everything to be just exactly the way they are suppose to be. If I look towards life from His perspective, the beauty in His creations are the first sites I see. Look for the beauty in people, places and things around you, and you will be amazed at how much more colorful the world will become.

Thoughts and Revelations:

I Am Redeemed

♥

Isaiah 44:22

"I have swept away your offenses like a cloud, your sins like the morning mist. Return to me for I have redeemed you."

They told me in sobriety that resentments kill. They said that if I did not learn to forgive those people who had harmed me, thinking nothing of what they had done to me, I would drink again. When God's word tells us that "if we ask for forgiveness, we are forgiven" it means exactly that. It doesn't mean that at some later date God is going to take everything you've ever done and throw it back at you. It is over and forgotten, never to be remembered again. This is the same attitude God wants us to have with other people. He doesn't want us making lists of past offenses so that as things happen to us we can add it to our list saying, here we go again. He wants us to forgive and forget. Resentments are heavy. Who wants to carry around tons of smelly garbage? Let go and be free. It is truly a life changing experience.

Thought To Meditate On:

When we go before God, sorry for the things we have done, He not only forgives us of those wrong doings, He promises to never remember them again. Wouldn't it be a great experience if we were given this same ability. I know we are not God and because He is perfect He is far more capable of responding Godly than we are. But he did say if we asked Him to help us, He would. So ask God to give you a forgiving heart. Ask Him to transform you by the renewing of your mind making it possible for you also to forget.

Thoughts and Revelations:

by Lacy Enderson

The Great Defender

♥

Ephesians 6:10-13

...be strong in the Lord and in his mighty power. Put on the full armor of God so that you can take your stand against the devil's schemes. For our struggle is not against flesh and blood, but against the rulers, against the authorities, against the powers of this dark world and against the spiritual forces of evil in the heavenly realms. Therefore put on the full armor of God, so that when the day of evil comes, you may be able to stand your ground.

Satan does not need to attack us overtly. He simply has to bring little distractions into our lives to make us lazy or busy or tired. If he can do this, we will stop reading the Word. We will cease to pray. We will take off God's armor of protection and be vulnerable to the world with all of its deception and lies. The only defense we have against the enemy is to stand firm in the truth. Pray daily, read the Word and trust that God is stronger than any evil that may taunt us. The enemy has always wiggled his way into my life through my bank account. When I cannot make ends meet and I am worried about where our mortgage payment will come from I stand naked before the enemy. I allow him to creep into my life every time I succumb to worry and anxiety. Worry is heavy but God's armor is light. The enemy would have you believe the opposite. So put on the armor of God. It cannot be penetrated by any fiery darts of the devil. You will overcome.

Thought To Meditate On:

Never let your guard down. Remember, we have an enemy who lurks around every corner waiting for our weakest moment. The Word says the devil came to steal, kill, and destroy. Resist the devil and he will flee from you. But you must be prepared. Don't ever think you can walk out of the house without your sword of the spirit or your shield of faith. You will be sorry you did. Stand strong and be ready.

Thoughts and Revelations:

Take Every Thought Captive
♥

Titus3: 3-5

At one time we too were foolish, disobedient, deceived and enslaved by all kinds of passions and pleasures. We lived in malice and envy, being hated and hating one another. But when the kindness and love of God our Savior appeared, he saved us not because of righteous things we had done, but because of his mercy.

Obsessive thoughts are powerful! They begin small and grow quickly into monsters that we cannot control. I have spent my life being controlled by obsessive thoughts. The nagging conversations that have gone on inside my head are enough to drive a person crazy. I found out in recovery that I am not alone and I am certainly not crazy. Obsessive thoughts are part of this disease we all share. But I do not have to be in bondage to these thoughts anymore. I was told I never had to live with such torment in my mind again. God would take these thoughts away. So I tried it, and it worked. I asked God to remove the obsessive thinking going on in my head and He did. Ask Him today to bring you the peace of God that surpasses all understanding. If you do, He will. And don't stop there. Everytime the thoughts come back, battle them with God's Word. The Bible says we have been given a sound mind, so stand on the Word and let your thoughts be few. There was a time we used alcohol to drown out the thinking. Without the pain reliever of alcohol the thoughts can run rampant. But you can stop them. You can make them go away. Let God help you today to clear your mind and allow it to be renewed.

Thought To Meditate On:

Because of past painful experiences my husband has a very difficult time on the road. He witnessed so many bad accidents he has a hard time driving. He hates trains, planes, buses and he is never a passenger in a car. It is sad to see him so afraid. I feel bad for him and what his mind puts him through. The worst part is he is continuously filling up his children's minds with these same fears. He believes if he tells his kids all about the accidents he has seen it will make them safer when they drive. But all it is doing is creating fear in them. If you have a fearful mind because of something in your past, get help. You don't have to live with the torment anymore. And you don't have to continue tormenting others.

Thoughts and Revelations:

Beyond Our Understanding

♥

Hebrews 4:15,16

For we do not have a high priest who is unable to sympathize with our weaknesses, but we have one who has been tempted in every way, just as we are - yet was without sin. Let us then approach the throne of grace with confidence, so that we may receive mercy and find grace to help us in our time of need.

I know it is hard for some of us to understand the part in the Bible which tells us that Jesus was tempted in every way just as we are. I mean, for goodness sakes, he was God! But, if one believes in the whole Word of God, as I do, than one must believe that Jesus really does understand what we're going through. For me, that is the most comforting news of all. I go to alcohol recovery meetings so I can be a part of a group of people who are going through the same things I am. It helps me to know that I am not alone. How much more reassuring it is for me to know that Jesus knows too? To be a part of Him, well, that's the best part.

Thought To Meditate On:

God understands everything you are going through. It says so in His Word. So be encouraged. The same strength God used to raise Jesus from the dead is the strength He gives to you today. We are overcomers through Him who overcame the world.

Thoughts and Revelations:

He Will Cover You With His feathers

♥

Psalm 28:7

The Lord is my shield; my heart trusts in him, and I am helped. My heart leaps for joy and I will give thanks to him in song.

Psalms 91:11 & 12 says; "For he will command his angels concerning you to guard you in all your ways; they will lift you up in their hands, so that you will not strike your foot against a stone." If the Bible tells us God is a barrier around us, than He is like an iron wall. If God tells us He is our help, than He is our help in every situation. So trust in Him and believe in His awesome ability to protect you from everything. Wherever you are in your journey through sobriety, trust that the God you call Lord will put a hedge of protection around you. Not only for today but forever. If you need to be carried, His arms are strong. If you need to be dropped so you can learn a few things, He will not hesitate. He knows what you need and you can rest in that knowledge. But you must get beyond simply calling Him God. You must trust that He is also your Lord. He is your protector. But He cannot protect you unless you trust Him to.

Thought To Meditate On:

God has a hedge of protection around you. That is a barrier wall of His love that keeps the evil out. He shields you from everything that would harm you. He is your glory and the lifter of your head. It is normal for humans to feel all alone, because in reality we can't see God. But He is there. He promises to stay by our sides, helping us and delivering us from all opposition. The Bible says that God will raise up a standard against the enemy, when the enemy comes in like a flood. How great is that?

Thoughts and Revelations:

by Lacy Enderson

Love Builds Up

♥

Ephesians 4:29,31,32

Do not let any unwholesome talk come out of your mouths, but only what is helpful for building others up according to their needs, that it may benefit those who listen. Get rid of all bitterness, rage and anger, brawling and slander, along with every form of malice. Be kind and compassionate to one another, forgiving each other, just as in Christ God forgave you.

It would be nice if we could move forward in our journey without lugging around all the baggage from our past. But sometimes the baggage is attached to the people we love. We handed it to them in a fit of rage. We tied it to their wrists during an alcoholic binge. We slung it upon their backs with mean and nasty words. My son Shaun is carrying some of that baggage. Shaun was a very busy child. He was stubborn and always getting into trouble. He was eventually diagnosed with ADHD but that was before we knew much about it. There was a time in my life when I had trouble saying anything nice. I was filled with self hatred and anger. I woke up each morning in a bad mood. I hated my life and resented Shaun for making my life miserable. I nicknamed him "Little Shit," and he lived up to his new title. The more I yelled the more defiant Shaun became. So I yelled more. This went on until he was four. By this time he was having problems in preschool, was acting aggressively with other children and was lighting fires in the backyard. My pediatrician recommended a family counselor for Shaun. So I made an appointment and the two of us went. By the grace of God a therapist showed me my part in his unruly behavior and I made changes. I quit calling him names and I stopped yelling at him. Today Shaun is a great kid. He is highly intelligent, even-tempered and loves me very much. But I do not pretend that he won't have a lot of baggage to deal with in his future because of my drinking and my rage. I will continue to move forward in my journey but I will never forget to be sensitive to the pain I have caused.

Thought To Meditate On:

When we are feeling good about ourselves we tend to say things that make others feel good also. Likewise, when we are troubled and in despair we tend to say things that are ugly and hurtful. The Bible tells us to make sure the words of our mouth are acceptable and pleasing. Not only to God but to others as well. If good words are hard for you to find, make a list of them and practice them often. If in a fit of rage you find it hard to remember the good words on your list, turn around and walk away.

Thoughts and Revelations:

Patient Endurance

♥

Romans 15:1,2,7

We who are strong ought to bear with the failings of the weak and not to please our-selves. Each of us should please his neighbor for his good, to build him up. Accept one another, then, just as Christ accepted you, in order to bring praise to God.

Before I got sober I was the world's biggest drama queen. I would spend hours on the phone bellyaching to my friends about how horrible my life was. I'd say," You'd be wacko too if you had my life." I would call a friend and bend her ear until she had heard my story two or three times. Then I would get off the phone and proceed to call the next friend so I could start all over again. I was miserable and I had no clue how to make myself better. Today I try not to tell everyone about all the prob-lems I'm going through. I strive to take them to God and lay them at his feet. He told me in His Word to cast all my cares on Him, so I do. Only He can fix them for me anyway. As far as those people God puts in my life who still don't quite get it. I just listen. And then I pray for them. Recovery tells me to practice patience, toler-ance, and kindness. I'm told I should treat these people as if they were sick. Would I be any more or less compassionate with a friend who had cancer? I'm told I should not. So today my motto is Love. Playing the victim is only a surface problem. These people have serious pain going on inside them. I know I did, so I must assume they do too. I believe those who hurt find comfort in sharing their stories with others. It helps them process it into something tolerable. The more I told my stories and the more people I got to agree with me, the better I felt. Right, wrong, or indifferent, that was just the way it was.

Thought To Meditate On:

We all need to remember that at one time we too were the weak one in need of help. Therefore, be patient with those who are needy and always be ready to give back what was so freely given to you. Humble yourself and don't worry aout that selfish pride. When you least expect it you might need a friend. And what happens at that time if you pushed them all away. I have a friend who tells me he made fun of fat people and became fat, he made fun of poor people and became poor. Don't make fun of those whose hearts are downtrodden. You could be next!

Thoughts and Revelations:

by Lacy Enderson

The Battle is Mine

♥

James 4:1-3

What causes fights and quarrels among you? Don't they come from your desires that battle within you? You want something but don't get it. You kill and covet, but you cannot have what you want. You quarrel and fight. You do not have, because you do not ask God. When you ask, you do not receive, because you ask with wrong motives, that you may spend what you get on your pleasures.

I keep trying to find a more delicate way to put this, but I suppose there isn't one. I am a control freak. I used to believe that as long as I was doing my best to treat others with love, kindness and respect, they should treat me the same way. In fact, I demanded that they did. I had "great expectations" of those in my life. I have a few defects of character that have played a big part in my actions. I am jealous, I am controlling, and I have a hard time trusting. I once heard it said that most of what we feel is either based on love or fear. I believe that my need to control others is based on fear. The fear that you will hurt me. The fear that you will leave me. The fear that you will disrespect me. The Lord says, "Fear not for I am with you." He also says, "Perfect love casts out all fear". It seems like every time I turn around I am faced with another monster of self I must overcome. I have been taught that the only one that I can change is myself. What you do is none of my business. That was a hard lesson to learn, but one that has proved to be a great benefit. I have so much more time to do the things I like to do now that I am not focused on you. I am not responsible for making sure everybody behaves properly, so now I can read a good book or watch a great movie. You can eat anything you want, drink as much alcohol as you feel you can. You can watch R-rated movies if you choose. That is between you and God. It is no longer my job to control you. What a relief.

Thought To Meditate On:

Let love be your motivator and not fear. Just because one person hurt you doesn't mean all people will. It was hard for me to tear down my walls. I was afraid if I became vulnerable you would hurt me. If I could control you like a puppet on a string than I didn't have to be afraid. You did what I said at all times and then I was happy. But the world doesn't work that way, and it didn't take me long to realize people don't like to be controlled. And you know what, I don't either.

Thoughts and Revelations:

Forgive For Your Own Sake

♥

Matthew 6:14,15

For if you forgive men when they sin against you, your heavenly Father will also forgive you. But if you do not forgive men their sins, your Father will not forgive your sins.

Sometimes when I find it hard to forgive, I take a look back over my life and remember all those people I have hurt who have forgiven me. I have selfishly done hurtful things to many people and they still love me. I said mean things about them and attacked their character, yet they forgave me. The fact is I am an ugly alcoholic. While under the influence of alcohol my behavior is hurtful and selfish. Yet, I cannot think of one person in my life today who holds a grudge against me. To all of you I have hurt, I am deeply sorry. To all of you who have hurt me, I forgive you. We offend God on a daily basis yet he forgives all of our sins. How dare I hold a grudge against a friend when Jesus came to erase all sin. God, help me to be forgiving. Help me to accept that nobody is perfect. Help me to be grateful for the mercy you have shown to me and be willing to pass it along to others. Help me to forgive. I heard it said, that unforgiveness is like taking poison and hoping the other person dies; you are the only one getting hurt.

Thought To Meditate On:

One of the requirements for recovery is making a list of all people we have harmed and being willing to make amends to them all. At first this sounds ridiculous. I mean, what does forgiveness have to do with sobriety. But it has much more purpose than you would think. How many times did we pick up a drink in anger over what someone had done to us? When we forgive that person of the offense we lessen it's power and the reasons to drink, thus ensuring our chances for lifelong sobriety. It does work.

Thoughts and Revelations:

by Lacy Enderson

Gentle Instruction

♥

2 Timothy 2: 25,26

Those who oppose him he must gently instruct, in the hope that God will grant them repentance leading them to a knowledge of the truth, and that they will come to their senses and escape from the trap of the devil, who has taken them captive to do his will.

I have heard it said, "If Jesus is not your God then the devil is." I have heard it said, "A man who does not believe in God will believe in just about anything." Before I came to believe in God, I was lost. I was unhappy and depressed. I constantly searched for happiness in nightclubs, in bottles, in boxes of cookies or in unhealthy relationships. I have heard it said, "God has put a void in our lives that can only be filled by Him." I used to walk around with emptiness inside me the size of the Grand Canyon. My problem was that I didn't know how to let God fill it. The Bible says, "Knock and the door will be opened unto you. Seek and Ye shall find." Thankfully, God put people in my life that taught me how to find Him. And when I deeply desired to find Him, He was there. If you are having a hard time with the God thing, just ask Him to reveal Himself to you and He will. That is His promise to all who seek Him.

Thought To Meditate On:

I had someone ask me once why I believed in God. I remember having lots of answers but none I could put into words. I told him it was better felt than telt and I meant it. God is a feeling I have. I just know He is there. Nothing in this whole world could ever convince me otherwise. If you want that kind of confidence in God ask Him to become that real to you. I am not quite sure how I was blessed with such an awesome relationship with God, but one thing I know, if He gave Himself to me He will give himself to you also. I'd like to think I am more special to Him than any of you, but I know I'm not.

Thoughts and Revelations:

He Ransoms My Soul From Hell

♥

Psalm 103:2-5

Praise the Lord, O my soul, and forget not all his benefits - who forgives all your sins and heals all your diseases, who redeems your life from the pit and crowns you with love and compassion, who satisfies your desires with good things so that your youth is renewed like the eagle's.

One of the controversies in Christian circles is the subject of healing. Some believe that when the Bible says, "By Jesus' stripes you were healed," it means a physical healing. Others believe that the healing referred to in this passage is of a spiritual nature. I have prayed for the sick many times and have seen miraculous healing. I have also prayed for healing and those people remained sick. I truly believe that God calls us to pray for such healing regardless of the outcome. This opens the door for Him to work according to His will. The last thirteen words that Jesus spoke before ascending into heaven were "… and you shall lay your hands upon the sick and they shall recover." I believe this to be a command that requires full obedience. It is not up to me to decide the outcome, that is God's job. Recovery teaches me our deliverance comes as the result of an inside job. The healing that must take place in the life of an addict is a spiritual healing. The Bible directs us to pray. Don't miss out on the many promises God has for us because you are unsure of what He would want. His word tells us "forget not all his benefits, He heals all your diseases." Pray against all doubt and unbelief and let the Lord reveal to you His many precious promises. He is waiting for you. Will you come?

Thought To Meditate On:

The benefits of God's love are endless. Every promise in His Word is true and for you today. Be willing and ready to receive them and He will bless you with them. Lift up your hands and your hearts unto the Lord so that he might fill them with all good things. God's promises are His prophecies to us. And remember, He believes everything in His Word whether we do or not. So His promises are not based on our belief, they are real regardless.

Thoughts and Revelations:

Instead of writing in this space, close your eyes and pray for those who are in need of a spiritual healing. Pray that they might believe that Jesus is the only healer they will ever need. If this describes you, pray for yourself.

by Lacy Enderson

The Lord's Purpose Will Prevail in the End

♥

Romans 12:2

Do not conform any longer to the pattern of this world, but be transformed by the renewing of your mind. Then you will be able to test and approve what God's will is - his good, pleasing and perfect will.

Did you know that God can restore you to sanity? When I came to believe that there was a God that could restore me to sanity, something happened. My life began to change. He began to pull out those weeds of corruption and evil and replace them with the beautiful flowers of God's Holy Spirit. But sometimes as one weed is pulled another grows up in it's place. For example: I was finally able to stop drinking but my language was horrible. Four-letter words flew from my lips like a sailor. I simply was not convicted in this area of my life. Until one day, God revealed my sin to me. I'm not sure when it happened, but I can no longer tolerate vulgarity. It truly offends me. God pulled that weed in His time. But I must play a part in this divine gardening. I must seek Him and believe that He is capable of cleaning me up. Be patient with yourself and remember the motto: Progress, not perfection. Now that I have given up cigarettes, I feel almost perfect. But then I'll have a bad thought or I'll fight with my husband. So no matter how hard I try, I am reminded each day that I am only human. But don't get discouraged at your continual lack of self-control. God already knew you would fail, and He has already made provision for you to get back up. I am happy with who I am today, faults and all, because I know I am exactly the way God wants me to be. And if there is some other area of my life He wants to clean up. I am sure He will hand me the hose.

Thought To Meditate On:

I am amazed at the transformation that has taken place in my life. My mom sees it, my kids see it, even I can see it. It is an amazing feat, and if you knew me before, you would consider the change an absolute miracle from God. The change in myself gives me hope for those people in my life that seem so hopeless. I know that if God changed me He can do the same for them. No matter how difficult a person seems for us, they are nothing to God. Believe me, He can do all things.

Thoughts and Revelations:

228

Supreme Wisdom

♥

James 3:13-18

Who is wise and understanding among you? Let him show it by his good life, by deeds done in the humility that comes from wisdom. But if you harbor bitter envy and selfish ambition in your hearts, do not boast about it or deny the truth. Such "wisdom" does not come down from heaven but is earthly, unspiritual, of the devil. For where you have envy and selfish ambition, there you find disorder and every evil practice. But the wisdom that comes from heaven is first of all pure; then peace loving, considerate, submissive, full of mercy and good fruit, impartial and sincere. Peacemakers who sow in peace raise a harvest of righteousness.

I often sit in recovery meetings wondering how I got there in the first place. I was Vice President of my senior class. I was the first co-captain of my school's drill team. I was a straight-A student. I was even homecoming queen for goodness sake. But I realize now that I spent most of my life doing whatever I chose to do and nothing that God commanded. I have had to come to terms with the fact that all of my best ideas landed me with a lot of apologizing to do. If I had truly went to God about my children I never would have sent them to live with their father. I have suffered with that decision for seven years. It was a very selfish decision made in fear and haste and I wasn't taking into consideration what was best for them. Only what I felt was best for me at the time. Had I prayed about it and waited on the Lord's answer, I would have done things completely different. But not me. I was in a hurry. My agenda was too important to wait. If I had heeded the warnings of the Holy Spirit in the first place I might have been married once instead of three times. If I had abided in Him I would have never taken that first drink after two and a half years sober. But I gave no thought to that drink at all. I had no spiritual defense against that drink because I hadn't spent any time with God in days. I don't always know what to do, and that is OK. I am not God and I cannot always know the future. He never asked me to. All He asked was that I rely on Him. He asks me to turn to Him in all my confusion and allow him to lead me to the place that is the best. He asks me to give Him first place in the morning. Now, is that really so hard to do?

Thought To Meditate On:

Selfishness and self-centeredness was the root of all our problems. Stop trying to run the show. That is how you got in all your trouble in the first place. Don't be wise in your own eyes.

Thoughts and Revelations:

by Lacy Enderson

Bridge Over Troubled Water

♥

Psalm 34: 17-20

The righteous cry out and the Lord hears them; he delivers them from all their troubles. The Lord is close to the brokenhearted and saves those who are crushed in spirit. A righteous man may have many troubles, but the Lord delivers him from them all; he protects all his bones, not one of them will be broken.

Have you ever heard the saying, "Worry is like a rocking chair, it keeps you very busy but gets you absolutely nowhere?" As long as I was filled with worry, I couldn't stop drinking. As long as I was drinking, God couldn't help me. As silly as it sounds I actually created storms in my life so I would have an excuse to drink. Alcoholics are great at creating reasons to drink. Sometimes the torment I put myself through was so horrible I would have preferred to die. And yet I continued doing it over and over again. Of course when my husband pointed this out to me I thought he was crazy. Why would I do a thing like that? Why would I purposefully create chaos? That was the most ludicrous thing I had ever heard! But, when I look back at my actions with a clear mind, I can see that this was exactly what I did. Since I've been sober I have learned to turn over the problem areas to God. Through prayer and more prayer God has been able to transform my worry into trust. Bad habits are hard to break, but one by one the cares and worries of this world seem to vanish. So get off the rocking chair and stand firm on the road of recovery.

Thought To Meditate On:

God understands our human nature to worry. If it wasn't going to be a problem for us, He wouldn't have mentioned it in the Bible. The Word says, "Do not worry." How much more clear could it be? He knew we would worry, because He created us. And He knew we would struggle, so He came to help us. If God didn't think you could get along without worry, He wouldn't command you to quit doing it. But He does command you not to worry, because he knows it is nothing more than a waste of time.

Thoughts and Revelations:

The Valley of Decision

♥

Isaiah 55:8,9

"For my thoughts are not your thoughts, neither are your ways my ways," declares the Lord. "As the heavens are higher than the earth, so are my ways higher than your ways and my thoughts than your thoughts.

There is a scripture in the Bible that says, "Many are the plans in a man's heart but it is the Lord's purpose that prevails in the end." There is very little more frustrating than to think I have an awesome and bright idea only to have it fail before I ever get started. I have been told in recovery, to pray for God's will and then pray for the power to carry it out. I was also told to go ahead and make my plans, but not to pack my bags. It has been suggested that when I set out to do something, always pray first. If God is willing, then I will do this or go there. It really is such an easy concept to understand, but a hard one to practice. Impatience creeps in unexpectedly. It just seems sometimes I must know better than God, because if He truly knew best, wouldn't He be doing things differently? And when I really want to do something, why would I pray about it just to have God tell me no? I have discovered that if God doesn't want me to do something, He's going to tell me no anyway. When the Bible says that God's ways and thoughts are higher than ours, that's exactly what it means. Save yourself a lot of wasted time. Spare yourself the heartache of a bad decision and take it to God first. Find out before you begin if it is a project or plan God approves of. He said in His Word, commit your ways unto Him and He will make your plans succeed. But make sure they are God's plans first. Success starts with obedience. And when God rewards your faithfulness, it will be far better than any plan you ever made yourself.

Thought To Meditate On:

When it seems you have tried everything else, and nothing seems to be working, give God a chance. You might be surprised with the outcome. Don't let stubborn pride stop you from receiving God's best. That is old behavior that needs to find it's way out. So open the door and show it the way.

Thoughts and Revelations:

by Lacy Enderson

He Has Set You Above Your Companion

♥

1 Corinthians 15:33,34

Do not be misled: "Bad company corrupts good character." Come back to your senses as you ought, and stop sinning; for there are some who are ignorant of God - I say this to your shame.

After my second husband left me I surrounded myself with women who were in my exact situation. They were divorced, lonely, lost, single mothers. We had the time of our lives. We celebrated our independence in nightclubs. We pacified our loneliness with ungodly conversations. And although I knew I had a drinking problem, the alcohol was still working for me. The hangovers were never as bad as the fun I was having. These women were my life and I looked forward to our crazy adventures. And then one day I knew I was done. The partying began to interfere with my job and my children. The hangovers became terrible reminders of the foolish things I had done the night before. I had to stop. I tried to continue being friends with these ladies but each encounter ended the same, drunk and disappointed. So I had to cut the relationships off. I could no longer go places with them or even spend time at their homes. I now have a whole new set of friends. These are recovering alcoholics just like me who are living sober today. I now have a true support system. I have the kind of support that leads to life and not to death. Be careful when you choose your friends. Choose those who want the best for you.

Thought To Meditate On:

Nothing changes until we change it. Sometimes that means we must change who we hang out with. Who is in your life today that does not contribute to your sobriety? It might be hard, but get rid of that person. Choose your companions wisely. If you are an alcoholic, it is detrimental to your success. It doesn't mean you have to hate people or even be rude towards them. If they are really your friend they will understand. I know my best friend wanted me sober, so when it came time to pick my remaining friends, it was people like her I clung to.

Thoughts and Revelations:

Nearer My God to Thee

♥

James 4:7

Submit yourselves, then, to God. Resist the devil, and he will flee from you. Come near to God and he will come near to you. Wash your hands, you sinners, and purify your hearts, you double-minded

During the summer of '78, when I was fifteen, I went to Catalina Island with a group of friends from school. I had just returned from a week at church camp and had rededicated my life to Christ. I promised God that I would quit drinking and smoking pot and I prayed fervently that God would help me get through the weekend on the island without drinking. During the day it was easy. I laid out in the sun and swam in the ocean. But when evening came and the alcohol was readily available, saying no was once again impossible. I drank enough beer to last all night and then some guy made me Hawaiian drinks with vodka and fruit juice. In the morning I felt so bad for drinking, I got up early and went to a Catholic mass with some friends. I wasn't even Catholic. I really did mean it when I told God I would quit. Every time I drank from that day forward, I promised I would quit, and I really meant it. Fortunately, I had a God in my life who understood my disease before I ever did. With each failed attempt came one more chance, until one day I was able to say no for good.

Thought To Meditate On:

A double minded man is one who lives in confusion about what is right and what is wrong. Picture an angel sitting on one shoulder encouraging us to do good, and a devil sitting on the other shoulder tempting us to sin. If we hold on tight to God and seek to do his will, the power of the devil will cease to have control over us. We will walk in God's righteousness. We will prevail in His power.

Thoughts and Revelations:

by Lacy Enderson

Power of His Might

♥

Galatians 61:9,10

Let us not become weary in doing good, for at the proper time we will reap a harvest if we do not give up. Therefore, as we have opportunity, let us do good to all people, especially to those who belong to the family of believers.

There was a guy I liked when I was in high school by the name of Tim. I met him at a gas station in the summer before tenth grade and the infatuation lasted for three years. He had a girlfriend on and off during this time, and when they were on the outs, he would look me up. Being "the other girl" was hard on me, but I liked him enough to deny my true feelings. In our senior year he got his girlfriend pregnant. When she told him she was keeping the baby, he left her. Once again, he looked me up. That year I was voted homecoming queen and I asked Tim to be my escort. As they announced my name, Tim and I walked across the football field towards the bleachers. Directly in front of me was Tim's ex-girlfriend. She was eight months pregnant and she looked very sad. She had dropped out of school and I hadn't seen her at all, until now. I felt terrible. Here she was about to deliver his baby and he was with me. I knew at that moment I could not continue seeing him. My conscience wouldn't let me. I wanted to, but God had other plans for both of our lives. They eventually got married, only to prove what I already knew. Had I not dated him they might have stayed together all along. That was a pivotal moment for me. I put someone else's needs above my own. Imagine that. A selfless act. And when I did, God changed my heart.

Thought To Meditate On:

Doing what is right is not always easy, and I can't say that is always what I did. I made a lot of bad decisions based on selfish reasons. Today I try to do what is right. I try to consider other people's feelings in all my choices. I might not always get it perfect, but I am a lot closer to it than I ever was before.

Thoughts and Revelations:

Be Self Controlled

♥

Proverbs 29:11

A fool gives full vent to his anger, but a wise man keeps himself under control.

I used to live next door to a lady who beat her son. We lived in a duplex. Her studio apartment and my house were separated by a wall. I could hear her on the other side yelling and hitting him. This went on for a long time. One night she asked me if I would watch him for her so she could go out. I said yes. She pulled up his shirt to show me some strap marks and told me not to worry. She said she got a little carried away. The next day I asked her over to my house and confronted her about the abuse. I told her I would report her to the authorities if she did not stop beating her kid. Her comment was, "What about you? You beat your son too." She had made it clear that if I reported her, she would lie and report me. I had been standing at my front door with my two month old son in my arms and the next thing I knew I was hitting her up the side of her head with my fist. I don't know what happened. I saw red and we were fighting. She was a big woman and I went down fast and hard. I allowed my anger to explode. In fact, I had so much suppressed anger in me, when I was insulted the anger was at full vent. I didn't report her. I will live with that guilt forever. I lost control of my feelings that morning and got in my first and last fist fight. I pray that God took control of that little boy's life. I pray that he has grown up to be a Godly young man. I pray that you will be more courageous than I was if you find yourself confronted with the issue of child abuse.

Thought To Meditate On:

Looking back over my life, especially at the times I was drinking, I see that I could have been a much better parent. Although I yelled a lot, I would not define my behavior as abusive. There were a few instances when I might have been overly harsh, but those times I remember clearly and will live with the nightmare forever. I think if that were the norm, I would remember more times like that. People who abuse children or animals seriously need help. If you find yourself lashing out at those around you because of your own anger and frustration, seek help. You can learn how to deal with the feelings in a more productive way. Hitting a kid never produces anything good.

Thoughts and Revelations:

by Lacy Enderson

Labor of Love

♥

1 Thessalonians 1:3

We continually remember before our God and Father your work produced by faith, your labor prompted by love, and your endurance inspired by hope in our Lord Jesus Christ.

After my second marriage I was introduced to a counselor who specialized in relationships. I began to see her because of the confusion I was feeling towards my husband. He kept leaving me and I kept letting him come back. It was becoming quite unhealthy. After a few sessions it was apparent to me that she had her own control issues. She told me that my husband had the S.R.B. syndrome, (spoiled rotten brat) and if I gave her six months of my time I would not want him anymore. So I met with her twice a week and she began to counsel me away from not only my husband, but everyone else in my life too. I needed someone to teach me how to be patient, tolerant, loving and kind. She taught me how to criticize, judge, and hate. She took out her machine gun and began blowing everybody away who did not meet up to her standards for me. She did not know how to love. She was a woman who had been hurt before and her mission was to protect me from others. Instead, I hurt a lot of people. When pain and anger are involved, there is seldom room for love, and yet God's number one command is to love. Be careful who you accept council from. If the advice feels wrong, it probably is. Weigh the words against scripture because God is always the final authority.

Thought To Meditate On:

Everybody always seems to know the answer, but most people base their opinion on their own experience. If you go to a restaurant and your food happens to be bad, you will tell others not to dine there. Even though all the thousands of other meals were delicious. Isn't it in our own best interest to try things out for ourselves and make our own decisions based on facts? We must learn to be responsible for your own choices. That counselor counseled me to divorce my husband. Right, wrong, or indifferent, I never should have divorced him just because she told me to, but I did.

Thoughts and Revelations:

My Soul Will Be Satisfied

♥

Isaiah 55:1,2

"Come, all you who are thirsty, come to the waters; and you who have no money, come, buy and eat! Come, buy milk without money and without cost. Why spend money on what is not bread, and your labor on what does not satisfy? Listen, listen to me, and eat what is good, and your soul will delight in the richest of fare.

One of the hardest things to comprehend is an addict who gets paid on Friday, is broke by Sunday. I am an alcoholic and I don't have this problem. He tries talking himself into staying home with his family, but the alcohol and drugs are too tempting. The money starts burning a hole in his pocket, and the voice in his head starts to taunt him. If you've ever seen a person like this, you would swear he was possessed. I have a friend who behaves this way. It is sad to see how his wife and children suffer. He fills them up with false hope all week. "We'll go someplace special," he says. "I'll buy you a new toy," he promises. But in the end, he always lets them down. I would think after living with this behavior for awhile they would wise up and stop expecting anything from him. But they just don't seem to learn. They continue believing his false promises and set themselves up for disappointment every time. A drug-addict alcoholic who is not in recovery is driven by the obsession of the addictions. It isn't that he doesn't love his family, He loves them very much, but he is sick. He works very hard for his money and then spends it on a temporary fix. A fix that will never fully satisfy him. Every week his intentions always start out good, but always end in disappointment. I pray that my friend will discover that God is the only one who truly satisfies, but my biggest prayer is that he gets sober.

Thought To Meditate On:

The most important lesson for the family of an alcoholic addict is to find out why they behave the way they do. It will make it so much easier on you to gain a little understanding. I am not saying you should hang around and take the abuse, but if you are planning on staying it would help to have a little knowledge. It is hard to understand what the alcoholic addict goes through when you are not one, so of course you will never fully comprehend. But any knowledge is better than none. So, seek some information. It will help you if you decide to stick around.

Thoughts and Revelations:

by Lacy Enderson

How Great Thou Art

♥

Deuteronomy 3:24

"O Sovereign LORD, you have begun to show to your servant your greatness and your strong hand. For what god is there in heaven or on earth who can do the deeds and mighty works you do?"

If I had to relate my life to a movie I've seen, it would definitely be Groundhog Day, with Bill Murray. Bill wakes up each morning just to find that he has to relive the same day over and over again. Because he knows that certain things are going to happen, he manipulates the day by changing his actions, which ultimately changes the circumstances. He finally lives the perfect day and gets to move on with his life. I have moved back into my parents house three times since I left home at the age of eighteen. Each time I've been there, I have been in a different place emotionally. Each time I'm a little bit stronger than the time before. I can't help but feel I will continue to move back home until I get my life right. My problem is I'm not always sure what right is. My intentions are always good, but I still keep making the same mistakes. I know there must be a path God wants me to take that somehow I keep veering off of. I pray for the ability to stay on God's path. God knows how tired I am of always starting over. It's about time I go forward and move on.

Thought To Meditate On:

I have always been grateful to my parents for their unconditional love. They never judged me. Each time I went home it was because of some mistake I made, yet they never made me feel bad for making it. I guess they knew that nagging wasn't going to help. I've always set out to please my parents. I loved doing what was right but somewhere along the way alcohol entered the picture and all my best intentions went right out the window. I haven't had to move back home in a while and I hope I never need to. But I do know that if the need arises, their door would always be open.

Thoughts and Revelations:

Be Imitators of God

♥

3 John 1:11

Dear friend, do not imitate what is evil but what is good. Anyone who does what is good is from God. Anyone who does what is evil has not seen God.

I went on a two day trip to San Luis Obispo with my Speech and Debate team when I was in high school. We drove four hours on a bus to Cal Poly University and stayed in a hotel called Divinity. We spent the afternoon playing pool, bowling, watching television and eating ice cream. It was all normal teenage fun. But that night the party began. They filled the bathtub full of beer and wine and everyone was smoking pot. We had quite a few rooms reserved, so we traveled from one room to another drinking and smoking. The party went on all night and then we had our speech competition the next day. I didn't do very well, but that was OK, because the party the next night was even better. Someone brought in bourbon and scotch and we had shooter contests. I remember hating the taste of hard alcohol, yet drinking it anyway. Our chaperone kept catching me wandering the halls and telling me to go to bed. I was so drunk, I often wonder why the adults who watched me stumble around the hallways never did anything to help me. I wonder how many were alcoholics themselves. When we got back to school, the teacher never mentioned my behavior at all. Did he know? Did he care? Was he too drunk to notice? I guess I will never know.

Thought To Meditate On:

I feel sorry for teenagers who still haven't discovered the damaging effect of drugs and alcohol. I wish they could bypass the whole process, as I am sure some will. I had good friends in school who went to parties with me to keep me safe, but they themselves never drank. I am unsure how this was possible for them since I couldn't go anywhere liquor was served without getting drunk. I guess they didn't have an alcohol problem. I guess not everybody does. I guess that is a real good thing, for them.

Thoughts and Revelations:

by Lacy Enderson

Find Rest, O My Soul

♥

Matthew 11:28-30

"Come to me, all you who are weary and burdened, and I will give you rest. Take my yoke upon you and learn from me, for I am gentle and humble in heart, and you will find rest for your souls. For my yoke is easy and my burden is light."

Eight years ago, during a time when I was alone and lonely, I kept a journal about my feelings. I pulled it out the other day to see how much I'd grown and I was shocked that the whole book was written in panic and desperation. I entitled my entries, "Dear Jesus." I wrote to God daily for help. I obviously depended on God a great deal but I hadn't fully learned how to trust Him. My heart cries were hopeless and full of despair. I wrote as if I was the most miserable person alive. Maybe I was. I didn't like remembering that time of my life. Reading my thoughts made me feel uncomfortable. Feelings of worry and confusion were brought back to the surface and I became terrified of where I used to be. It was almost like reliving the moment all over again. Everyday I waited for God to answer the questions I had. I spun around in circles at the mystery of my life and I could not sit still in my own skin. Frustration and anxiety filled my mind each and everyday. I couldn't escape it no matter how hard I tried. I was in a hurry for answers and God wasn't quick enough. I hated that feeling. Today, I can be still knowing that God is working. I have a greater faith in His power and the future He has for me. I have grown some since those days, thank God, and I am grateful for the growth. I must continually remind myself that God is in control and His hand is upon my life. His peace will guard my heart and mind.

Thought To Meditate On:

When I tell the stories about my troubling life and then follow the stories with 'just trust in God', I am not discounting the fact that fear and desperation are very real feelings. I still cry and yell and try to get God's attention. I still roll around on the floor begging God for what I think I need. I just don't do it as often anymore. I am not saying those moments of despair will all of sudden go away just because you trust in God. What I am saying is slowly over time you will learn that God is working even though you can't see Him. And even though things are not happening as quickly as you'd like them to, they are still happening. Fear and desperation will slowly disappear, over time.

Thoughts and Revelations:

240

Worthy of Respect

♥

Titus 3:2

To slander no one, to be peaceable and considerate, and to show true humility toward all men.

On a family vacation a few years back my sister and I got into a horrible argument. My brothers had brought a cooler of beer and placed it in the motel room. I decided I would have a few. My sister didn't think it was a good idea for me to drink. She asked me not to. I got very angry. How dare she ask me not to drink but not say a word to my brothers about their drinking. That hardly seemed fair since they consumed far more beer than I ever did. And how dare her think she had any right to judge me. I was not her daughter and my drinking was none of her business. My sister and I began to yell at each other and things got ugly real fast. We began shouting hateful words back and forth. I told her I never liked her and she said her feelings were mutual. Her children were present in the room during our argument listening to our slanderous words. This unfortunately only added fuel to the fire. Her girls were very angry with me and rightfully so. I spent the remainder of the day on the beach drinking beer. And it was two months before I spoke a word to my sister.

Thought To Meditate On:

When I think about the arguments I've had in my life, whether with my husband, my mom, my kids, or in this case, my sister, it never fails to amaze me that alcohol always had something to do with it. Or else the fight was because I had been drinking. Either way, it just compounded the truth that alcohol to an alcoholic is a poison and a disaster.

Thoughts and Revelations:

by Lacy Enderson

Effective Fervent Prayer

♥

Colossians 1:9,10

For this reason, since the day we heard about you, we have not stopped praying for you and asking God to fill you with the knowledge of his will through all spiritual wisdom and understanding. And we pray this in order that you may live a life worthy of the Lord and may please him in every way: bearing fruit in every good work, growing in the knowledge of God.

I worked in the Dental field for over seven years. I quit when I decided that I couldn't be around the temptation of the drugs anymore. The cupboards and drawers in some of the offices were stocked with samples of narcotic pills. The dentists gave them away to the patients. For a long time I had no desire to take them. In fact, I had two major mouth surgeries and asked for non-narcotic pain killers. My pill addiction came years later as a result of emotional pain. I had heard of people in recovery who had a pill problem. Because I had never taken narcotics, I never understood why. I heard it mentioned that narcotics were wonderful sedatives for numbing emotional problems. I hadn't had a drink in a while and my life was becoming extremely uncomfortable. I decided to try a Vicodin. It was wonderful and it worked. It numbed my emotional pain just like they said it would. But before long, those pills had become a huge problem. I found myself taking them everyday. I had a good friend who suffered from major back pain. He had been on prescription drugs for over a year. I used to bring him pills home from the office where I worked. After realizing the stronghold the pills had over me in such a short time, I quit providing them for my friend. I realized he had developed a strong addiction and instead of pills he needed prayer. As I prayed for him, God delivered me.

Thought To Meditate On:

I am not one to judge the behaviors of others, and I definitely don't like telling people what to do, but if I am providing an addict with his drugs, I have every right to make the decision to stop. I didn't understand the addiction to pills. I had no idea they could become a habit just as the alcohol had become. But when I took that very first pill and I stayed up all night cleaning my house and feeling good, I knew I was in trouble. Take my word for it and stay away from narcotic pills. If you take them, eventually they will bite you in the ass. And believe me, they bite hard.

Thoughts and Revelations:

The Lord is Our Judge
♥

Romans 14:13

Therefore let us stop passing judgment on one another. Instead, make up your mind not to put any stumbling block or obstacle in your brother's way.

I had a friend who was having marital problems. She was tolerant of the strife in her home for a while, but when she had, had enough, she kicked her husband out. She had two children to raise, no job and no income. So she decided to earn money by planting a marijuana tree in her backyard and selling the buds. I had never seen a pot plant before. This one was most impressive. It was huge and quite the tree. She babied the plant like it was of great value. It turned out to be. With the sale of the buds she was able to support herself during the separation, and remodel her kitchen. It's amazing what a desperate person will do. It was a high risk endeavor taken to meet the immediate need she had, and it worked. It is probably not the first initial response for most people in need. But how can anyone judge the actions of another without fully understanding the situation they are in? It's important to me to leave judgment to God. My friend needed someone to talk to and a friend who cared. She didn't need someone telling her what to do. This was years ago and in the end everything worked out just fine. Her husband returned home and they have been married for over 25 years. In my opinion, God took a bad situation and turned it into good and the whole family now lives happily ever after.

Thought To Meditate On:

It is interesting to me what desperate people will turn to in their time of need. I can't say I have ever been in a completely desperate place, so I am not quite sure what I would do in such a situation. I met a man on his very first day of being homeless. He was clean, well dressed and a man of great respect. He was begging for money outside of a Blockbuster store. He said he had just gone through a divorce, lost his job and his home and was recently forced to the streets. It has been at least eight years since then and the man is still on the street. And he has learned to survive all these years. I bet if he'd been asked ten years ago if he thought his life would ever come to this, he would adamantly have said no. But he has done what he needed to do to survive, and given the same lot in life, I probably would too. In a desperate situation we turn to God and he helps us through it. We try to make good choices doing the best we can. No judgement involved.

Thoughts and Revelations:

by Lacy Enderson

God's Servants

♥

1 Peter 2:13,14

Submit yourselves for the Lord's sake to every authority instituted among men: whether to the king, as the supreme authority, or to governors, who are sent by him to punish those who do wrong and to commend those who do right.

There are those people in my life who know more than I do and have experienced more in life than I have. Most of them are older and wiser, but some are actually younger than I am. It has always been hard for me to take suggestions from people no matter how old they were. I was stubborn and selfish and thought myself completely capable of handling anything. Even when others had gone through the same trials and had the answers for me, I didn't want to hear it. This happened all the time in my relationships. People on the outside could see the potential disaster I was walking into before I ever could, but I told them to keep their opinions to themselves. My relationships were none of their business. So I continued to date whom I wanted, doing it my way, and the end result was always destructive. But I am not the only one. I have friends caught up in bad relationships who don't heed my warning. They call me up crying about the neglect, or the emotional abuse, and the next day tell me how glorious everything is. You've heard the saying, love is blind? Well, I think it is deaf and mute also. I never say a word to them. I never tell them what I think they should do. I just listen. If they were strong enough to take advice, they wouldn't need it. Their strength would be the answer to end the relationship. I know. It wasn't until I became strong that I was able to submit to another's suggestions. When that happened I didn't need their suggestions anymore. Some people are addicted to relationships just as they are addicted to drugs and alcohol. They need them. It is amazing the character defects that get overlooked just to stay in a relationship. Just amazing.

Thought To Meditate On:

In the Bible Paul prayed to God and asked Him to save him from wicked and evil men because not everyone had the faith. Now, if the Apostle Paul was living in a day when he needed God's protection from people, why is it we are so gullible? Why do we allow just anybody to come into our lives? I have justified relationships I would not have wished on my worst enemy, all because I didn't want to be alone. Someone was better than no one, no matter what that meant. I have had more abusive relationships than I care to admit. But one day I realized I deserved better. And you do too.

Thoughts and Revelations:

Let There Be Light

♥

1 John 1:5-7

This is the message we have heard from him and declare to you: God is light; in him there is no darkness at all. If we claim to have fellowship with him yet walk in the darkness, we lie and do not live by the truth. But if we walk in the light, as he is in the light, we have fellowship with one another, and the blood of Jesus, his Son, purifies us from all sin.

After my second divorce I invited a friend of mine to move into my apartment with me. She was married to a drug addict and grew increasingly tired of the craziness he brought into her life. She was a recovering alcoholic who had discovered Jesus. She was trying to make positive changes and his drug use was hindering her growth. On her birthday I really wanted to make her feel special, so I took her to my favorite dance club. Since the two of us had alcohol related problems, I don't quite know what I was thinking. Didn't I have a favorite restaurant? What was wrong with a nice dinner? Within fifteen minutes of walking into that night club I was passed out on the back couch and her birthday was ruined! It only took me three drinks to fall into a blackout and into an evening I will never remember. My friend asked some guys to drive us home in my car because she couldn't drive and I wasn't able to. So two men we didn't know drove us home to my house, came in and hung out for quite awhile. I don't remember any of it. My intention was to celebrate my friend's birthday, but the alcohol turned the night into a celebration of immorality and shame. Alcohol ruins our best intentions. Alcohol perverts everything good. Alcohol is the enemy and is best left alone.

Thought To Meditate On:

I wonder if God was pounding me on the shoulder that night trying to get my attention before I made my plans. He knew the outcome of the evening before it ever happened, so I am sure if I was listening I might have heard Him telling me to do something else. But I was so excited about going drinking and dancing if God was speaking to me, I wasn't listening. In fact, I probably had that speaker dial turned all the way down. I wanted no interference. You see, it's not God's fault when we end up in bad situations. It is our's because we don't heed His warning. God tells us things but we don't hear because we are too busy doing everything our way. I am not completely sad that the night ended the way it did. I don't think I ever went back to that night club. So if the outcome was good, I won't completely discount the night. But wouldn't it have been better to just not have gone again in the first place? And the saga continues.

Thoughts and Revelations:

by Lacy Enderson

Let the Poor Say I Am Rich

♥

Ecclesiastes 5:19,20

Moreover, when God gives any man wealth and possessions, and enables him to enjoy them, to accept his lot and be happy in his work—this is a gift of God. He seldom reflects on the days of his life, because God keeps him occupied with gladness of heart.

I read a story in the newspaper about a man who shot his wife, his children, and then himself because he could not provide for his family. For him, it was easier to have them dead than to watch them go without. Isn't that sad? He quit. He gave up. I don't know his full circumstances, but I know that what he did was not the best answer. Actually, to me and to God, it was no answer at all. The stronghold that money has on some people can cause devastating results. The love of money truly is the root of all evil. Statistics show that money is the cause of most divorces. Most of my drinking when I was alone was because of financial reasons. It seems ironic now how much money I spent on alcohol to drown out my financial fears. If I added up all the money it cost me to escape from uncomfortable feelings of fear, I probably would have been able to pay the bills. That is the insanity of alcoholism. I took my last few dollars to buy cigarettes and alcohol and then complained I couldn't buy food. One of the hardest principles I had to learn in recovery was that fear of economic failure would leave me. They told me I no longer had to be motivated by fear of finances. That didn't happen overnight. That was a long process. I couldn't imagine being free from financial fear. It was what I thought about all day long. But today, if I wake up in the morning and thank God for His provision, I might not receive a new boat, but I have food, and clothes and all my needs are met. There is a contentment in my life today I never experienced before.

Thought To Meditate On:

I think financial insecurity is the norm for most people. Not too many people have a huge savings account and an endless supply of money. God knows we all wish we did, but that is not a true reality for most people. It seems for those who do have more, they just have bigger expenses and more bills. So in the end, we are all doing about the same financially. But God doesn't want our focus to be on what we have and don't have. He wants us focused on Him. He is our provider. He will meet all of our needs. If you put God first, He will put you first. The Bible says that God wants you lacking no good thing. He wants your vats to be full and overflowing.

Thoughts and Revelations:

Beauty For Ashes

♥

Jeremiah 31:13,14

"Then maidens will dance and be glad, young men and old as well. I will turn their mourning into gladness; I will give them comfort and joy instead of sorrow. I will satisfy the priests with abundance, and my people will be filled with my bounty," *declares the LORD.*

I have learned more about myself through other people's character defects than I have in all of my attempts at self awareness. I had a lot of problems I could not see. I was full of anger, rage, pain, and resentment. I don't know how I functioned on a daily basis with all of the baggage I carried around. I would come home from work so heavy with life's burdens that I would just lay down and fall asleep. I could do nothing else. I met a person who was exactly like me. He was plagued with every one of my character flaws. It was as if I was looking in a mirror. I did not like what I saw. It was the ugliest picture I had ever looked at and I ran from him to escape myself. But he was exactly what I needed in my life. I could not see my faults until I saw them in him. It is sad to see another person suffer the same torment I have gone through. I would not wish those feelings on my worst enemy. My prayer for those who cannot see their own faults is for God to introduce them to someone else who struggles with the same heavy load. Look around you. Is there somebody in your life who reminds you of yourself? Do they make you feel uncomfortable? God will use them to change your heart, so get ready.

Thought To Meditate On:

God doesn't want us suffering. He wants us happy, joyous and free. God will do whatever He has to bring us to a peaceful place. Sometimes He uses other people. I was told once that if God sends someone into my life to teach me something about myself and I run away from that person, He will send another person just like the first, until I quit running. So take off your running shoes and put on your listening ears. Become teachable and start learning.

Thoughts and Revelations:

by Lacy Enderson

And the Word Was God

♥

Psalms 19:8,9

The precepts of the LORD are right, giving joy to the heart. The commands of the LORD are radiant, giving light to the eyes. The fear of the LORD is pure, enduring forever. The ordinances of the LORD are sure and altogether righteous.

God knew what I needed before I was ever created. Although He had better ideas of what he wanted for me, He knew I would fall and need His help. So He inspired the men of old to prepare a book called the Bible, showing me the provision of God and His ability to deliver me from all my troubles. Unfortunately, I chose a different path, one in which I thought I'd have more fun. I allowed the lies and deceptions of the enemy and the world to crowd out what was right. I suffered the consequences of my mistakes. Going to parties and getting drunk was common for me. In high school I developed the nickname sleazy. Not because I was being taken advantage of, but because passing out all over people's houses and hanging on guys I didn't know set up a rather poor picture of myself. The image they saw of me was exactly what I portrayed, a sleaze. I had to learn to accept that, or make changes. When I decided to quit going to parties, everyone was disappointed. They didn't have anybody to talk about anymore. As much as I enjoyed drinking, I was tired of getting drunk and being labeled. I wasn't what they said I was and it disturbed me that they would all stoop so low. Didn't they know, they too were at the same parties? What did that say about them? Today it doesn't matter. Because today I don't drink. Sobriety means I never have to do anything that I wouldn't normally do. Those drunken behaviors are no longer who I am. If you want to put a label on me today, how about, a recovered alcoholic, a blessed and loved child of God, and a victorious overcomer.

Thought To Meditate On:

God doesn't ask us to do something unless He feels we are capable of doing it. He isn't a mean spirited dictator. He is a loving God who cares about you more than you will ever know. It wasn't that God didn't want me having any fun, He just didn't want me to be the object of other people's ridicule and scorn. He thought higher of me than that. And it wasn't that He wanted me bored and lonely. He just had better plans and people for me. So after I gave up the parties and the labels, I discovered God was telling the truth. It has been nothing short of remarkable.

Thoughts and Revelations:

Perfect Unity
♥

1 Corinthians 1:10

I appeal to you, brothers, in the name of our Lord Jesus Christ, that all of you agree with one another so that there may be no divisions among you and that you may be perfectly united in mind and thought.

My second husband and I had seen a sobriety advertisement on television and we decided it was time for us to quit drinking. We didn't join any clubs or support groups. We simply decided to give up alcohol. The difference in our relationship without alcohol was amazing. He actually came home from work on time and he spent more time with the family. I was less angry and we got along extremely well. One day after four months of alcohol abstinence, my husband called me at work to tell me a friend was coming over to watch a fight on TV. He wanted to know if it was OK if his friend brought beer. I had a sick feeling inside my stomach. When I got home his friend was sitting in the front room with a six pack of beer. My husband asked my permission to have a couple. So I sat there and watched them each drink three beers. I was shaking on my insides. I could hardly stand the torment. I felt like I was going to crawl out of my skin. I couldn't believe that four months of bliss was about to go right out the door. I knew what the marriage was like with alcohol and I couldn't believe we were going back there. I was crushed. When his friend left I jumped in the car and ran to the store and bought two 16 ounce cans of beer. I brought them home and drank both of them really fast. The shaking and the torment disappeared and I was left with a feeling of unbelievable dread. My husband and I did not drink well together. We fought everyday, and alcohol only magnified the problems. It is sad to say, but once again, we were off and running.

Thought To Meditate On:

Problems are much easier do deal with sober. Alcohol has a way of intensifying even the smallest problems. The imagination I had while drinking was incredible. I could fathom a story in my mind when I was drunk that made absolutely no sense when I was sober. It was these vain imaginations that got me in so much trouble. I hate alcohol. I hate the way it called my name and I hated it more when I'd give in. I am so incredibly grateful that I don't drink anymore. In fact, I am so glad to be an alcoholic because alcohol is never an option. Life without alcohol is the greatest life I know.

Thoughts and Revelations:

by Lacy Enderson

Blind Faith

♥

James 1:2-4

Consider it pure joy, my brothers, whenever you face trials of many kinds, because you know that the testing of your faith develops perseverance. Perseverance must finish its work so that you may be mature and complete, not lacking anything.

I pray for faith like a thirsty man prays for water. When I am walking through a hard time and I can hardly find the strength I need to continue, my need for faith becomes all I think about. It reminds me of these song lyrics, "I'm going to walk by faith and not by sight, 'cause I can't see straight in the broad daylight. I'm going to walk by faith and not by fear, I believe in the one who has brought me here." There are no mistakes in God's world. Everything happens for a reason. I have gone through two very painful divorces. I cannot explain exactly why this keeps happening to me, or even if it will happen again. What I do know is I have persevered through each one and came out on the other side stronger. Although I don't believe divorce is a good thing because the Bible says God hates divorce, God used it for my good and everything turned out alright. I have often wondered why some couples get together and stay together forever, and why this seems impossible for me? Of course I pray this never happens again, but they say the only guarantees in life are death and taxes. So I'll do the best I can, and I'll continue to pray for faith. Faith is the ability to believe in something I cannot see. And the future is one of those things I cannot see. So I pray and ask God to grow my faith so I am able to believe in His hand on my future. Because no matter what my life brings, if God's hand is on my future, then it can't go wrong. So in spite of the divorces and all the other storms in life I've walked through, God is always with me. He will never make me walk alone.

Thought To Meditate On:

I'll say for the record, I am eight years into my third marriage and all is going extremely well. I won't say it has been great for the entire eight years, but it is now. Maybe someday I'll write a book on relationships. I think I might have it figured out. Don't beat yourself up because you've been divorced. Yes, the Bible says God hates divorce, but you are forgiven. If the Bible says your repented sins are forgiven then your divorce is also. It is God's will that people learn to live together in marriage. It is His ultimate goal to see married couples happy. But sometimes it is not as easy as we would like it to be. Don't give up. It does take time and given the time you need, you too can learn how to be married, and happy!

Thoughts and Revelations:

A Star is Born

♥

Daniel 12:3

Those who are wise will shine like the brightness of the heavens, and those who lead many to righteousness, like the stars for ever and ever.

I had a friend who was addicted to crystal meth. I had never gotten involved in uppers so I wasn't familiar with her problem. Some days she was the happiest person in the world and other days she was extremely depressed. These were symptoms of her drug addiction. She filed for divorce from a husband of many years and her children remained with their father. She couldn't keep a job very long so she hooked up with different guys who would provide her with her drug. It was sad watching her go through such torment, but I understood the drive and I knew I couldn't help her. One day she called and asked me to come over and pray with her. She knew I had recovered from alcoholism and I was a believer in Jesus. At one of her lowest points she cried out for help and I prayed with her. I haven't seen her in a long time. I couldn't tell you if she was clean or not. But I do know that God heard her prayers. And I believe eventually God will deliver her from crystal meth just as He delivered me from alcohol. Something happens on a persons insides when we pray. Even though we don't see the outward manifestation, it doesn't mean there wasn't an inside transformation taking place. Prayer changes things. It always does.

Thought To Meditate On:

I have a friend who has asked me why it seemed like some people had a better relationship with God. She wanted to know why it seemed easier for some Christians than it did for other's? I don't know the answer. I know at one time my walk with God was difficult, but today it is easy. Maybe it isn't that God makes it easier for some. Maybe it is that some have climbed higher up the hill. I haven't always had a relationship with God that was this close. At one time He was far away and many days I could not find Him. So if God seems far away, give it time. Eventually He will make Himself available to you on a more personal level. That is His goal.

Thoughts and Revelations:

by Lacy Enderson

Rise Up

♥

2 Timothy 1:7

For God did not give us a spirit of timidity, but a spirit of power, of love and of self-discipline.

I was at a bar one night with some friends and I saw a man I wanted to meet. I was tired of being alone so I waited until he left the bar and I chased him down the parking lot. Can you believe it? I had a few cans of liquid courage in me, so I was able to put on the charm and ask him for his phone number. I never could have done that sober. Actually, if I was sober, I never would have wanted to meet a guy in a bar. I called him the next day and we began dating. The strange thing about this guy is he didn't drink at all. He said he didn't like the way he felt the next day. That's funny, neither did I, but that didn't stop me from drinking. Ironically I found myself drinking more because he was sober. I guess I didn't have enough confidence in myself to think a sober guy would find me attractive. I always went out with drunks who thought I was a ravishing beauty. His sobriety made me more nervous, and gave me even more reason to drink. That relationship ended abruptly. I wasn't much fun to be around, drunk all the time. Looking back I am surprised he didn't dump me a whole lot sooner. No matter how hard I tried to drink socially, I always turned into a drunken idiot. I discovered that drunk women are not attractive and I tried hard not to be one, but I failed every time I picked up that first drink. When I think about the guy I met in the bar, I get embarrassed. I pray I don't ever run into him.

Thought To Meditate On:

I do not have one story to tell of a successful dating relationship between myself and a man I met in a bar. Not one. I guess that should tell us something. I would tend to believe that the statistics of relationships lasting between two people meeting in a bar are low. I am not saying that nice people don't go to bars. I went to bars and I was a nice person. But the majority of people who go to bars are not the type of people I would want a serious relationship with, not even when I was drinking. Maybe you should take up a sport or a hobby and find people with similar interests. I think the chance of a successful relationship might be higher this way. Just for the record, I met my third husband in Alcoholics Anonymous. It wasn't on the list of places I wanted to meet a man, but it worked out OK.

Thoughts and Revelations:

Fallen Angels

♥

Mark 11:25

"And when you stand praying, if you hold anything against anyone, forgive him, so that your Father in heaven may forgive you your sins."

I attended the same church for six years. It was a new church, so the pastor answered phones and did all of his own counseling. I had the opportunity to get to know the pastor quite well. He helped me through one of my divorces. I was also heavy into my drinking and we had conversations about that issue too. I told him he couldn't possibly understand how hard it was living in the world. He had always been isolated within a church. His father was a pastor, he went to seminary and started as a youth pastor, married a young girl in his church and then started his own fellowship. Everyday he went to work at the church, so he had no idea what it was like living in the real world. He actually agreed with me. He had not been tempted as some of us were. And he admitted he didn't understand all the problems his congregation were facing. Many years later I learned that my pastor friend had fallen into an adulterous affair. It was with a woman from the church. He was tempted and he gave in. I felt really bad for him. The congregation was very unforgiving. Half the members of the church left. I try to remember the scripture that says, we are only qualified to take the sliver from our friends eye when we have removed the plank from our own. Where was the grace? I was amazed at the lack of tolerance in the people from that church. Who did they think they were to judge a man so severely? Did they actually think the pastor was God himself made perfect? A pastor is only human just as we all are. In fact, they are tempted even harder because of their position in the Lord. Try to extend compassion to the pastor who falls. Or better yet, pray for him before it happens.

Thought To Meditate On:

People can be so critical and condemning. Most of the time I can't understand why. People are all human no matter what place of authority they are in. A person doesn't go to school and earn credentials to become perfect. No, it doesn't happen that way. People need to be more tolerant and extend more grace.

Thoughts and Revelations:

by Lacy Enderson

I Will Sing To Him A New Song

♥

Exodus 23:25,26

Worship the LORD your God, and his blessing will be on your food and water. I will take away sickness from among you, and none will miscarry or be barren in your land. I will give you a full life span.

A few summers ago my step daughter and her friends hung out in my apartment. I had a passion for teenagers and I loved their company. My teen years were difficult, so I felt like I could relate to them. I understood what they went through because I went through similar circumstances when I was their age. They talked and I listened. I always welcomed them in my home because I knew they needed a safe place to hang out. My home was safe. I knew as long as they were with me, they were behaving. One of the boys that spent time at my house was in a very bad car accident. He was out one night drinking and drugging and he ran into the back of a parked car. He was in a coma for three days before he died. That was very difficult news for me. The pain in my stomach was tremendous. I was literally sick for four days. A lot of what I felt was the sorrow I saw in my daughter and her friends. I felt so bad for them. I knew there wasn't anything I could do to make it better. The grieving had to run it's course. God knew our pain, and he cared. But he also knew that worship would bring peace during the torment. So I prayed and sang songs to God, and eventually the pain left my stomach. I still don't understand the death of that boy and probably never will. But it has motivated me to increase the prayers I pray for my own children. Every morning I thank God for protecting them from all harm. And so far He has.

Thought To Meditate On:

God asks us to remain in an attitude of worship during each and every situation, whether good or bad. With each song of praise, God brings peace and serenity. The Bible tells us that God inhabits the praises of his people and that God's abundant blessings bring long life and health. So try it today by making a joyful noise, unto the Lord.

Thoughts and Revelations:

254

Beloved, Let Us Love One Another

♥

John 13:34,35

"A new command I give you: Love one another. As I have loved you, so you must love one another. By this all men will know that you are my disciples, if you love one another."

My sister's husband was sharing a story with me about a couple of homeless people, when he began to cry. The spirit of God had moved on his heart with such compassion, that to tell the story still brought tears to his eyes. He went to lunch with two of his co-workers and saw a homeless man yelling at his wife outside the Taco Bell. He and his friends went in, ordered their food and sat down. A few minutes later the homeless man and his wife came in and sat down next to the men. My brother in law had only recently given his life to Jesus and his co-workers were unbelievers, so he was a bit uneasy when the Spirit called him to pray for this couple. "What will my friends think?" went through his mind, but the Spirit was strong and my brother in law was obedient. He asked the man if he could pray, and then he laid his hands on the man and asked God to take care of his needs. The power of God was so strong it was as if there was no one else in the room. He was aware only of God's presence and this man. When he was finished praying he said one of the man's teeth fell out of his mouth and landed on the table. It was an uncomfortable moment to say the least. My brother-in-law reached into his pocket and handed the man some money. After he did, his co-workers each took out what they had and offered it to the man as well. When God speaks of love, this is the love he speaks about. Love your neighbor as yourself even when he is a dirty, poor, homeless man.

Thought To Meditate On:

God is the exact representation of love. His love is perfect and unconditional. That means that God's love isn't based on what we do. We don't have to earn God's love. He loves us no matter what. God's desire is for us to love this way also. He wants us to love other people the way He loves us. This unfortunately isn't always easy to do. The Bible asks us to be an example of God's love so others might see God's love in us and believe in Him.

Thoughts and Revelations:

by Lacy Enderson

Majestic in Power

♥

Zechariah 4:6

So he said to me, "This is the word of the LORD to Zerubbabel: 'Not by might nor by power, but by my Spirit,' says the LORD Almighty."

I had gone out with friends to a billiards hall to shoot pool and drank quite a few pitchers of beer. I don't remember getting too incredibly drunk, but I knew I had drank way too much. I watched a guy on cocaine acting very weird and I became concerned for myself. Even though I didn't do hard drugs I saw the altering effect the drug had on him and I wondered what I must have looked like when I was drunk on alcohol. I never seemed to care before, until I saw this guy all strung out. I don't think I ever saw anything like it. It must have been the Spirit of God, who opened my eyes at that moment to what was really going on. I was an alcoholic hanging out with drug addicts and I had no business being there. God had given me a life. I had kids, a home, a job and things were going well. What was I doing there? If Jesus was in my heart like He said He was when I invited Him in, was I bringing Jesus to a billiards hall to shoot pool? It was time to leave. And it was time to quit drinking. The next day I did.

Thought To Meditate On:

Don't depend on your own strength and power. Rely on God's power and you might have a better chance of success. We must be willing to allow His Spirit to provide the power we need. The Spirit enables us to accomplish things self-will could not do. Let God's Spirit be your helper. Let the Spirit be your guide. The Bible says it is not by might or by power but by God's Spirit. He is an ever-present help in time of trouble.

Thoughts and Revelations:

Wise Men Store up Knowledge
♥

2 Peter 1:5-8

*For this very reason, make every effort to add to your faith goodness; and to good-
ness, knowledge; and to knowledge, self-control; and to self-control, perseverance;
and to perseverance, godliness; and to godliness, brotherly kindness; and to brotherly kindness, love. For if you possess these qualities in increasing measure, they
will keep you from being ineffective and unproductive in your knowledge of our
Lord Jesus Christ.*

About once a year when I was growing up my Aunt and Uncle and five cousins
would come to visit my family. It was my father's brother who followed in his parents footsteps and became a Pentecostal preacher. They drove around in a motor
home full of band equipment and sang in churches all over the United States. The
kids were home-schooled and brought their schoolwork with them. They would set
up their band equipment in our living room and sing Jesus songs for us. They had
awesome power and something different than what I had, being raised in the Baptist
church. I'm not putting down the Baptist's, I'm just saying the Spirit of God never
moved there like He did in my front room when my relatives sang. It was truly
amazing. My grandparents were two other extraordinary people. My Grandma
would come to our house often. She was such a happy woman. She shined with the
glory of the Lord. I remember wanting what these people had. I saw a relationship
with God in them I had never experienced, and I wanted that. Although it took years
of doubt, frustration and ignorance, I have finally been blessed with the same
knowledge and power of God as they had. He was there all the time just waiting for
me to call on Him. I just didn't know how.

Thought To Meditate On:

There is a list of qualities we must develop in order to produce a fruitful Christian
life. These are found in the Word of God. We walk in faith, love, joy, self-control,
goodness, kindness, mercy and Godliness. We need to possess a genuine reverence
towards God. We should acquire an attitude of selflessness so we are able to make
sacrifices of ourselves for the good of others. It sounds like a lot of hard work, and
it is, but it is worth it.

Thoughts and Revelations:

by Lacy Enderson

Divine Appointment

♥

Habakkuk 2:2,3

Then the LORD replied: "Write down the revelation and make it plain on tablets so that a herald may run with it. For the revelation awaits an appointed time; it speaks of the end and will not prove false. Though it linger, wait for it; it will certainly come and will not delay.

Sometimes when I drank, I became very spiritual. At least I thought I was spiritual. One time a girlfriend and I went to a bar to have a few drinks and dance. I had always referred to my friend as my spiritual advisor. When we drank together we talked about God. So in my humble opinion, drinking was not a problem for us. I heard it said once that if something brings you closer to God than it must be from God. Well the drinking brought us closer to God, so I justified it as being OK. This particular night we decided to enlighten the drunks in the bar and began to preach the Word of God while standing on barstools. It was probably a very funny sight to those who were listening to us. We were two drunk women going on and on about the Lord in a bar. We were on our soapbox and we were very proud of ourselves. I don't know how proud God was of us. He may have preferred for us to wait until we were sober to represent Him. Or maybe God touched someone that night and they went on to get saved. I can only hope so. Today, I spread the message of God sober and I stay out of the bars, but I am not completely convinced that God didn't use me in those situations. Drinking was never God's best for me. I always knew He had better plans. But while I was still growing in my knowledge of God, He used what I had at the time. I don't suggest you run out and get drunk so you can start preaching. I don't recommend that at all. But don't underestimate the power and grace of God. He can do miracles anywhere He chooses.

Thought To Meditate On:

It's hard for me to preach Jesus to people because I have social anxiety as I have mentioned before. When I was drunk, I had no problem at all. It is too bad I had to be intoxicated to be any good for God's Kingdom. But someday my hope is that I will be given an inner confidence. Someday I hope to be preaching to a stadium full of people.

Thoughts and Revelations:

258

Notes:

_____

_____

_____

_____

_____

_____

_____

_____

_____

_____

_____

_____

_____

_____

_____

_____

_____

Notes:

_____

_____

_____

_____

_____

_____

_____

_____

_____

_____

_____

_____

_____

_____

_____

_____

_____

_____

Notes:

_____

_____

_____

_____

_____

_____

_____

_____

_____

_____

_____

_____

_____

_____

_____

_____

Notes:

_____

_____

_____

_____

_____

_____

_____

_____

_____

_____

_____

_____

_____

_____

_____

_____

Notes:

_____

_____

_____

_____

_____

_____

_____

_____

_____

_____

_____

_____

_____

_____

_____

_____

_____

_____

by *Lacy Enderson*

Notes:

_____

_____

_____

_____

_____

_____

_____

_____

_____

_____

_____

_____

_____

_____

_____

_____

_____

_____

_____

_____